A Mischief of Mice

Secrets, Lies, and Love
in the Sand Hills of Minnesota

CYNTHIA BLOMQUIST GUSTAVSON

Other Books by Author

Poetry

Scents of Place: Seasons of the St. Croix Valley
Please Use This for Children and Not for War and Guns
Between Tahlequah and Tulsa
Excellent Feathers: Painting and Haiku (with R.B. Bieber)

Poetry Therapy

In-Versing Your Life: A Poetry Workbook for Self-Discovery and Healing
Re-Versing the Numbers: A Poetry Workbook for Eating Disorders
Re-Versing Your Pain: A Poetry Workbook for Those Living With Chronic Pain
Con-Versing With God: Poetry for Pastoral Counseling and Spiritual Direction
Fe-Vers: Feeling Verses for Children

Fe-Vers: Feeling Verses for Teens
Bully: The Big Book about Bullies and the Bullied

Children's Fiction

Ballad of the RagMan

Previously published

"7 (First Language)", *"15 (Grounding)"*, *"17 (Opening Doors)"*, originally published in *Between Tahlequah and Tulsa* (2014, Blooming Twig Books, NY).

"A Man Named Joyce" in *River Images*, Vol. I, Issue III, fall 1996.

"Back Roads", *"Haiku"*, *"Rockhound (Crystalized)"*, *"Selma's Ice Cream Parlor (Respect)"*, originally published in *Scents of Place: Seasons of the St. Croix Valley* (1987, Country Messenger Press. Marine on St. Croix, MN).

"But I Need More (Moving On)", *"I Don't Write Love Poems (Tending)"*, *"Paisley Dress of Purple (Wounded)"*, *"Patience of the Cross Timbers"*, originally published in *Con-Versing With God: Poetry for Pastoral Counseling and Spiritual Direction* (2006, Blooming Twig Books, NY).

"Dialysis", reprinted by permission, Dec. 12, 1984 edition of *The Christian Century*.

"Easter Lil" in *River Images*, Vol. II, Issue II, Winter 1997.

"Empty Ice Cream Bucket (Secret)", *"Prisoner (Memory)"*, originally published in *Please Use This For Children and Not for War and Guns* (2010, Blooming Twig Books, NY).

"Frozen Ground (Frozen)", *"To Roxanne (Silence)"*, *"Train to an Inner Lake: Voyageurs National Park"*, originally published in *In-Versing Your Life: A Poetry Workbook for Self-Discovery and Healing* (1ed. 1995, Families International, Inc.; 2d ed. 2006, Blooming Twig Books).

"Old Annie's Ghost" in Sidewalks, No.3, Aug. 1992.

"Timeless" in *Re-Versing the Numbers: A Poetry Workbook for Eating Disorders.* (2006, Blooming Twig Books, NY).

A Mischief of Mice

Secrets, Lies, and Love in the Sand Hills of Minnesota

Copyright © 2023, Cynthia Blomquist Gustavson

Published by Blooming Twig

New York / Oklahoma

Hardcover ISBN 978-1-61343-150-4

Paperback ISBN 978-1-61343-151-1

E-book ISBN 978-1-61343-152-8

Dedicated to

Dorothy Knoblauch Blomquist Jorgenson (1924–2008),
Dr. John Gustave Adolph Blomquist (1912–1960),
Roxanne Blomquist Bieber, and
John Leigh (Wink) Blomquist.

To Dr. Ed Gustavson, my courageous and engaging
husband of over 50 years, and to my children for whom
I wrote this memoir: Britta Joy Gustavson, and
Kent Samuel Gustavson.

And to Svea Brook Gustavson, born on 1/11/11,
on whom the future rests.

Table of Contents
—— ▫O▫ ——

Searching

After crows stole the baby wren from its nest
I knew why they were called a murder of crows,

and watching doves cooing and doing what they were doing
I knew why they were called a piteousness of doves,

but what did 15th century Englishmen know of wombats
to call them a wisdom, or cobras to become a quiver?

I understand a clowder of cats or a business of boars,
hunters who named them knew those animals well —

I particularly like a shrewdness of apes, those prototype
ancestors using tools to survive and become kings.

But as a child I was the hunted, lying awake in my bed, listening,
terrified of the scratching in the hollow, thin wall

in wintertime when mice in the cold country came inside,
through cracks in century-old brick and holes in the dried wood,

to nest and raise their families on the inside of my bedroom wall.
Sometimes they died there, making my room reek with a stench

unequaled by any other stinking thing and, unable to get at them,
I went to sleep holding my breath, head in the pillow's feathers.

Those who first named these invaders called them a mischief of mice,
having seen their playful scratching, sniffing and skittering

across sand hills and vetch-vined meadows, traveling through
dark walls, closets, and cabinets — searching.

introduction

Marsh Marigold
[*Caltha palustris*]

In 1964, I memorized sandy-haired Swedish-American writer Carl Sandburg's poem "Four Preludes on Playthings of the Wind", from his 1920 collection, *Smoke and Steel*.

> *... And the wind shifts*
> *and the dust on a door sill shifts*
> *and even the writing of the rat footprints*
> *tells us nothing, nothing at all*
> *about the greatest city, the greatest nation*
> *where the strong men listened*
> *and the women warbled:*
> *Nothing like us ever was.*

As the Vietnam war raged in the mid-1960s, I recited Sandburg's ironic words in high school Speech contests, with dramatic effect, for classmates and friends. Afterwards, some of them were drafted into service, and never returned. "Nothing like us ever was" exclaims the Swede's haunting refrain, written shortly after World War One.

War and peace had their hands on me in those years, and throughout my early adulthood, as I traded my rural home in the St. Croix Valley of Minnesota, for St. Peter, a college town. Then, I went east, called by the siren song of Boston, where my eyes opened. Folk music's humanness and realism in those years, as well as its simple poetry, drew me in, as did the passion of anti-war demonstrations on Boston University's campus.

Surrounded by visions of war and demonstrations for peace, I thought constantly back to the Valley.[1] Not with nostalgia or homesickness; far from it. I loved city life and its cultural experiences, diverse classmates, and high-level lectures. But I began to realize how the people of the Valley handled war and peace differently. And I began to see their stories, and mine, in a different light.

The characters I describe in these pages are indelible and real to me, from Old Annie to Easter Lil, and even little Lillian, the Native American foster child. These were my neighbors and friends. And though, in hindsight, they were dramatically dissimilar in status, education, belief system, politics, and everything else, they had learned to live together on our sand hills, in peace.

I first heard the late bard, Pete Seeger, at Boston Common, wielding his banjo as a weapon against hatred. He sang about flowers given to young men, and young men donning uniforms, who were only to end up in graveyards, and graveyards nurturing flowers, a circle song depicting the never-ending cycle of love and hatred. "We shall overcome," he encouraged all of us to sing, together.

---

[1] I have capitalized the word "Valley" throughout this book because it acts as a character in my story.

But now I see that we have not overcome.

I was born in the first half of the most warring century in the history of humans on Earth.

But I'd like to think that we singers and poets have planted a few flowers on those graves.

And there is something we can do.

There is something I can do.

Let's all continue to write and read poems, tell and listen to stories, and sing and hear songs.

This is how poets, singers, and all of us, together, can take action to save our communities, our countries, the planet, and ourselves.

Poetry will keep us honest.

– Cynthia Blomquist Gustavson

Tulsa, Oklahoma, March 2023

"I'm a **lonely little petunia**
in an onion patch…**"**

– Popular 1946 song by Kamano, Faber & Hartmann

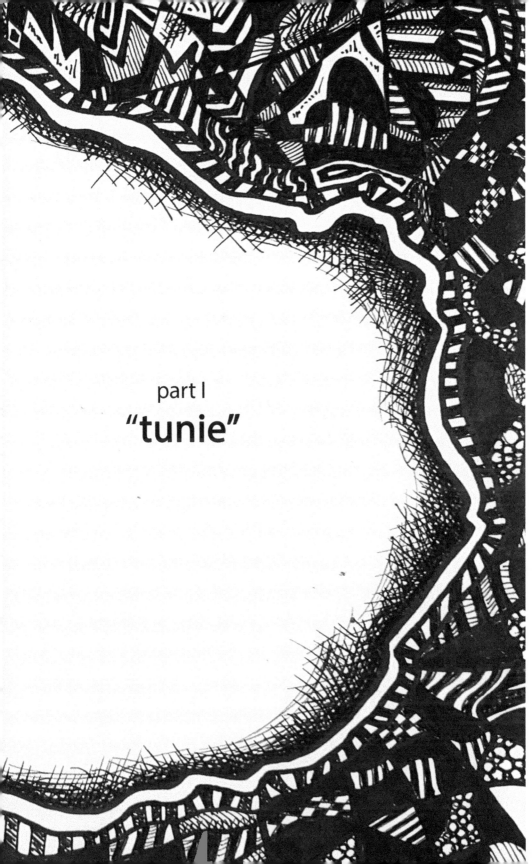

part I
"tunie"

But I Need More

I once lived
in a hundred year old house

its creaking walls
enlivening dreams
of dead farmers

who starved
growing corn
on its sand hills

They stayed around
lost in pioneer dust
and tobacco smoke

in silent vigil
to see how it all
turned out −

each hundred acres
carved into fives
McMansions peeking

through remaining white pines
that for centuries thrived
on hills of glacial sand

Ghost farmers now
drift in the wind
as brick mansions

dwarf the old wooden house
tall bluestem prairie plowed under
for manicured lawns

and towering pine
I planted in rows
decades ago are
all that's left of wild

White pines
and suburban plots
survive on

hills of sand −
but I need
more

chapter 1
the first secret

Aster
[*Aster amellus*]

I guess I'm a storyteller. Or a poet. You decide which.

Let me start with a story from a long time ago, back when I thought the bottoms of my feet came from God with a tar-coating, and when my brother and I brought berries and rabbits back from the woods to supplement Mom's vegetables from the garden.

I was never a mischief-maker, but that doesn't mean I never got in trouble. I could just blame the Anderson boys, or my sister, or later my friend Pat, but I hereby consent to my misdeeds, as if I had initiated them myself. Because some of them haunt me to this day, so many years later.

I've kept this story secret all my life. And maybe I should still keep the secret, but I can't bear to take it to the grave with me.

It's time for you to hear what happened to Old Annie, and what we did.

——————— ∘O∘ ———————

Like rats, we all followed our Valley's own Pied Piper – tall, sweet-talking Chuck Anderson. He was only three years older than I was, but already, his developed musculature and bearing exuded a sense of authority for the rest of us kids.

"It's so perfect," Chuck said proudly through his toothy grin.

I didn't understand what he meant until I saw him swinging a rope over the low branch of a box-elder tree, with what was clearly a tightly-woven noose.

We all had seen bad guys hanging from nooses in the town square on our black-and-white television screens, where you could barely make out a face or even an outline. Even as a kid, I couldn't imagine how the townspeople in these cowboy shows could be callous enough to see a hanging as a happening. But that's what we saw on TV. And despite everything we teach our children about kindness, peace, and love, I guess it's human nature.

I now live on bloodied soil in Tulsa, Oklahoma, where the Tulsa Race Massacre took place just over a hundred years ago, and where the hangings and burnings of African-Americans, their homes, and their businesses were subsequently nearly erased from memory.

How can such inhumanity take place? Such violence?

Well, I certainly don't have an answer, but I can say that none of us from the Valley has spoken of our own dark secret until now.

We buried our shame deep inside, covered up like sand beneath the Valley's hills, hidden away like rotting muskrat stoles in Old Annie's dresser.

——————— ◦O◦ ———————

"I suffer so," Mom would say about days like these.

It was a hot, muggy July day in 1958, too hot for friends outside the Valley to bike the winding tar road down to our house, set among tall pines along Valley Creek Road.

I was a country kid, not because I lived on a farm, but because my parents wanted land outside the city. Originally a mink farm, our property evolved into a tree farm with rabbits, birds, dogs, and cats as our animals. Deer, skunks, squirrels, and chipmunks roamed freely through our back prairie.

In the Valley we were used to hanging around with the closest neighbors we had. Where else would we go? So on this hot day, by mid-morning my sister, brother, and I had gathered the gang. And like a caucus, we were trying to agree on a plan for the day.

Chuck, fourteen, lived next door in a dilapidated farm-house, and was the oldest of the three Anderson boys being raised by their single mom, Alice, who was gifted with a scrappy spirit.

Every once in a while their dad, Mel, a TV repairman, drove over to visit, careful to leave before Alice came home from work. Chuck, tall, chiseled and handsome hadn't inherited these traits from his dad, especially not the swimmer's physique. (He didn't especially look like Alice either, come to think of it.)

Chuck suggested playing Hide and Seek, winked at my 13-year-old sister, Roxy, and laughed. At this, Roxy groaned, and suggested that we instead go through our box of raggedy dress up clothes, and rip and sew them into exotic outfits to wear to imaginary balls and ballets. Or if the boys wouldn't do that, maybe we could dress up like cowboys, Indians, and saloon girls.

"Yeah! I love those saloon girl outfits," Chuck said with another wink at Roxy. She scowled.

Those were the days when girls were supposed to be pretty, dumb, and non-athletic. Neither Roxy nor I went along with that cultural norm, and tried to be smart, fast, and ready for any adventure, but that also didn't always turn out well.

That morning, Chuck's younger brother, Brent, and my brother, Winky, both eight years old, had their own agenda, wanting to organize a baseball game, but then they decided it was too hot, and maybe fishing in May's Lake would be better.

Now things were getting political. Four boys versus the two of us. Roxy decided we needed to go find another girl, so we called Carol, who lived kitty-corner in the other direction, in the old converted schoolhouse.

Despite the addition of Carol, as Roxy and I feared, the boys took charge, our voices ignored. No big surprise.

Carol and I sat in a cool patch of clover looking for four-leafers. Better to look for luck where we might be able to find some.

Carol was my best friend, even though she was two years younger. If it were up to us, we would have chosen to play school, or take out my dad's sheet music and play. She took piano lessons, and even at age nine, could pick out simple accompanying melody and chords, as I sang hits from the 30's and 40's.

"It's gonna be the crick today," Chuck finally announced. "Only way to stay cool," he said with the finality of a baseball ump.

"Yah, Brent and I'll catch minnows," said Winky as he ran down the road to the bridge with Brent trailing after him. They were best friends – did everything together, from tossing a baseball back and forth for hours, to teasing the neighborhood dogs, to doing anything they could to disrupt the lives of girls like us.

Brent lived with two boys who had experienced everything a younger brother would want to know. I realize now that Winky, on the other hand, survived despite cohabiting with older sisters who constantly belittled his beloved sports, and who each set a scholarly example that was impossible for him to match. Unlike most of the neighborhood's dads, our dad was a musician, and he also wasn't much interested in sports.

Luckily, Mom was Winky's biggest fan. Maybe that was due to his sparkling brown eyes and impish grin. It was true, there didn't exist a cuter boy anywhere.

"Okay. I'll play tag in the crick as long as I don't get my hair wet!" answered Roxy. Our mother, who later became a beautician, had warned us over and over about our fine, thin hair, that didn't keep a curl or bounce back to normal after it got wet.

Carol and I nodded to one another. Water tag was a good enough idea. But first we played our own game, looking for shiny agates in the clear water.

Bolles Creek bubbled up through a limestone spring on top of Meisner's Hill, and even though it tumbled a mile to the bridge, it hadn't yet warmed a whit. There was no way for our skin to get used to this creek water that always felt like melting glaciers. That was part of the fun of it.

As soon as everyone arrived, Chuck chased his middle brother, Mark, under the bridge, and the game of tag got under way.

Mark, a fast and impulsive boy, was in my 5th grade class at Afton Lakeland Elementary School. Even though I tried to help him on the bus ride to school, he never could manage to finish his simple assignments. I watched daily as our teacher was tricked by his giggling and playing dumb, but somehow, his charm always worked for him.

Mark was what my mom called foxy. He had none of his older brother's good looks, only average, but his silly giggle got us all smiling. More than his giggle, he had a way of tipping his head sideways and opening wide his puddle-brown eyes, the way dogs do with their owners, a won't-you-take-care-of-me look that melted women. Well, it didn't work with me.

Mark also always wanted to play marbles, which I didn't understand, because he lost most of his marble collection to me. He was a terrible aim, just didn't take the time to position his fingers or think about where the marble might end up. It made no sense that he wanted to keep playing, and losing. I guess he thought he might win them back again, along with the rest of my collection of aggies, cat's eyes and even steelies my grandpa had made for me.

Grandpa Blomquist was a tool and die maker at a foundry in St. Paul. When I showed him my marble collection, he suggested it might be even more fun to play marbles with my classmates if I had steelies. The next time I saw him, to my amazement, he handed me a dozen steel marbles that I used to rack up a nearly unbeatable record.

When I think about Mark, in hindsight, it is clear he just wanted my attention. I would see him standing at recess or in the hall staring at me, with a grin plastered on his face. At that time, I thought his grin was nonsensical, but I think all he wanted was for me to acknowledge him.

We were both middle kids, and maybe that connected us. I got my attention from excelling in drama, band, scholastics, but I'm not sure Mark ever figured out how to get attention at all. At our 25th class reunion he gave me that same grin, but wouldn't come to me. He waited for me, as always, to find him in the crowd.

Anyway, there was Mark, alongside Brent, Roxy, Winky and me, in the cold creek. Our toes were immediately numbed in the water, so we lifted our feet high with every step, allowing our toes to momentarily roast in the summer's heat, before dipping down again.

The sounds of our echoing laughter, around and around like wind in a conch shell, sailed through the Valley. After a while, exhausted, our bodies still only partially accustomed to the cold, we crouched in a deep water hole.

All summer long we had watched the creek divert its swollen waters into an eddy as it approached the cement bridge. Now it had formed this deep sink, slightly warmer than the creek, yet still unbearably cold.

Winky yelled, "Bet I can stay in longer than any-a'-ya."

"Bet not," retorted Brent and Mark simultaneously.

"I don't bet," said Roxy, in her refined I-don't-get-my-hair-wet voice, "and I'll get out when I want to."

"Yah," I agreed with her and nodded. I hated that everything had to be a competition.

Winky doubled down on his bet. "Bet I stay in longer-'n Chuck. Otherwise, let him dunk me ... if he can."

"Ha! Not likely," said Chuck with a grin. "But I'll take the bet, 'cause I can't wait to hold that stinkin' little noggin of yers under 'til it turns blue!"

Okay, now it was serious. No one budged.

In those days no one wanted to be called a "pansy," especially the three girls. After all, we were country girls, and we all considered "being tough" a prized character trait. We didn't complain, didn't cry, loved getting dirty as much as any boy, and even dug worms, stuck them on hooks, and went fishing for fun.

Well, we expected this kind of brief pecker-check among the boys. It happened every time.

But it was worth it. There was a reason we girls stayed in the frigid creek, and dealt with the inanity of the boys.

We knew that at some point soon, Chuck, infinitely wise in our minds about the workings of the world, would recall one story after another, about hopping railroad cars as they slowed down next to the near-by Stillwater Prison's farm fields, and then riding them to White Bear and big city Minneapolis, about hitchhiking to St. Paul, and exploring its limestone caves tucked into the banks of the Mississippi, where gangsters made moonshine and hid from police.

It was worth shivering in this cold creek, no matter how blue our lips got.

But Chuck's best stories were about Old Annie, the reclusive, wrinkled old woman who lived just across the bridge from where we shivered in the creek.

We leaned in so we wouldn't miss a word.

He began each story the same way: "I woke at midnight, looked out my upstairs window, and watched her lantern glowin'."

He had regaled us with stories of watching Old Annie flay raccoons and rabbits, skinning them, then washing their pelts in this very creek, and hanging the hides out to dry on her twine clothesline.

Her shack had no running water, and no electricity for running motors or furnaces, so you could hear everything. And Chuck swore he had heard Old Annie talking to someone on those silent, cold nights when the moon was full, and he said her floorboards creaked as she rocked in her chair.

How did Chuck know about her rocking chair? How close had he come to her cabin?

More than once, Chuck told us he had seen the glow of a kerosene lantern at night. Of course, we still all had kerosene lamps for when the electricity went out from storms or tornadoes in the summer, but for Old Annie, that was all she used.

Scariest of all, Chuck told us he had heard faint, eerie tones of what sounded like an organ playing funereal songs late into the night.

In fact, just that morning, in the light of dawn, he had watched as a tiny, black-draped figure placed her high-buttoned black boots out to dry on her front door jamb.

We kids couldn't tell truth from tall tale. But Chuck sure did sound like he spoke from experience.

We knew Annie lived alone in the woods next to the creek. And we knew that no one but Chuck had ever seen her. It wasn't hard to believe his ramblings about her primitive way of living.

The Anderson home stood opposite a dirt drive, in those days used by trucks for picking up sand and gravel from an enormous gravel pit carved out of a sand hill out back. On its way, the road wound around a couple of mostly dry ponds (except in rainy years when they filled and we used them for skating rinks in winter), and then headed back toward the pit, where on weekends we'd spend hours searching for agates in the gravel.

Across the dirt drive, only a short distance from the creek bridge, a thin, bramble-edged path led to Annie Beutel's haggard shack. There was no driveway, and no car had ever been owned or used by the Beutels, as far as anyone remembered. And only Old Annie used the half-hidden path.

The deeper part of the creek, where we were sitting rapt, listening to Chuck, wasn't even 200 yards away from Old Annie's home, so our fear and trepidation was real.

Twice I'd followed the stream east and hidden behind a wide oak, just short of Annie's house, and peered around it to see the rotting timber roof that barely held up her cabin. Her place wasn't really big enough to call it a house, but Old Annie had lived there for decades, protected by the ancient, sagging box-elder trees.

———— ∘O∘ ————

Mother had warned me with a stern face, "She's a private person, Tunie."

Mom often called me Tunie, short for Petunia, and that was okay, because I knew Mom loved flowers. But when Roxy heard it she started calling me Loonie Toonie. It stuck for a long time. My sister was convinced I was looney, and it was her job in life to sophisticate me.

With a kind, yet sour face, Mom continued, "She lives in another world. You leave her alone. Hear?"

I figured that "other world" she lived in must have been a century behind me, but it existed right here, just down the creek, on the other side of the bridge, in my Valley, rubbing up against my nearly-sophisticated world.

We considered the 1950's to be modern times in Afton, Minnesota. All of our homes had a telephone, television, electric appliances, and most of us had indoor plumbing. But Old Annie's home had none of those conveniences.

Our neighbor, Betty Bradshaw, truly one of the sophisti-cates of the Valley, told us that Mr. Beutel, Annie's husband, had been a muskrat trapper, but he was long dead. Years of drought had sucked the remaining water on their property into fields of cattails, with only an occasional muskrat house reaching skyward, like a teepee out of the reeds.

All that remained of her dead trapper's paradise was her falling-down cabin, the cattails, the kerosene lamp, and Old Annie herself.

Chuck told us she was 100 years old, but I asked my Mom and she said, "I only saw her once, at Betty's house, and she asked me about my kin. She didn't know my dad, but knew his uncle. I'm pretty sure she's around 80 or so."

Chuck's stories had her visiting nightly with her husband's ghost, as he trapped long-tailed muskrats among the cat-tails, or later, as together they skinned and boiled the furry rodents in a witchy cauldron. With the Anderson's house's windows wide open on hot summer nights, Chuck swore he could smell the leather curing from across the street.

Each story ended the same. "Old Annie'll curse ya, if ya get too close."

Then he'd throw forward his head, closer to us, and whisper, "and watch out! Nobody knows her better'n me, 'cause anybody who gets closer to her place than my house, disappears."

Even though I loved the stories, most of the time I disregarded Chuck's warnings. He was prone to exaggerating, and I'd seen him hang around with a gang of shady characters. So I took it all with a grain of salt.

Lately, though, I'd been thinking more and more about Old Annie. When I'd been down playing at the creek, I'd never seen anyone enter her house, or even her yard. Even my mother, Dorothy, who was known in the Valley for checking on all its vulnerable residents, didn't visit Annie. How could that be?

Maybe Chuck was right. Maybe this old woman who lived two houses down from us really was a witch. That would explain things, wouldn't it?

While we all shivered in the creek's cold waters, we jumped as the Anderson's dogs began to bark loudly. That signaled either they were chasing squirrels, or they detected the approach of human or animal.

I leapt up the bank on my almost-numb limbs, jumping high enough to avoid touching the stinging nettles. I squinted my eyes, and was just able to make out a black outline in the distance, moving slowly towards us.

Could it be? The vague image of a tiny woman, no bigger than I was, came into view. From behind my hiding place, I watched as she approached, and I took notice of her white, wispy hair pulled tightly beneath a black bonnet tied with a bow beneath her chin. I had seen pioneer women wearing bonnets like that on Wild West cowboy shows, but no one wore them any more.

The ancient woman's pale wrinkled face displayed skin pulled tightly over cheekbones and chin, her mouth taut, showing no sign of friendliness. Her full-length black dress, entirely lined with tiny silk buttons down its front, was smaller than a size one, and could not have been found in any local stores, or even in the Sears-Roebuck catalog, but had to have been hand-sewn.

Beneath it all was a well-worn pair of high-buttoned leather boots. Probably the ones Chuck had seen drying on Old Annie's doorstep. This woman, emerging from the past, was marching straight into our lives.

"Git up here. Quick!" I whisper-shouted to the others, waving my hands to get their attention. No one else had noticed the dogs, and no one noticed me.

I didn't want Annie to hear, so I ran down the bank again and said a little louder, "It's Annie! She's comin'! She's in all black. Teeny thing. Can't be anybody else! I know it. Ya gotta git up here now!"

We scooted up the bank into the ditch and hid behind a couple of huge, wide-trunked burr oaks, hoping the old woman didn't see us staring, or notice us at all.

"Hurry, Winky and Brent! Stop lookin' for water spiders and git up here before she can see ya!"

As this apparition from the past came toward us, my eyes fixated on her child-sized, tight, black leather boots. No one I knew had boots like that, not even my grandmother, but I knew settlers had worn them, because I had read about it in my favorite book, Little House on the Prairie.

Chuck had called Old Annie a witch, but she appeared to me more like a harmless ghost. Her skin had no color, not even a flush from the day's heat. How could it be that an eighty-year-old woman had walked two miles from downtown Afton on a 98 degree day in July in those tight boots, in that black, full-length dress, and that bonnet?

Winky giggled. Roxy kicked him in the shin to shut him up.

There she was, Old Annie, clutching a bag from the grocery store. It meant that her errand had indeed required a four-mile round trip, in those tight boots.

I knew she could see all seven of us peering out from the woods. Nevertheless, she looked straight ahead, with eyes as silent and sour as shriveled gooseberries, staring into the beyond.

I never saw her again. None of us did.

———— ∘O∘ ————

The following summer we heard that Betty Bradshaw resettled Annie Beutel into a nursing home across the

St. Croix River in Hudson. I was still afraid to go near her shack, but sometimes I'd stand at a distance, in the cold creek, and feel it taunting me to come nearer.

Chuck finally led the expedition. "I got a great idea! Let's put Old Annie's stuff on. She's got corsets and mink stoles in there. And I wanna hear Roxy play that old pump organ."

I gasped, quietly. Chuck must have been there, touching her things. How else would he have known about mink stoles? The thought of it gave me the creeps! I wasn't sure I wanted to go, but I had a taunting, ceaseless gnawing in my gut.

Something pulled me closer. I needed to know more about her. So I slowly followed the others down the overgrown path.

Chuck led us to a broken window, where he smashed out the remaining glass, and crawled in.

One by one the others followed.

I finally squeezed my wiry frame through the empty window of Old Annie's tiny cabin, and was immediately overcome with the heavy scent of mold. With clouds covering the sun, and no light inside, at first I saw only vague shadows.

My own breath scared me, and the planked floor creaked beneath the weight of my bare feet. A mesh of dust and spiderwebs caught my face, and before proceeding I wiped my eyes and hair free of the dirty silk, hoping no spiders had landed. Looking up, I noticed hundreds of dense cob-webs seeming to hold the corners of the ceiling together like some primitive glue.

Then the music began, faint at first, with increasing volume. No, I tell myself, this can't be real.

I soon recognized the eerie tonal melody of "Moonlight Sonata" as it vaporized into the damp air.

Then I saw her, atop the dusty, three clawed stool, her feet pumping and fingers sliding over the yellowed ivory keys of a wooden reed organ. The small hairs of my arm stood at attention. It was Roxy, playing her favorite memorized sonata on the abandoned instrument.

At age 13, my sister had already attended the Minneapolis Symphony and gone to see every traveling ballet troupe that came through the Twin Cities. Few could compete with Roxy's grace and strength when she danced en pointe. I was clumsy in comparison. Not only did she dance, and play the piano and French Horn, but she also knew how to sew, really well, and a blue State Fair ribbon for her 4-H sewing project hung on her wall.

But that day, Roxy showed off what a great musician can do with phrasing, volume, and mystique. I'll never forget the haunting sound.

As I was listening, my bare foot slid on a massive pile of fur lying in a heap on the warped floor. It looked like a pile of dead rats. I immediately leaped backwards.

"Don't ruin those!" Chuck called, "They're mink, and probably worth a bundle!"

I knew better. Mom had a mink stole, and these were nothing like it. This was a cruder fur, long-haired, thinner and not as soft. These had been wild animals, like the ones I had seen hundreds of times swimming around the huge stick-mounds in the swampy areas around May's Lake. These were old, moldy, disintegrating muskrat hides.

My own mother and father, as part of their whirlwind romance, had bought acreage and moved out to the Valley a decade earlier to start a mink farm, hoping to cash in on the expensive hides. But soon after, a mink bit my mother, and that ended the whole venture. We stayed on the land nonetheless, and planted pine trees instead.

The Beutels had bet on a different pelt. Muskrat hides brought a much lower price, and were not farmed, but trapped in the wild, and were used for muskrat coats in the Roaring Twenties, but that market had dried up during the Depression.

We found more stoles stored in drawers in the dark cabin. They mostly fell apart in our hands as we draped them dramatically across our shoulders.

I was appalled when Mark found Old Annie's cotton long johns, and with delight held them up, giggling. Then he found a corset, tiny, but sturdy — made of bone. I'd seen ladies on television westerns wiggling into corsets like that, but I'd never seen one first hand.

I grabbed it away from him and wrapped it around my own waist, pulling the drawstring tight. "I take back everything I ever said about wanting to wear those gorgeous Miss Kitty dresses. This is torture!"

Chuck hooted. Then his face turned to stone, and he whispered, "Let's make these clothes into a dummy."

"Yeahhhh." Everyone let out a collective affirmation.

First the boys filled the corset with old cotton socks and frayed towels. Roxy found Annie's long, black, pioneer dress and pulled it over the humble stuffed corset, carefully buttoning dozens of dark satin buttons. I searched the room for her high top shoes, but couldn't find them.

I finally noticed a small pointed toe sticking out from under her faded, but apparently home-made quilt. It was patched together from various calico prints and hand quilted in a "crazy quilt" pattern, just like the ones my grandma was teaching me to make.

Kneeling in the dust, I pulled the old boots out from their hiding place, along with an array of crisp beetle carcasses and dead flies. I brought the boots over to the dummy, and pinned them to the bottom edge of the skirt.

Carol finished the dummy of Old Annie's clothes by tying her black bonnet onto a wadded head made of towels.

I suddenly wondered what Annie was wearing at the nursing home, since we had all her clothes. These were her high-mileage walking boots, and her black mourning dress.

At the nursing home, did they have her wearing a hospital gown, even though she wasn't sick? Did they make her wear a sweatshirt and pants, as if those kinds of clothes would feel comfortable to her? Could she see out a window from her room and pretend she still lived in the woods?

Did they feed her fresh trout and wild onions and blackcap jam? And was it ever silent there?

When the dummy was finished, we all stared at it, transfixed, not knowing what to do next. I thought it should sit on Old Annie's rocker, staring out the window into the yard, but Chuck, excited by the possibilities, had another idea.

Chuck led all of us, including Roxy who was carrying the dummy, back out the broken window. We stopped in the shade of one of the ancient box-elder trees, in what used to be Annie's yard. Then Chuck instructed us to wait outside while he retrieved something from his house. On the way he mumbled something about how, "it would be perfect."

We swatted mosquitoes and traded Old Annie stories while we waited. I was just happy to be outdoors. The cool breeze and shade helped me relax. We could breathe again, freed from the decaying air inside the small cabin.

Chuck arrived with a rope. "We'll hang her in effigy," he announced. "Then she'll never bother us again."

The others jumped up and down, cheering and yelling wildly, "Never! Never again!"

Together we hoisted the dummy up and into the noose.

I stood silent, a knot forming in my stomach. I had learned it was as bad to think evil thoughts as to act on them, and here we were, doing both.

All I could say to myself was, "Forgive us, Annie. We ought to know better."

We hanged Old Annie's dummy there, her black high-buttoned shoes kicking in the summer breeze.

Her towel head, in its black bonnet, tipped to one side, as if resting.

A mix of summer heat, wild feelings, and bubbling guilt led the three younger boys to punch at each other and giggle. But the giggling abruptly stopped, as we all felt an eerie, heavy silence spread.

A vacuum like the absence of sound after a thunderstorm, before insects and birds recover enough to chatter.

———— ∘O∘ ————

The next week a Washington County Sheriff's car drove into our driveway. Our family wasn't one that ever came into contact with the law, so when the sheriff's deputy came to our door, we all crowded around to find out what was going on.

Mother answered the door with a concerned look.

"Sorry to bother you, ma'am. Just wonderin' if you've seen anything strange around Annie Beutel's place lately?"

My sister and I exchanged wide-eyed glances. Then Roxy took hold of Winky's arm and my hand, and started backing us up, hoping the deputy could not see the expressions on our faces. We retreated to the kitchen where we could hear, but not see the interaction.

"No, but I never go that way myself," Mother replied. She didn't walk anywhere, so she wouldn't have seen anything by the creek. And Annie was not on her list of shut-ins that she visited.

The officer replied matter-of-factly, "Seems she died last week in a Hudson nursing home."

"I'm so sorry to hear that," replied Mother with genuine concern.

The officer wasn't finished. "Thing is, her relatives wanted an old pump organ she had in her shack over there," he said as he pointed down the street toward her shack. "But the organ's gone."

"Oh no!" said Mother. "I didn't even know she had relatives."

"Well, yes, she did, and they want to know who took the organ. Do you have any idea?"

"No. We have our own organ, a Hammond. My husband's a musician, you know."

"Yah, I know Johnny. I see him sometimes bass fishin' on the St. Croix."

Mom nodded, and added genuinely, "I can't think of anyone who'd take somethin' like that."

"I just came from over there, and the window's been broke into, and the place's been vandalized." He shook his head. "And the darndest thing ... there's old clothes, towels and rope layin' in the mud under the old box-elder, and I'd swear it looks like a body."

"Oh, my!" Mother replied.

"Well, if you hear anything, Dorothy, call me. And, thanks a lot."

Mother closed the door with a concerned look, and we all scattered.

It wasn't hard to figure who'd probably taken the organ, and sold it. I know, you're not supposed to accuse anyone without giving them a fair trial, but Chuck had boasted the day before about a new leather jacket he'd just bought.

Well, as far as I was concerned, the pump organ was probably in the hands of someone who would enjoy it, and keep it from rotting. So I figured it wasn't so bad. That's what I told myself, anyway.

And it seemed to me that Old Annie's relatives could have been a little more interested in her a lot sooner than after her death. I mean, was she out there completely alone?

I was worried about my complicity in the stunt. I had been just as excited as everyone else about entering someone else's house, going through her things, hanging the dummy, calling her a witch, and treating Old Annie as an alien. I hadn't done anything to stop it.

Was I still a good person?

I had helped keep it a secret. A secret – wasn't that proof itself that something was wrong?

The officer had said that Old Annie had died the previous week. But which day, what time? We never asked.

To this day, I believe it happened in that moment, when Old Annie's head hung down, and her black boots kicked freely, as she swung from the noose on the box-elder tree, in the clearing by the cold, cold creek, as the swamp inhaled dust, mold, and muskrat rot …

... held it in silence ...

... then exhaled its cleansing breath through the corn-silk hair of its children.

Timeless

Summers seemed eternal
the year my lithe body
turned nine.

Solitaire and scribbling
within the lines
of coloring books

took up time,
but not easily,
so I wandered worn paths of deer

and raccoon, following
their lead
anywhere,

and found sprays of wild
black raspberries,
stayed all day,

picked amidst the thorns,
then traipsed home
with cheeks

and hands stained
from berries
and blood.

Now I follow paths
on yellow paper
pads

finding phrases of wild
description. I pick
and choose

words amidst confusion,
slowing time
enough

to write them
into poems arriving
home

with tattooed fingers
stained from ink
and age.

chapter 2
trusting

Butterfly Weed
[*Asclepias tuberosa*]

L ow pressure air, and its musk-filled wind, blew through the Valley on 08/08/08, the day my mother died. The day of Lion's Gate. The day of lucky eights.

Thank you for the present I most wanted in the world.

I found the inscription that sad day, as my sister-in-law and I went through Mother's belongings. It had been written by my dad to her after Winky was born, carefully tucked inside the cover of her treasured, white leather, Eastern Star Bible. The words whiplashed me.

"Most wanted." What about Roxy and me? His firstborn daughters?

My dad had already been gone for 48 years on that day. Why did those words anger me so much? I knew my dad had loved me. I could tell he loved me when I had sat in his lap, and laughed, as we simultaneously shouted the correct answers in front of *Name That Tune*.

And yet, something about that inscription made my heart bleed, as if there was more to that story. Much more.

I was a girl, and what did he think I could accomplish? I felt rejected again.

I tried to imagine the 1940's male stereotypes that he lived with. But then again, I knew his step-mother and sister were both college graduates and scholars. I knew that his biological mother had been a concert pianist. And I knew that as a child we would take Sunday afternoon rides to Minnesota colleges, showing us where we might attend some day, because he had made it known that high school was not the end, and that we were expected to go to college, and maybe even graduate school.

So many questions.

———— ◦ O ◦ ————

"Ha! Ha! You're not the baby anymore!" Roxy sneered.

Just shy of five years old in 1950, she had crawled into the front seat of the car where we waited. Already understanding family hierarchy, I, at three years and 45 days of age, was now being replaced.

I squirmed in the back seat of the navy blue '48 Nash, peering out its high rear window. It was one of those boxy cars, with narrow windows, and I felt claustrophobic.

It had already been a couple of hours, and Roxy and I had waited patiently in the July heat. Even with the two front windows open, we were sweating and itching to get out. But when Dad says STAY, you stay in the car until he returns.

It wasn't unusual to wait in the car back then. And of course, children couldn't go into hospitals, so we waited outside. Even when Mother went to grocery stores or pharmacies, she would often leave us in the car. Because of convenience, I suppose.

That day our Nash was parked in a small lot outside Lakeview Memorial Hospital, a tall brick building overlooking Stillwater's Lily Lake, as Roxy and I waited to see our new-born brother. This is, in fact, my oldest memory. Later in life I'd live in a ranch style house overlooking that same lake, where I transplanted ferns from the surrounding woods, and I would ride bikes with my children to Mom's house, out in the country.

They called my sweet-smelling, three-day-old brother, John Leigh. But Dad immediately christened him Winky, for what, to us, seemed like no reason at all.

Did he wink? Did he blink? I think Dad just liked the sound of it.

Roxy called him "Mama's little man-child." And from the moment of his birth, Winky, in fact, became both Mama and Daddy's little manchild.

I was the unseen middle one, not the eldest, or the baby, or a treasured son, but more like a middle name that no one uses except when their identity is questioned. Like my own middle name, Marie, which for my generation, was and is vanilla, standard, and normal.

On a late November day, in the same year, I had my second memory. I stood barefoot in the kitchen helping Mother feed oranges, apples, and cranberries into an old meat grinder.

In my day, there were no fast-food chains. When you wanted meat from a farm, you would get butchered live-stock. If you wanted hamburger, you used one of these meat grinders to grind it yourself.

This silver device looked kind of medieval, with iron teeth, and a mechanism to force the meat into the cogs, tearing fat from muscle and pulverizing it. This grinder was made of heavy cast iron, with a long, curved, wooden handle, and a vice to bind it to the countertop.

We used our grinder a little differently than most, to make Minnesota country relish, tearing flesh from cranberries, apples, and oranges. When we added sugar, and maybe a little cinnamon, it created the most wonderful side dish for our Thanksgiving dinner. My mom had learned this technique from Grandma, and it wouldn't have been Thanksgiving without it.

My job was to stuff quartered pieces of fruit into the mouth of the large grinder, holding my hand over the top to shield their escape. As Mother cranked the handle, the red-orange juice ran down the cast iron grinder, dripped along the cabinet door, and followed the laws of gravity into an ever-growing puddle on the floor.

I had earlier discovered a reddish crack under my fourth toe. It usually only hurt me when I tried to lift my toe too high. And of course, we went barefoot around the house. We went barefoot everywhere!

As I stepped into the acid pool of orange and cranberry juice, puddled on the floor beneath the grinder, it filled that crack in my toe, and shocked my body as if I'd stepped on a frayed electrical cord. Like a match struck and ignited, the acid burned. Its stabbing pain sent me screeching out the kitchen door.

I ran up the back hill, past my best climbing tree, a leafless box-elder, and finally stopped on a patch of frozen ground that only partially numbed my throbbing toe.

It was in that moment of relief, on that hill, my bare foot on the snow, when I saw the secret door.

I was even with the rooftop of our house, looking down from this knoll, seeing clouds of smoke rising from our brick chimney. The neglected gutters were all clogged with soggy and frozen fallen leaves. But then I saw something I never expected to see. My eyes fixed on this small triangular door, just above the lower roof, where it opened into a hidden gable. I'd never seen this door before, because it was visible only from this very spot, this back knoll of autumn-brown prairie grasses, black cap briars, and vetch. My knoll. This frozen patch of ground.

I couldn't claim much as my own. I wasn't the eldest child, or the youngest. I wasn't the wished-for boy. I wasn't the prettiest, smartest, or even loudest. I shared an already too-small room with my sister, who had successfully convinced Mother that she would never, under any circumstances, hurt or tease me, no matter how much I complained that she did. So I created my own world.

Since no one else wanted the back knoll I discovered up on the wild prairie, above the house, I claimed it as my own. As we grew older, Roxy wouldn't even think of going there, because her fancy shoes got tangled in vetch vines, and the hundreds of pollen-collecting bumblebees circling around their purple flowers scared her. And Winky only wanted to spend time on mowed lawns playing football and baseball. So, thankfully, my siblings would never know about my treasures. They didn't even notice the intricate weaving of vines and wildflowers, the fox dens, and deer trails up there.

And they didn't know about the hidden door.

I imagined it contained treasures from the 100 previous owners of this old farmhouse: priceless relics, spinning wheels, butter churns, lace curtains, porcelain dolls, and maybe even old money.

We knew there were 100 owners listed on the deed, who had all tried, and failed, to farm these sandy acres. And I was the only one who knew.

No matter what season, I'd trek up the back knoll, to the prairie and sand hills that stretched for miles and miles beyond it. In winter, locals took a well-trodden trail to the ice skating swamp, but none wandered off course to look for paw prints in the snow, or pussy willows at the first sign of spring.

I learned to discover the earliest crocuses around Easter-time, and then trillium, hepatica, May flowers, and trout lilies. Then finally, around Mother's Day, waxy, golden cowslips. Treasures unseen by anyone but me and the wild creatures.

In May I hunted elusive stalks of wild asparagus. Mother steamed and creamed their tender tips in her family's German style, and served them on toast.

In June, I broke through a jungle of vetch, in order to access an enormous patch of wild strawberries in the valley below the knoll. I picked for hours, accumulating quart after quart of tiny, extra-sweet wild berries, needed for jam.

These were wondrous hours of sunshine, accompanied by friendly bands of clicking dragonflies. I expertly flicked off each berry stem with my fingernail, before its flesh fell into the yellow Tupperware pitcher. That way, the berries needed only to be washed clean of an occasional bug or grain of sand before being boiled into jam, with a little sugar and pectin, poured into Mason jars, and stored in our cool root cellar.

July brought "blackcaps", our name for the black raspberries of Minnesota. These seedy cousins of the red berries grew wild, mostly next to deer paths and fences. Usually swarms of mosquitoes, little black flies, and thistles protected them. Even though Roxy and her friends considered them too uncultivated, they were my favorite. In my wild-taste, Mother's garden-grown raspberries were good, but blackcaps have an untamed flavor that begged me to collect them, despite heat, thorns, humidity, and even snakes.

Gooseberries, blackberries, and chokecherries ripened in August, and also made good jam, though not as sweet as raspberry. If we cooked and canned more than we could spread on pancakes, toast, and ice cream, over the long winter ahead, we'd wrap them up with a red bow and give jars away at Christmas.

Wild bittersweet berries lured me deeper into September's cool woods. I found a few isolated trees whose branches were gnarled with this exotic, woody vine, filled with small, bright orange berries. I learned at a young age that bittersweet was poisonous, so there would be no jam there. But I still loved them. I'd arrange fiery stems in a waterless vase, and the brilliant berries soon dried to grace our table all winter.

Year after year, after each adventure, harvest or pilgrimage up to the prairie, or woods, I would climb the small hill behind our white house, and stare at the hidden door, dreaming. I thought up countless ways to get up to it, open the door, and finally claim my secret treasures.

My favorite box-elder tree grew not far from the edge of the roof. Once, I tried climbing it, with hopes of jumping from the tree to the roof. While perched on the outer limb my fears crept in, and after a few minutes I realized I didn't have enough monkey muscles, or squirrel brain, to accomplish a leap that far.

I even thought about bringing out a tall chair for Roxy to stand on, so I could mount her shoulders and climb onto the roof. But I quickly changed my mind. She would want to claim the treasures behind the wooden door for herself.

Then, one June, shortly after my tenth birthday, I took out my old tennis shoes and trekked out over the muddy knoll, and into the spring prairie, searching for new discoveries.

As I returned home, I noticed Mother standing on a six-foot ladder, reaching her lean arms up to wash the outside of the picture window that looked over the Valley. My dad didn't do jobs like this because he was always busy, or sleeping. He held down at least two jobs, or a job and school, both which required a lot of driving time from our rural home. Mom never questioned being in charge of all the odd jobs around the house and property, a true farmer's daughter.

We didn't own a ladder, so I figured Mother must have borrowed it from the Meisners across the road. From up on the knoll I watched her as she slowly backed down the rungs, carrying her bucket and rags, storing them by the back door, and going inside to prepare lunch.

Filled with anticipation, I seized the moment, ran to the back of the house, and dragged the heavy wooden ladder around the corner. I set the ladder's feet squarely in a lily-of-the-valley patch, and climbed the steep steps upward to the gently sloping roof. I flopped my body onto the tar shingles, far above the ground, and negotiated my legs off the ladder and onto the roof.

A rush of joy flushed my face as I viewed the distant horizon from this new vantage point. I could see my wild berry patch in the distance, and trace lines of deer trails leading to places beyond where I had ever explored.

I stood up, stooped forward on the steep roof, and inched up the steep shingles carefully, placing my hands on the edge of the black tar shingles ahead of me, for balance. I felt strange walking with slanted feet; my muddy, worn-soled tennis shoes barely gripping the sloped surface.

The triangular door was now straight ahead of me. My secret door. Wooden and painted white, its paint had partially chipped off. As I inched closer, I noticed it was missing something else, too. A doorknob. How would I open it?

I stuck my fingernails into the black-gapped space between the door and house, and pulled. It wouldn't budge. I pulled harder, until my fingernails felt as if they were lifting from my skin. It hurt, but I wasn't going to stop until I got that door open.

Then a quick, sharp stab hit my neck. It hurt worse than pulled-out fingernails. It hurt worse than cranberry juice in my toe. One shocking, painful needle, and then another in my arm. I looked up in confusion, and saw a round, gray, foreboding wasp's nest in the crook of the roof gable. We'd all been stung by wasps and knew how they took out their revenge. I saw its swarming residents moving toward me with lightning speed, and circling my head.

The pain intensified as my arm and neck swelled up like a water balloon filling with water. I whimpered and held my arm, at the same time trying to keep my balance, swat away wasps, and retrace my steps down the slanted rooftop to the tip of the ladder.

The ladder! Where is it? Am I in the right place? It wasn't lying on the ground. It couldn't have fallen, because it was nowhere in sight. I could hear Mother inside the kitchen rattling pots and pans, so I knew she hadn't taken it for window cleaning. Then it dawned on me.

"Roxy, you creep. Git that ladder back here. Now!"

I screamed hysterically. "I know you did it. Gimme that ladder. Winky, help! I need the ladder. I gotta get down!" They both appeared within seconds, laughing so hard they fell into the lily-of-the-valley patch, holding their stomachs and patting each other on the back.

When Mother appeared, her face taut with pursed lips and lowered eyebrows, all laughing stopped. So did the screaming.

"What's going on here? They can hear you all the way to Afton!"

Between my sobbing and screaming I said, "Wasps ... stingin' me. Get me outta here! I need a ladder!"

Mother knew who the main culprit was and turned her I-mean-business eye toward my sister. "Roxanne, where is the ladder? Get it NOW!"

Without answering, she and Winky slipped around the corner of the house and retrieved the ladder.

"You too?" She asked, looking at Winky.

"Yup. Sorry." Winky tried to suppress a smile. "But it was so funny."

"Not so funny if it was you getting stung! Now put that ladder up against the house, and the two of you go to your rooms!"

The ladder was carefully raised.

I was lowered.

Mounds of baking soda paste were slathered on my wounds. And not another word was said.

Mother and I were the only ones to eat our chicken noodle soup that day, as my sister and brother thought about their "shenanigans". The stinging still hurt, but it was kind of cozy, just Mom and me at the table.

Things changed that day. Not for the wild places whose soft deer paths still lead in and out. Not for the vetch and bumblebees and wild berries that cover the prairie. Not for my favorite box-elder tree, that just keeps growing. Not even for my brother and sister, who continued to lead their own lives.

That day everything changed for me, how I looked at people, and unknown places, hard-to-get-at-places, and deserted areas. While they still sounded the call of adventure, I now felt a ghostly, different uneasiness about them, and a lingering gnawing about whom I could trust.

So what about the little, magical, triangular door? To this day, it's never been opened. When Mother came to visit years later, and I asked what was inside the door, she said hesitantly, as if she didn't understand why I was asking, "I don't know. There was no doorknob, so I never opened it."

She had lived in that house for over sixty years. I can only guess that she thought it was just an empty space.

After Mother died I realized that none of us had ever looked inside that door, despite the fact that in later years both my sister and my mother owned antique stores, and could have rescued any treasures that were hidden there.

Mother and Father are gone, and now the house is too.

The new owner, despite saying that she would reuse the Swedish stone foundation and wooden floors, bulldozed the house to the ground.

Any answers are now buried in the sand.

The back knoll, shaded by my ragged box-elder, is still covered by a sprawling garden of perennials among the stones. Iris, phlox, johnny-jump-ups, and daisies bloom without need of a gardener.

These forgotten flowers, untamed, have gone wild.

Grounding

I wrote Valley Creek into my will
and those left behind will
pour my dust there, and it will
travel east to the untamed St. Croix, join
the Mississippi past apple orchards
on the cliffs of Point Douglas, flow
rhapsodically past Minneapolis mills,
through canals and cities,
to finally enter the oceans of the earth.

These ancient waterways
bubble up times past when I searched
our birch and cedar woods to find
this old meandering stream full
of red banded agates, thickets of
thorny black capped berries,
soft deer tracks in the sand, and
trailing orange bittersweet in the treetops.
Pockets full of treasures, I followed the creek
home, arriving late, unnoticed.

Get along home, Cindy, Cindy.

I see in my mind that creek –
how it leapfrogs down the north hill,
juts east under the bridge
toward the rising sun,
heading with the brilliance of childhood
toward the tannin-toned St. Croix.
I know all other places by this flow,
this momentum, this heart map.

chapter 3
translucence

Petunia
[*Petunia violacea*]

A hundred owners in a hundred years.
One hundred owners, would you believe it?
That's what was listed on the deed when my dad, red-cheeked and newly married to my mom, bought a little white clapboard house and farm in the Valley.

They really thought they could grow rich from farming mink. That was the dream. Ours was the latest of a hundred names of those who had tried and failed to make a living from that land.

I imagine what it must have been like for the other 99 families, skimping on food to save for seed, and plowing up deep vines of prairie vetch to make rows in the soil.

But this was soil that had little in it but limestone sand. When it rained too little, the water seeped away down their sand hills. When it rained too much, the seedlings, having only these grains of sand to cling to, would lose their grip, washing out and dying.

Heartbroken, each farmer would sell the land and our little white house to the next hopeful farmer.

To be honest, our Valley, with its sand hills and gullies, was never meant to sustain agriculture. The region's real farms were south of us, towards Hastings and Miesville, where the land was flat and the soil black, where my Grandpa Knoblauch farmed, and where my mom and her brothers had learned the value of hard work.

But here in our Valley, only two plants really thrived, poison ivy and pine trees.

Then, here and there, where they could gain a foothold, a variety of thorny, wild berry brambles scattered themselves about, and mice ran freely from one plant to another, food for hawks and snakes in summer.

Our neighbors' yards were littered with large deciduous trees, mostly oak and maple, whose leaves changed to burnt orange, red, and amber each October. But their abandoned fields, and ours, grew mostly tall prairie grasses and tangled purple vetch.

That was it.

Valley Creek was the name settlers gave this land between Afton to the south, with its population of 100 hearty souls in the 1950's, and Interstate Highway 12 (later known as Interstate 494) to the north. The highway headed west, to the cities of St. Paul and Minneapolis, and to the east, over the river, to Wisconsin.

Valley Creek was a perfect name for this stretch of land, traversed by fingers of streams, and resultant valleys. To its east the Valley bordered crooked State Highway 95, running along the wild and beautiful St. Croix River, that in the previous century had transported enormous white pine logs and their log-rolling lumberjacks to downstream lumber mills.

On the west, the Valley's rim was outlined by a gravel road, spanning a high glacial ridge that passed by several, enormous Indian mounds that seemed to appear out of nowhere. At the time, everyone thought they were ancient burial grounds, but archaeologists never discovered any remains. It turns out they were actually high hills built by local Native American tribes in order to observe the river, which they saw as sacred, from a distance.

Early colonists from the East Coast tried to farm this land, with their European methods, but their approach was never successful. These sand hills have never been hospitable to such crops.

On the western ridge, one small brick church still stands. It housed a strict German Lutheran congregation that served the Valley's first poor, prairie farmers. The land on this western prairie was more suited to farming, and the immigrant Germans with their strong work ethic eked out a living there.

In my childhood, two one-room, white clapboard school-houses stood as well. But after "consolidation" of schools in 1953, these buildings were sold and transformed into homes.

The forerunners of our creeks first cut through the hills when the last glacier retreated 10,000 years ago. The departing mass of ice deposited its sand and gravel into several long ridges, forming valleys close to the river, a few miles to the east.

Unlike our Valley, the southern half of Minnesota boasted southern prairie, where fertile rolling hills would be interrupted by an occasional oak, scattered in fields populated by black and white spotted dairy cattle. The state's northern wetlands were known for iron ore exploration and tourism.

Valley Creek, much like a middle child, sits at the boundary between the two, and its geography is more like the reclusive, green, rolling mountains of Arkansas or West Virginia. Maybe that's why I've always felt so close to the folk music of the Appalachians, songs about valleys and hollows, and people left behind.

Years later, when I first attended university in Boston, I tried to teach my New York roommate how to pronounce Valley Creek like a proper Minnesotan.

I'd say, "It's 'crick', as in 'pick-a-tick-off-quick'."

She sneered, and said it was ignorant to pronounce "creek" as "crick". I didn't say it, but I'm sure she had no idea how "ignorant" my Minnesota ears interpreted her flattened New York "a"s either. The argument never went away because there were words in every one of my sentences that bothered her. The next year I chose a kinder roommate.

I still say "Valley Crick" to this day, but you can say it how you like.

———— ₒOₒ ————

No one I knew resembled the fictional families we saw on 1950's television. But my parents might have been another level of out-of-the-ordinary.

My father, John, slept until late in the day, having arrived home from work at two in the morning. We didn't dare wake him until noon, even on weekends.

Dad wore a trimmed mustache, smelled of original, musky Old Spice, and his gray-blue eyes sparkled out above his wide Scandinavian cheekbones, surrounded by pale, translucent skin that showed off the spider-veins in his face.

He was overweight, and he knew it. He carried 210 pounds on his five-foot-ten-inch frame. At home, in his sleeveless white t-shirt and colorful plaid shorts, you could see the varicose veins in his pale, hairy legs. That, and his bulging midsection, were hard to ignore. But he knew how to cover all of that up, and when he dressed for work, donning his bow-tie and suit, he looked dashing, charming, and the height of sophistication.

John Gustave Adolph Blomquist was an intense, charismatic man, who felt deeply about music, and equally deeply about everything else. I could tell when to stay away from him by the escalating tone of his voice. He displayed a peculiar tensing of the left side of his chin, as he would descend into anger. I remember he was harsher on Winky than on Roxy and me. Maybe he was trying to initiate him into the world of men.

Silence was strictly enforced on those mornings as Father slept. He also insisted on absolute quiet on Sundays at noon, as he listened to live radio broadcasts of the Mormon Tabernacle Choir, singing their lush choral arrangements, or the Gunsmoke radio drama. I particularly remember that he loved to hear the gallant French horns portraying the galloping of cowboys' horses. As we all gathered in the living room, we could see his joy. Dad had been trained in classical music, taking lessons at Hamline University and learning to play their cathedral organ with multiple stops and registers.

My dad emoted his way through the world, before that was en vogue, for men. Sure, I remember his angry tirades, but also his great warmth. Most of the time I was scared to do anything wrong. But at the same time, I always sought out his bear hugs, and there was no greater joy than sitting on his lap, with his thumb smoothing back and forth over my delicate hand, as if I was the one he cared about most in the world.

But Dad was only at home for short periods of time. In his absence, Mother took the role of executive director in our house. She became an expert repair person, taking care of not only the cars, but also the mowing, raking, yardwork, painting, wall-papering, and every other odd job, alongside her nearly full-time work as a nightclub waitress and hostess.

Dorothy Elvira Knoblauch grew up on a farm, and she would make sure that we would not be run-of-the-mill farmers' children.

Instead of cattle or horses, we kept rabbits, birds in a cage, cats, dogs, and an occasional guinea pig. And instead of the endless fields of corn her two brothers maintained, she cultivated only a one-acre garden on the side lot.

Mother took the few dollars we saved on produce, and used them to introduce us to the cultured world. She not only bought us tickets to the ballet and the Minneapolis Symphony Orchestra, she also paid for our music, ballet, and tap lessons. Both she and Dad encouraged us to look beyond the Valley in every possible way.

I realize now, I actually didn't see my mother. She was always around, but I don't remember ever really looking at her. I could tell you that she wore cat's eye glasses, and that I never really liked them. She was slight, somewhat tall, and had beautiful, naturally curly hair, which had a red-cocoa-brown color to it that matched her eyes. But that is all I can think to describe.

Mother didn't do much touching. Hugs were rare. Kisses were non-existent. But she did drill proper phrases into our brains.

"Use your head."

"Do what needs to be done."

"If you can't say something good, don't say it at all." This last one is probably why she never said anything about her own childhood.

She was our mother-without-a-history, always busy.

Nevertheless, she inspired us to become whomever we wanted to be. She loved saying, with dead seriousness, "Remember, we all pull our pants on one leg at a time."

———— ▫O▫ ————

Looking back, I consider myself lucky to have had interesting characters living in our Valley, all of whom cared for one another.

My friend Carol's father, Don, worked in the big city for the telephone company, and woke up extremely early on weekends to cook homemade, yeasty cinnamon rolls for his neighbors. I loved staying overnight there with Carol, and waking in the morning to the smell of yeast rising, sweet cinnamon filling the air, and sugar frosting melting onto just-out-of-the-oven rolls. My stomach growled in anticipation.

The Whites and Nelsons let everyone enter May's Lake through their properties, for swimming and fishing, even providing the fishing boat. I remember many Sunday nights, quiet in the boat, while fishing with Dad for crappies and sunnies. Sometimes they were so plentiful we'd just lower the bobber, and immediately watch some little yellow-bellied critter begin tugging. I loved the silence, the calls of red-winged blackbirds, and the soft grunts of dinosaur-looking great blue herons, who all shared the lake with us.

The Barnes family invited the Valley kids for movies in their specially designed home theater. My Dad also enjoyed listening to music with Dr. Barnes, Vice President of 3M, in his all-room-quadraphonic stereo, before any of us knew that kind of thing existed. When their extraordinary home was built, the engineers dammed up the creek to form a cold lake, surrounded by limestone steps. We were invited to swim there whenever it was hot enough outside for us to endure the cold creek-lake water.

Several families allowed us to use their personal tennis courts, including the owner of the most popular television station in the Twin Cities, KSTP. Because our Valley is so beautiful, close to the St. Croix River, and only 1/2 hour distant from St. Paul, we shared the Valley with these kinds of ultra-rich, land-owner families that used many of their mansions only as summer homes, but also with poor farmers, and those, including us, who just loved the beauty and accessibility of the Valley.

Everyone, except Old Man Sauers, allowed us to run around and explore their back acres. None of us, even our parents, knew why Mr. Sauers and his sons valued their privacy over friendliness, but we stayed away.

What's more, it was very inspiring, growing up as a girl in the 1950's, to see several women who worked full time, when the norm was to stay home with kids. Gloria Haslund, a teacher, college graduate in Home Economics, volunteered her expertise with both 4-H and Valley Creek Women's Club. Others, too, had degrees, and used them in professions, or in volunteer work.

Winnifred Netherly was our Valley artist, who came to picnics dressed in hippy-looking skirts and silk scarves, and didn't know much about cooking, and didn't care. She let her fly-away hair turn gray and wore it long.

Sisters Jen Nelson and Marge White had been USO comediennes during WWII. They'd been around the world, and could make anyone laugh. We'd all seen them do their hilarious routine, using the music "Mule Train." They had a little statue of a mule, and every time the music lyrics said, "Mule train, Haw! Haw!", they'd whip the mule with a shoelace. I still laugh when I remember it.

Jo Olson helped run their family farm, but she also volunteered a lot of time with our 4-H Club. She wrote and directed our one-act plays that almost always won a medal at the competitions. She was another woman who knew the value of laughing, and when I think of her, she always has a smile on her impish, Irish face.

Carol's mother, Helen, was in charge of the financial books for the wealthiest woman in the Valley, Mrs. Stoltz. Who said mathematics wasn't for girls?

You'd never guess any of them had tasted success, because all of these women consistently spoke to us children as if we were adults, honest and forthright. It was an early lesson in feminism. I understood there were no limits to what I could become.

These neighbors, not just the ones in mansions, were mostly educated (or self-educated) and valued the arts. But mostly they all just eked out a living, same as my family. Our homes were small, old buildings with poor insulation and one cramped bathroom. If families were lucky enough to own two cars, the second was a junker, just to get to Afton and back. Second helpings were rare, except for Thanksgiving and Christmas dinners, and secondhand and homemade clothes were the norm. But we had few complaints.

In Valley Creek, our lives might have been humble, but we were surrounded by the riches of pristine streams that bubbled out of glacial till and limestone, flowing alongside wildflower meadows and rolling, pine-treed hills. The elite of St. Paul soon discovered this virgin beauty, building their summer mansions upon acres of landscaped lawn, with majestic hilltop or lake views, many times larger than our mostly wood-framed farm-houses. Thinking about our small home, centered around its living room fireplace and round kitchen table, I often wondered how a family could feel warm or united in a rambling stone Tudor.

The owners of one Tudor mansion employed me for a few years as a teenager, so I got to know them well. "Cynthia, after you cook dinner, you'll serve it to the adults in the formal dining room, and you'll eat with the children in the kitchen."

"Yes, Ma'am." In Minnesota we never said sir and ma'am, but this family's matriarch came from Shreveport, Louisiana, and demanded it.

Can you imagine? The children didn't even eat with their parents! No warm family conversations around the kitchen table. I did my best to try to make the kids smile and laugh, but it wasn't easy.

I would nod and smile to our other upper class neighbors, as they rode their Tennessee Walking Horses along the tar road that passed in front of our house. They'd make a 45-degree pivot there, riding up the gravel road, still named Indian Trail, which led to the west side of May's Lake. They would trot up its steep hills, and down again to marshy lowlands.

If I followed close behind, I could watch them stop there, witnessing rookeries of white egrets, great blue herons, and other ancient-looking birds that made their homes in private, secluded marshes. Sometimes we watched our other neighbors from the city too, as if they were another species, slowly strolling along the road on a cool summer's evening. So odd. The idea of taking a walk for anything other than getting to a specific place, for a specific reason, was beyond my comprehension. And when I thought about their Tennessee Walking Horses, it seemed exorbitant to own any horses for no other reason than to walk them. They were entirely opposite from the thick-bodied work horses that pulled hay wagons and plows on my uncles' farms.

Even though they could afford fancy clothes and hairstyles, the city women seemed to me to be completely ignorant of fashion, at least from what I saw in magazines and on TV. They pulled their hair straight back into a bun, or wore it unfashionably short and straight. Their clothes were colorless, and so, too, were their faces, except for a cured-leather tan, the unfortunate result of too many years relaxing in the sun.

We lived in different worlds. Unless one of us worked for them, as maid, carpenter, or babysitter, we mostly forgot about them. And even if we had wanted to, their world was not ours to enter.

But my family's own world seemed rich enough. We traveled to the city several times a year. Roxy watched newspaper ads for visiting ballets, while I searched out any touring Broadway musicals. We put away pennies to get the best tickets we could afford. Both of us knew the Nutcracker music by heart and could dance to most of the songs. I'd stare at those colorful ads and escape to dreams of princesses, swans, and dancers of the Russian Bolshoi and Royal Canadian ballet companies. We also memorized the show tunes we heard on records and radio. I especially liked "June is Bustin' Out All Over", with June being my birthday month, from Rodgers and Hammerstein's "Carousel."

Music was always part of my world. I got that from Dad.

As a teenager my father had earned money improvising organ music as a backup to the silent movies that played in the ornate movie theaters of St. Paul, his home city.

Before we were born, Dad played jazz piano and organ in the traveling big bands of the 1930's and early 40's. And after coming off the road, he made a living playing Hammond Organ at expensive restaurants and nightclubs in the Twin Cities. For a while he even played at a private club in northern Wisconsin, staying in a closet-sized log cabin for tourists, and only coming home on Sundays.

One Saturday afternoon we drove there to visit him. Dad put me high on a stool at the dark polished oak bar that smelled of dark German beer. He served me 7-Up with red grenadine, a tiny straw, and a maraschino cherry.

At first I thought I could peer out a window behind the bar, but on second glance, I realized it was a photo that appeared three-dimensional, lit up from within a shadow-box frame. I giggled as the bartender allowed me to switch the picture's light on and off, and on again.

"This is so beautiful! I think Grandma Knoblauch would love this!" I said. I thought Grandma would like it because she loved her tall pine trees she had planted, and this picture was full of pines. And of course, it lit up.

"Cindy," replied Roxy. "That's a beer light! Grandma would have a fit if she knew! You are so stupid!"

That was nothing new. "Stupid" was Roxy's favorite word for me.

"No, Roxanne," Mother said with a smile. "I think Cindy has a good idea here. Your Grandmother has no reason to know that these lights are used in bars. She'd just think it was beautiful, as Cindy said."

Dad replied, "I agree. I'll order one, and we'll give it to her for Christmas." We all laughed.

We did give her the "beer light" for Christmas, and it became our favorite family joke that Grandma, who hated alcohol, loved her on-off "Land of Sky Blue Waters" picture, and never knew it was meant to hang behind dark, musk-smelling bars.

Later, Dad played for a short while at the newly-opened Bayport Yacht Club, just up the road from Afton, in Bayport, Minnesota. I remember dining there one evening and seeing Mom and Dad dance together, cheek to cheek. That was probably the only time I saw them truly enjoying one another.

Dad finally settled into a nightly stint with his own band at the St. Paul House in Shakopee, an hour drive from home. For someone who had played in the jazz clubs of New York, Charleston, and New Orleans, it must have been a bore to play standards night after night for drunk dancers and small-time Minnesota mobsters. Especially thinking about the adventures he had experienced on the road, under his stage name, Johnny Brant.

Though jazz was his passion, Dad had been classically trained at Hamline University, and for him, music was as much an intellectual exercise as an emotional one. He often joked with us about radio stations that played country music, and made sure we knew we were not "country" people. And when it came to the new "rock and roll" music, there would be strictly no listening, no laughing, and no discussion.

The night Elvis Presley appeared on the Ed Sullivan Show, I recall my dad shouting at the black and white set: "Ignorant! What a fool!" His eyes dilated into black saucers. "No subtlety. This is noise, not music!"

Dad's voice rose until it was at the decibel level he used when he was fed up with his children's misbehavior. "You don't play drums on every beat. I won't let him hammer this crap into my head."

He turned the set off and stomped out the door, presumably to visit some musician friend with whom he could vent his anger. It seemed so strange to me that he'd gotten that worked up about music, but it was more important to him than anything else. Many times in his short life he had chosen "music" over relationships, with his parents, his first wife (whom we only found out about many years after his death), and even with us.

Later, we got this lecture one more time. "You will not ever, I mean not ever, listen to that music. It is, in fact, not music at all. Noise, just noise! If I catch you listening to it, you will be punished."

Dad raised his left eyebrow, laser-peered out from under it with his stormy-blue eye, and said, "Understand?"

Of course we understood. It meant that if we listened to local rock radio station WDGY in the car, before getting out, we would change the station back to WCCO with its broadcasts of pop music and hog belly futures.

We would never hum rock music tunes at home, and if we went to a dance, it was presumed that we would leave the room whenever rock music took over.

This was my first lesson in learning how to attempt to out-wit adults. Unfortunately, I've always been a terrible liar. My skin is so transparent that it blushes red every time I try to hide the truth, embellish the truth, or outright lie. So when it came to rock and roll, I would just try to change the subject, and that worked most of the time.

Dad's hang-up was music. Mom's was speech.

The worst word we could possibly say was "ain't". According to Mother, it was used only by ignorant people. Being the granddaughter of immigrants, she was aware of the value of proper speech in society. Many of the Germans in our Valley couldn't pronounce a "th" sound, and it came out as "t", or they used an inverted sentence structure in their speech. In my youth I didn't understand that English was their second language. I only knew they were wrong, and I was taught that this made them sound unintelligent, and I was not allowed to talk that way.

So, ironically, I was a country girl who learned to use formal speech, and a country kid who didn't listen to country music. My dad also taught me to hear the sounds of the city in the jazz of Benny Goodman and Tommy Dorsey. But I also heard the sounds of my rural life in the classical music of Dvorak and Grieg.

———— ∘O∘ ————

The strange mix of people who lived in the Valley knew this fallow land contained a blessing, despite its poor, sandy soil. An eclectic community of neighbors lived here, who all ended up here for different reasons. Our neighborhood had: a musician, an artist, a museum curator, a teacher, an engineer, a carpenter, a waitress, a state-level judge, an owner of a Minnesota-wide dairy, a social worker, and a prison guard. We were all thrown together, an intoxicating cocktail.

What's more, Valley soil couldn't grow cash crops like corn or soybeans, but it could grow luscious pines, and meadows full of wild berries. And the Valley's limestone bubbled with icy, cascading creeks. All of this, plus its dry gullies and sandy gravel, gave us kids an endless play-ground for exploration.

Hidden in the gravel, alongside granite, quartz, and jasper, was the elusive, exotic red-banded agate, carried south by a glacier centuries earlier, from the distant north shore of Lake Superior. I spent hours searching for these unique gemstones, head down, waiting to find the "big one", even though the gem would be of no value to anyone but me.

My very own copy of the *Golden Guide to Rocks and Minerals*, a present from Grandma Blomquist on my eighth birthday, described the agate as "a kind of chalcedony with a banded or irregular, variegated appearance." The banded part I knew, its red-hued lines often surrounding pure white quartz. But I had to look up "chalcedony" in the glossary. The book showed its pronunciation as *kal-SED-uh-nih*. The definition made sense: *a group name for any waxy, smooth form of quartz.* These layered rocks were not only beautiful, but better yet, smooth to my hand.

Agates are found around the world, but the Minnesota ones are red-banded, the rich color deposited from rust leached out of iron ore deposits in the ground. For me, the most incredible aspect of an agate's beauty is that they are translucent, allowing partial light to filter through the stone.

The Valley echoes such translucence. It is, and was, a place of shadow and light: its blue creek that sometimes appears clear and white; towering blue spruce, at times black and dense; Indian paintbrush with its green handle dipped in red or orange fire; goldenrod that ripens from yellow to gold to rust. This Valley stands as a core of pure quartz, wrapped by layers of color and character.

Like the agate, the inhabitants of Valley Creek were also exotics, individuals escaping the crowding of cities, immigrants from countries like Germany, Sweden, and Finland, leaving behind poverty and war, and those just looking for a safe place to start over.

We were people, and sand, and objects, dragged from somewhere else — lodged here in the sand and fallow soil of this place, thriving.

Boundaries

Barely visible above
the polished ice cream bar
we see Selma's white, wispy hair,

and lean in to hear her whisper voice,
spinning stories about the raging
St. Croix River,

about fighting
its latest flood,
mud and mold covering the parlor,

and attacking her home in back,
Turkish rugs waterlogged,
Victorian furniture ruined.

She worked day and night
bailing out the wayward water,
mopping and scrubbing,

hoping to keep the parlor open –
to keep the children coming,
to keep the town alive

in the valley of the cold and lovely
lake-sized river that doesn't
respect its bounds.

chapter 4

preparing

Tulip
[*Tulipa*]

I'm Selma's godchild."

All through my childhood, and even today, in Afton and surrounding towns where Selma and her Ice Cream Parlor are legendary, that statement raises eyebrows. Nobody else knows her, the person, anymore, only her name that's on everybody's favorite ice cream parlor.

When Jesse Diggins, the Olympic gold medalist cross-country skier, was interviewed for television a few years ago, she and her friends and family recorded it at Selma's Ice Cream Parlor in Afton. There's a street sign now just outside the door that says, "Jesse Diggins Trail." Selma could never have imagined her little parlor being broadcast around the world.

Jet-setters, jet-ski bunnies, and city-dwelling owners of cabin cruisers now invade Afton on summer weekends, where it still nestles beneath the limestone cliffs that line the St. Croix River.

Afton Alps was developed, where the land was once considered a worthless ravine, in the 1960's by two brothers from Hastings, and it is now the largest ski area near the Twin Cities. And the local Afton marina, whose sole purpose, when I was a child, was selling gasoline to fishermen for their trolling motors, now houses ocean-going yachts that sail south through the St. Croix, the Mississippi, and finally into the Gulf of Mexico.

Busloads of tourists now visit our iconic village daily, attracted to its simplicity and its turn-of-the-century charm. The town is named after the famous song, Flow Gently Sweet Afton (written by Robert Burns in 1791). The song reminded its founders of the quiet nature of this river town, built on a flood plain, where the gentle St. Croix widens into a lake.

——————— ∘O∘ ———————

In the 1950's, about one hundred residents called the village of Afton home, but many more used it as their local hub. The town center consisted of The Afton House, an old stagecoach stop and inn, two grocery stores, Lerk's Bar, a family-type bar run by Lerk Lind, a Methodist, who was proud to tell you he didn't drink, Sill's Barber Shop, a lumber store on Highway 95, and a garage that housed the best car mechanic anywhere. It was also home to the Afton Volunteer Fire Department. At the south end, across from the town park, stood Selma's Ice Cream Parlor.

The village homes were mostly small wooden structures on limestone foundations, except for one lonely stone mansion south of town, owned by the inventor of the acetylene torch, Elmer Smith. I never met him, but people say he was just like everyone else. I did know his daughter, Mary Ellen, who retired to a house just south of the original mansion on the river. Jim Jorgenson, the man my mother married nine years after my father died, took care of Mary Ellen's property for years, and he even thought of Elmer's daughter as part of our family.

The town has changed, but never too much. The grocery stores are long gone, but The Afton House has become an exclusive Bed and Breakfast and restaurant. Lerk's Bar, later run by Lerk's daughter Bonnie, was a longtime destination for Twin Citians looking for a great burger. The garage and the lumberyard still stand, but they've been divided into various stores and artist lofts over the years, as well as home to the post office. The Smith mansion has been sold and remodeled to enormous proportions.

Selma's Ice Cream Parlor is the only place that remains close to what it was in 1913 when Selma and her husband, Ed Holberg, opened it. It is now the oldest ice cream shop in Minnesota. In the days before refrigeration, Ed sawed ice outside in their back yard in the winter, and packed it around the ice cream freezers. Ed was the town postmaster, and housed the post office in the building just north of the parlor.

When he died in 1938, Selma continued selling ice cream, and living in the back quarters. She was an inspiration to the town, and became almost the town matriarch.

Sunday mornings after church we often stopped at Selma's before we drove the two miles home. She never failed to fill a grab bag of penny candy for Roxy, Winky, and me. She had no children of her own, but being her God-child meant that our whole family was special to her.

My maternal Grandpa Knoblauch once told me how Selma Swanson had grown up in rural Miesville, on the farm down the road from his family's farm. Both of their mothers had emigrated from Sweden, and so on Sundays they attended the Swedish Augustana Synod Lutheran Church, different in many ways from the stricter German Lutherans who, he was careful to point out, wouldn't pray with anyone else, or join any organizations.

I've seen a confirmation picture of the 13-year-olds, Selma and Frank, looking older than their years, and very serious, seated at the front of Cannon River Lutheran Church. When Mother and Dad moved near Afton, where I was born two months later, Selma was the only person they knew. She turned out to be the best godmother any kid could ask for.

Selma always seemed ancient to me, older than my grandparents. Her hair wasn't gray, it was wispy and white. I don't know how tall Selma was in her middle years, but by the time I knew her, she had shrunk to the size of a ten-year-old.

Her voice wasn't really a voice at all. I never heard, but I figured she must have had an accident, or maybe an operation on her voice box. It was something no one talked about, mainly because it was no one else's business. She tried to whisper really loudly, but it came from the back of her throat and it sounded scary.

Once Winky asked her how much a certain candy cost.

"Two for a penny," she replied in her scratchy whisper.

Her voice obviously didn't scare Winky, because he replied, "Well, if it's two for a penny, then can I have one for nothin'?"

It took awhile for her to stop laughing, but she answered, "You bet'cha. Have a stick of licorice," and she handed the jar around for all of us.

I knew that sometimes arithmetic wasn't right, that sometimes half of two-for-a-penny really was getting something for nothing. If I picked only half the wild asparagus in the ditch, and left the other half to seed, we'd get free asparagus forever. And the jack pines on our back acres that we thought were destroyed forever by fire, later grew so thick the deer could hardly run through them.

That fire, probably started by a neighborhood kid experimenting with cigarettes in 1958, was a surprise to everyone. It flamed through the hundreds of trees we'd planted across our sandy prairie faster than a red fox racing a Corvette.

In those days, Smokey the Bear kept warning us how fires could destroy everything. We had little understanding of regeneration, renewal, and natural cycles. We only knew that the prairie fire had devastated our trees, and blackened the earth. The Afton Volunteer Fire Department fought a valiant fight, but the fire had everything it wanted, tall grasses, brown pine needles, and a drying summer wind that fed long tongues of fire.

We were crushed. Every year for ten years we had bought one hundred seedlings from the county extension service at a penny apiece, had hired Adey Schuster to plow rows, and then our family had painstakingly planted the tiny trees by hand. Some had been lost to moles and some to drought, but most had thrived on the sand hill and prairie where nothing else grew.

The devastating fire claimed three quarters of these trees, but the firemen fought hard enough to stop it before reaching our house.

That was spring. But by the time snow fell that year there were thousands of jack pine seedlings, surrounded by bright green prairie grasses and orange and violet flowers. I couldn't believe it.

Every week I'd trek over the soot-covered sand to discover the new blooms. Where one pine had been, now there were fifty seedlings surrounding the charred remains. The pinecones had opened and ripened from the fire's heat. Grasses and wildflowers that had been forced off the prairie by non-native invaders blew into the renewed soil and took root.

This was arithmetic gone wild.

We had other fires at our house too, fires that required much more of our attention. There was the lightning ball that rolled through the dining room, burning a path down the pine floor. And there was the lightning bolt hitting our electric meter outside the living room's picture window. That time, Mother had been standing just inside the window, ironing clothes, while Roxy read a book on the couch, and Winky and I played Pick-up Sticks on the floor next to the ironing board.

When the bolt hit, with its simultaneous flash and crash, we looked up in terror. It took a few stunned minutes, but we finally realized, as our hearts pounded, that none of us was hurt.

Despite the lightning charge completely ruining our house's wiring, miraculously it did not come through the iron's cord to Mother. You might say that we got "two for one" (the flash and the boom together) and we got "one for nothin'" in the unexplained gift of Mother's safety.

The big fire came in the summer of 1960. Dad was at work and the rest of us were at Bible school in Bayport. We left the church late that day because Mother had to gather things for the next day's lesson.

On the drive home it poured so hard we had to stop the car at the side of the road, waiting for the rain to let up enough to see clearly again. Minutes later, we started to drive again, but as we headed down the tall, winding hill leading to our house, terrified, we saw an electric bolt reach down from a darkened cloud, solder its finger to our house in a loud raucous blast, and then depart. By the time we pulled into the driveway, smoke streamed from the windows.

Again, the Afton Volunteer Fire Department came to our rescue, as quickly as if they'd been waiting next door. They saved the shell of the house, but most of the floors were burned, and the wiring and roof were ruined. Water damage was extensive, and every object in the house reeked of damp, smothering smoke.

I knew that once my dad came home he'd get us out of there, and make everything all right. I couldn't get myself to walk into the house again, so I ran down to the creek to get away. When I heard Dad's car, I meandered back home.

Dad walked through the house with a solemn face, as he and the fire-chief found out what worked, what didn't, what was safe, what wasn't, and then he came back to us. I wasn't prepared for what he said next.

"We're staying here tonight. He tells me the insurance would pay for us to go to a hotel until this is repaired, but I've decided not to. This is our home, and we're staying put."

He looked each of us in the eye as he said, "I know it stinks, and stings your eyes, but I want you to learn to live through anything. There's not always going to be an insurance company to bail you out. You just have to do whatever needs to be done. We'll do it together. We'll be all right. I promise. We'll be all right."

"No!" I was angry, beyond mad. Surely it wouldn't be so bad to have a good night's sleep in a comfortable bed. What was my dad preparing us for, some elusive future where I would need to be tough? I was a girl. I wasn't sure I wanted to be any tougher than I already was. I just wanted to get out of there.

Dad put his hand on Winky's shoulder as my little brother announced, "Smells like a weenie roast to me. Where're the buns?"

"Well, let's go get some in Afton, and stop at Selma's for ice cream too, okay?" Dad replied with a smile.

We must have smelled like wet chimneys when we arrived at Selma's. But she understood right away.

"Reminds me of the time," she said with her whisper voice, "lightning struck here and set my freezer on fire. Woke me right from the middle of a dream. Smoke everywhere, puddles of melted ice cream, middle of the night. I set out to cleaning it up the minute those firemen left. Had it open for business in two days."

Why did the adults around me try to teach this pride in being tough? What would be wrong with opening her store in three days instead of two?

Would it be a sin to sleep overnight at Carol's house tonight and get away from the smoke and chaos?

All I knew was that from my youngest days I was told it was not acceptable to cry, not even if I skinned my knee falling from the bike, and certainly not at a movie or TV show. Tough was expected, and tough is what they got.

I laid awake all that night in my bed, breathing the fumes of smoke, musk and wet insulation. My sheets and blankets had been washed next door at Carol's house, but I felt dirty. The air was dirty. I didn't understand. It didn't feel safe. This time, I felt my Dad expected too much of me, but I didn't argue. I knew I had to be strong, so I kept my feelings to myself.

The next day everything in our closets and drawers, on our windows and floors, was sent to the dry cleaner's. Eventually, wires were repaired, boards replaced, and walls painted, until the house felt safe again. Everything seemed back in order.

Two months later, in late September of 1960, as the Valley's Tartarian maples peaked with their bright orange and red canopies, I suddenly felt the interior burning of another fire. I had stayed overnight at my friend Pat's house, and even though it was a school day, when I awoke, her mother drove me quietly home.

I knew something wasn't right when I saw my grandparents' car parked in the driveway. When I entered our house, Mother was sobbing. My father's parents, usually seen only on holidays, sat stone-faced in the living room.

"You're not going to school today," said Mother. She motioned to me with uncharacteristic emotion, "Why don't you go sit over there on the couch next to Grandma Blomquist?"

I did as I was told, my heart pumping in my chest.

Mother swallowed hard, partially covering her mouth with her hand and said, "Your father had a heart attack last night."

There was a silence that overcame the room, as if the air had been sucked out.

Grandma gave me a squeeze and solemnly whispered, "Johnny won't be coming home again."

I glanced at my sister, who always knew how to act. She had her head down and wouldn't look at me. Winky had found his toy car and was nervously driving it around and around the living room rug. Grandpa's moist eyes stared into space, holding back the tears.

We thought my dad was 45 years old. That's what he'd told Mom. Grandma and Grandpa straightened us out, and informed us that he had really been 48.

We'd been told that Mom and Dad were nine years apart in age. I guess Dad thought it sounded better than being twelve years older than Mom. That was only the first of a pattern of lies that I've since discovered about my dad.

I was thirteen. But there were no hysterics from me. I knew what Dad would expect. I spent the rest of the day collecting and storing the dozens of cakes, casseroles, and breads brought to our house by concerned friends and neighbors.

This was a costly double tragedy, the fire and then Dad's death. But through these trials, I learned more than a 13-year-old had a right to know about responsibility and survival. Even at the funeral, when the hearse door slammed onto my thumb, breaking it, I held it firm, with dignity, as it swelled and throbbed, knowing that it hurt only half as much as I hurt inside.

I didn't cry a single tear. I had become that tough girl my dad wanted me to be. My mourning would come later, in times and places when I was alone.

Selma, too, would come into hard times. In the spring of 1965, at age eighty-two, she was suddenly hospitalized. And the mighty St. Croix took that opportunity to flood its banks in what was called the flood of the century. Her parlor wouldn't be spared.

I volunteered like many, upriver in Stillwater, filling sandbags alongside Stillwater State Prison inmates, in their striped uniforms. Later in the week, I served food at a Red Cross station set up at the St. Croix Beach Firehouse, for those who were washed out of their homes. But in my busy-ness, I had forgotten my godmother, Selma.

The river devoured downtown Afton, and everyone evacuated. When neighbors wanted to know what was happening to the homes and buildings, Winky found an empty rowboat and maneuvered it around the flooded waters of Main Street. When he reached the ice cream parlor, he found water licking the top of the door. There was nothing he could do.

A local photographer, documenting the flood's damage, snapped his picture. Winky became national news that day, and a framed photo of my brother in his rowboat hung inside the door at Selma's for over thirty years.

By the time Selma left the hospital, the river had receded, but extensive damage to her home and shop remained. Too weak to fight back against the mighty river, Selma closed the ice cream parlor for good.

But Selma forgot about the "one for nothin'" part. No one could imagine an Afton without Selma's. And Afton wasn't about to let the river dictate policy.

Elmer Smith, from his mansion on the hill, knew how the ice cream parlor held the soul of his community together, and he personally paid for complete restoration, and made sure Selma's would survive any future bouts with the St. Croix.

Her shop stayed open until Selma's death, when a new owner, Laine Lonergan McGee, an old friend and college roommate of my sister's, took over.

Laine tells how she bought the store soon after Selma's funeral. When she moved into Selma's quarters in the back of the parlor, she felt an undeniable presence. Friends were afraid to stay overnight, or even work the evening shift alone. So one night she sat down at the ice cream bar and made a deal with Selma.

"I know it's you, Selma. This is your place. It always will be. It has your name, your furniture, your candy, and ice cream. My name is Laine, and you knew me as a kid. I'll be your friend, and I'll continue to keep this parlor alive with the laughter of children, but I need to live here, and I need to have my friends work here. Is that a deal?"

There were no sounds, no clanking of chains, no cold breezes. No one knows if it was Selma, or if it had anything to do with ghosts. Maybe it was just a sacred blessing. But after that, no one was afraid. After all, Selma was my godmother, friend of my grandpa's at their confirmation when they were only thirteen years old and just learning about life, the kind person who rewarded me with candy for attending church, a family friend who comforted us in hard times.

One for nothin'.

———— ▫O▫ ————

As I write this chapter, so many years later, I am inhaling smoke that has drifted 2000 miles from California and Oregon, from western fires burning out of control. Every year now, place-named fires dislocate families, whole towns, and sicken the lungs of people across the country.

Have we forgotten the cycles that renew? Are we listening?

With every choking breath, I remember my Dad saying with conviction, "We'll get through this. We are resilient."

Was he already thinking about the complications of his own life that would have consequences for our little family? Was he already anxious about our future?

Thinking about the world, I wonder, are we resilient enough?

I row my metaphorical rowboat to assess the damage. Flow gently sweet Afton, for there are difficult times ahead.

Silence

Beach-walking after
your daughter's wedding,
we jumped boulders,
like checkers on the board
stamped into the linoleum
of our bedroom floor.

Back then you chose
the bottom bunk, while
I climbed to sleep, but felt
safer there, for field mice
scratching the
inside of our bedroom wall,
would find you first.

Each time Mother sewed us
matching dresses
we'd wear them two years,
then I'd get yours,
old and faded, and wear it
another year, or two.

Later, your babysitting cash
bought clothes that fit you.
I'd roll your skirt waists
and drown in your blouses
whose darts fell flat
on my non-existent breasts.

You dictated the order of my
wearing, but I didn't mind.
I was a modern woman
in the style of the day, until
you went away to college
and cleaned out the closet.

It was a good trade,
losing clothes for losing you;

no more sneering, lying
to get what you wanted.
"She wouldn't do that,"
Mother always said.

So I became silent,
even when you stole my friend.
I never understood why
we couldn't have been three,
but you said no. That's
when I waged an inner war.

You got a B, I earned an A.
You acted in a play,
I directed one. You got
to regionals, I to state.
You went to a state college,
mine private, with scholarship.

You were beautiful.
I was smart.
You were musical.
I was literate.
And then I forgot you.
No longer needing

to put you down
in order to survive,
I remembered you only
as a springboard
that lifted my jumps
higher than expected.

But today at the wedding,
when everyone stared
at us, because
posh eastern you

and midwestern me
each wore the same dress.

And why not? It was you
who taught me style.
You who showed me
the softness of Capezios,
the subtlety of
fabric and form.

As we walk the beach
trail remarking
how rare it is
to find a friend,
we promise never
to let years pass again,

And we listen to waves fall
back from the sand,
whispering,
like the soft
scratch of field mice
in a familiar wall.

chapter 5
observing

Peony
[*Paeonia officinalis*]

T unie, I'm proud of you." Mother gave me a kiss on the top of my head.

Barbara's mother hugged and thanked me, saying, "Your watchfulness was a blessing."

Dick walked a mile to and from the nearest store and bought me a Baby Ruth candy bar. He admitted in a whisper-voice that even though his sister was a pain, now he knew he really did love her. That got me thinking about Roxy, but I came to no quick conclusions about our complex sisterhood.

Carol loaned me her sunglasses and hat for the rest of the afternoon. She made a place for me on her striped beach towel and rubbed my back with the rest of her baby oil. I even got to sit in the place of honor next to her mother, Helen, who had big, strong arms like no woman I had ever seen. Days like that were scarce, and I absorbed every moment.

Before that day, I'd never seen a live person appear white as a ghost, or at least as white as the bleached sheets we pretended were ghosts on Halloween. I felt a fragile vulnerability. I was ashamed that, only a moment before, when not breathing, this girl had been a faceless, nameless body to me, a curiosity, a real life science project. I was glad no one was able to read my mind. All anyone else knew was that I had alerted them to the danger. I was kind of a hero.

As Barbara Schaeffer sat up, I saw the rush of blood return to her face. I didn't know then that decades later I too would be surrounded by a cocoon of spectators, as I felt the blood rush to my face and hands and feet, also after almost drowning — in my case, due to a whitewater canoe accident. "I, I ... got out too far," she sputtered.

"Shh," Helen interrupted with a soothing, relieved smile. "Just relax now."

"The current must have ..." Barbara tried to explain.

"No need for talking. Just take a deep breath."

She coughed again, and gulped down air.

"Try to relax. It's okay. You'll get your breath back in a minute," Helen assured her.

"Where's my mom?" Barbara asked in a panic when she noticed the crowd around her.

Barbara's mother and her brother, Dick, rushed terrified through the crowd. Mrs. Shaeffer scooped Barbara up in her arms and hugged her, then recognized Helen, and looked to her for answers.

"She's okay." Helen gently placed her hand on her friend's shoulder. "We didn't let the river take her."

————— ₒOₒ —————

"Mrs. Rosenquist, I have to talk to you!"

"Cindy, what can I help you with?" The choir director of Memorial Lutheran Church spun around and peered at me through her half-moon reading glasses. "You can talk while I collect the sheet music from this morning's service, okay?"

"I don't wanna sing those dumb Sunday School songs anymore. I wanna be in your choir. The words are better, and you sing in parts, and everybody's faces look like angels when they sing."

"Well, Sweetie," she said. "I'm glad you like my choir. And we always need more sopranos. But you're only nine years old. Do you think you'll be able to read the words and the music?"

"No trouble! You know I can sing! I'll be there."

"You come Wednesday night and sit in front, and we'll see how it goes."

"I'll get Mom to bring me. Oh, and thanks so much. Really, thank you Mrs. Rosenquist. This is so cool!"

I ran out of the church and announced to my friends that I would now be a member of the adult choir. I knew I was a good sight-reader, and anyway, any time I didn't know something, I'd just drop out and listen until I memorized the words and the melodies. Sopranos almost always sang the melody, so it would be easy. And besides, I'd had piano lessons from Mrs. Borg, the pastor's wife, so I knew how to read music as well as anyone else.

I loved singing in the adult choir, especially my first song with them. It was an old gospel hymn about walking in the peaceful garden with Jesus. I sang it over so many times the words and melody got stuck in my brain, not just that week, but I found myself singing bits and pieces in my head the entire year, especially "and the joy we share as we tarry there, none other has ever known."

I looked up the word tarry, a strange word. It said to stay, or wait, or in particular, to stay in expectation.

That morning of the almost-drowning I had biked to the creek, parked it, then edged down the slope sideways to avoid the stinging nettles, and had picked a bouquet of tiny orange flowers that looked like lit-up lanterns suspended from an emerald green ceiling. Their name described these flowers perfectly, jewelweed.

After throwing a few sticks into the creek and watching them flow downstream, I rode back home and set the jewelweed in a water-filled, blue-tinted Mason jar. I shoved aside my brother's baseball cards to make a place for the bouquet on the kitchen table. Then I waited.

All of us hated to wait until late afternoon to go to the beach, but in those days, no one swam during the hottest part of the day. I'd heard adults with tight voices whisper something about polio and water and heat. It was hard to believe the river I loved could in any way cause polio, but it was an unwritten rule that no one dared test. Polio was a dreaded disease that had struck so many people around the world, and even in my community. And then, too, we were warned about getting cramps if we swam too soon after eating, so we waited.

Two o'clock seemed forever, but Mother finally gave us the okay. She loaded the three of us kids, along with our neighbors, Helen Appleby and Carol, into our rusty, yellow-green Studebaker. It was one of those old cars that looked as if it couldn't even make it to the junk lot. But we only needed it for short trips, so we crossed our fingers and took off.

On the drive south, Valley Creek Road (County Road 21) meandered over two creeks and a dry run, before it snaked around the blind curve by Spike Spreeman's stone house. It continued over hills that paralleled the lower creek as it flowed toward the St. Croix River.

It was always a slow ride, not only because of the winding road and hills, but because at any moment, deer could rush out and cause an accident. There were lots of tragic deer stories in the Valley, and none of us wanted to be the next sad tale. A half-mile before reaching the village of Afton, after rounding the last hill, we left the main road, took a 45 degree angle back north onto a dirt road, and followed it, with its washboard and potholes, to St. Croix Beach.

My sister, Roxy, ruled the back seat. Taller, stronger, and 22 months older than me, Roxy had somehow already acquired the tool of power-talk. No niceties when she wanted something, simply "Do it!"

Even without words, she would set her jaw in a slightly forward manner, raise her eyebrows, controlling any situation. Auburn hair fell straight around her white Scandinavian skin and gave her a princess-like quality, which of course fooled Mother into thinking Roxy could do no wrong.

She and I shared the same high, narrow nose bridge, inherited from the Blomquist side, as well as baby-fine hair and smoky blue eyes. From the Knoblauchs, we got Mom's high cheekbones. But we didn't look alike, and my blond hair was not the only difference. Her face was sculptured while mine was pumpkin-like, her body muscular and mine bony.

In the front seat, between Mother and Helen, sat Winky, the wiggly one, younger than me by three years, and as always, the only boy. He resembled the Knoblauchs, with his darker skin, hair, and eyes, and his more solid nose. He tanned so dark in the summer, everyone thought he was Native American, so different from Roxy's easily burned skin and my freckling.

Everyone loved Winky. I thought he was undeniably the cutest boy I'd ever seen, especially when his chocolate eyes sparkled. He had a natural athletic ability, and he always smiled.

I didn't. I often looked as if I were a passenger on some other spaceship than Earth.

Roxy let me know how embarrassing I was to her, especially when I sat glossy-eyed, open-mouthed, and twirled thin strands of straggly (what my mother, in frustration, called corn-silk) hair into a tight rope.

"Cindy, move over," Roxy ordered. "I'm squished. Git outta my way!"

I didn't move fast enough. Her elbow gashed me in the side, as she moved her butt alongside mine, and pushed until my bony ribs smashed against the door handle. She already took up half the back seat, having pushed Carol into the other door. Her feet straddled the center floor bump, and she had positioned her knees, one in each direction like pointed fence poles, that warned, "Do not enter."

"Stay there." She looked in both directions to make sure both Carol and I understood. We responded with stiff bodies and gazes directed out the windows.

Younger, thinner, meeker, and not having learned the word or concept of assertiveness until 1970's women's liberation, I sat quietly trying not to irritate my sister.

"And stop bopping your foot!" she yelled as her toe stabbed my shin. "Can't you just sit still?"

— ∘O∘ —

I was different from my siblings, as well as from most of our friends, in one significant way. I was always skinny. Not thin ... Emaciated.

Mother took me to the doctor months after I was born, because I never cried, even from hunger. I had barely doubled my weight in the first year of life, though today's pediatricians tell us infants are expected to triple their weight by age one.

Before I was twenty-five years old I never remember wanting to eat. I ate to stay alive.

On the rare occasion when Father drove us to Beno's, the filling station two miles north at U.S. Highway 12, to buy gasoline, he'd often get each of us a six ounce bottle of pop.

"I get Cindy's," Roxy would state matter of factly on the drive north.

"No fair!" Winky would pipe in. "You got it last time!"

Calmly she countered, "Too bad. I said it first."

"I think," Dad would say, "we ought to wait and see first if she can finish it this time. It's hers, you know. She can decide herself what she wants to do with it."

I would carefully choose Orange Crush, because it was less fizzy and less filling, but they were right, I never finished a 6-ounce bottle of pop, and I usually chose to bring it home for Mother.

I was also a fidgeter. It went hand in hand with frequent escapes to an alpha-wave brain state some call "La-La Land". Throughout school and college, and even now at church or a lecture, I move from hip to hip, cross and uncross my legs, and constantly bop my foot up and down to some imagined beat.

In second grade, that beat changed into an obsession with the rhythms of poetry, not a usual activity for a child from a mostly bookless home, but an activity common to dreamers.

Tall, black-haired Miss Kilkelly read to us from her favorite poetry book every day after lunch, and paraded us to the school library, where I discovered Dr. Seuss's rhymed stories, whose sounds delighted me even more than the characters or their exploits.

I don't remember seeing either of my parents read books. Mom's eyes were bad, and Dad wanted to read, but couldn't find the time. Mother dutifully brought us to the majestic Carnegie Library in Hudson, Wisconsin, where the building smelled like a combination of Grandma's old house and Uncle Russell's sweet hayloft. It was quiet there and in its tall ceilings and spacious interior I felt reverent. I loved standing in the center of the building, staring at the domed roof and breathing in the smell of old paper and leather. When it was time to leave, I'd check out an armful of books, and return them in two weeks, unread.

That behavior was repeated each summer when the Washington County Bookmobile parked at Afton Township Hall just down the road. It felt like magic in the converted bus that smelled of musky leather. I would carefully open and close books, seeking something of interest, find a pile to check out, and then walk home with books that never got opened again, unless they were volumes of poetry.

I knew how special books were. They told about the rest of the world, about places my dad had seen, about girls like myself in exotic countries, about all the important things I would never know if I stayed there in the Valley. In fact, sitting untouched on our living room bookshelves was an entire set of Harvard Classics that Grandpa Blomquist bought before World War II to educate himself. Grandma was a college graduate, and he was determined to be her equal.

I wanted to be like Grandpa, disciplined, progressing book to book in my knowledge, but for me it seemed impossible. Nevertheless, that set of classics served as a symbol of what we were expected to become. Those volumes are still prized, filling the top shelves of my living room bookcase.

———— ░O░ ————

That day we bounced over a dozen or so potholes at the bottom of the gravel hill, the old Studebaker having no workable suspension system. Something slipped out from under the front seat. I reached down to pick it up ...

"Stop it! You're squishing me against Carol!" Roxy loudly whispered directly into my ear. "I said, hold still!"

"But it's an agate. Under there."

I kept reaching until I had it in my hands. There is something unexplainable about an agate, so many shades of red, aligned alongside brilliant white quartz. My mind went back to the time when it formed, slowly, layer upon layer with each washing of different minerals, and then the crystallizing.

I wondered, did it happen when things got really hot, or under the pressure of an icy glacier, or when it all melted? I was sure it must have hurt, and I quietly thanked the rock for being its beautiful self, and taking the long journey to my Valley, and hiding just long enough for me to find it.

"Who cares? Git rid of that dumb thing!"

Roxy looked closer, saw its color and large size. "That's where that went! It's mine! I found it in the gravel pit last week, and then lost it. Give it here!" She grabbed it from my hand and gave me another positioning whack with her butt. "Look at those lines. You don't find many that red."

"Like blood," I said.

"Yah, like yours runnin' down your face if you don't shut up."

"Gee, Cindy," I turned my face to the window and mouthed the words under my breath, so Roxy couldn't hear. I noticed a turtle crawling off the bridge as we passed over the third creek. "Thanks for finding my favorite agate. You're such a great sister you know." I figured if I said it to myself it'd work just as well as if she'd actually thanked me.

"What're you doin'? Talkin' to yourself again? What an idiot!"

According to Roxy, being an idiot was my main role in the family, but I had another role as well, what I like to call Finder of Lost Things.

My brain kept a mental picture of how a room was supposed to look, and when anything was out of place, the misplaced object would appear to me, as if it were highlighted. It worked outside too. My eye could skim a patch of clover, and identify the differently patterned growth immediately.

One Christmas I surprised relatives and friends with gifts of stationery, packs of eight pieces of paper with a dried four, five, six, seven or eight leaf clover pasted onto each sheet. It took hundreds of them collected and dried in my dictionary for the project. It was not difficult collecting them. My eye picked out the anomalies automatically.

"There! Behind the birch," I shouted.

Still only half-way to the swimming beach, Mother slammed on the brakes, as dust clouded our vision.

"Two deer. One's a fawn." I pointed, "nibbling the water cress. That's an expensive treat!"

"Look! It still has its spots," Winky laughed.

"Oh, who cares? We've seen a ton of 'em. I'm hot. Come on, Mom," Roxy complained. "Let's get to the beach."

———— ◦O◦ ————

Running tiptoe across the scorching beach, we tried not to burn our bare feet. We dropped our towels and raced to the water's edge. Mother remained on the beach that day in 1956, lowering herself onto our biggest bath towel.

Though her figure was perfect, I could tell by her stooped posture that she felt self-conscious in her elasticized, yellow swimming suit. She was tall for her generation, 5 feet 6 inches, but nowhere near as tall as my grandmother, her mother, who at 5 feet 10 inches, was a giant among her peers born in the 19th century.

In July's humidity, Mother's hair formed sassy curls around her prominent cheekbones and high forehead. She reached into her purse, pulled out tortoise shell prescription sunglasses, and exchanged them for the black pointed ones she wore daily. Her light brown eyes were extremely sensitive, and the beach's glare added to the dryness and constant sting of her eyes. Mother dug her heels into the beach and unconsciously sifted her hands through the warm, loose sand at her side. Even though the rest of us would be in and out of the cool water all afternoon, she would remain on the towel until it was time to leave.

In contrast, Helen, the same age, but heavier and shorter than my mother, wore her suit with dignity. Her coloring was lighter, and her features finer boned. I thought Helen of Troy could not have been more beautiful than our Finnish-American neighbor. Once during each beach visit she would rise from the towel, stride confidently to the beach and dive into the water. The only mother I knew who could swim, she performed the Australian crawl with grace, looking like a young Esther Williams, the Olympian swimmer and movie star.

Though her only child, Carol, was two years younger than I was, we were best friends. As I watched Helen rub half a bottle of baby oil on Carol's fair skin, I envied her only-child status. Carol had her own striped beach towel, not just an old bath towel, and she had flip flops to keep her feet from roasting on the sand, real sunglasses, and a straw hat. Best of all, she didn't have a sister.

That was important, but then I started thinking about the advantages of living in a larger family. Carol swam as well as I did, but her mother watched her like a she-bear, never out of sight, and not only at the beach. It was different for me. As one of many children, and not the youngest, my mother didn't always keep track of me, making it easier for me to wander and explore on my own.

The beach was full that day. Perfect weather. The river water in July had already warmed as much as it would that summer, so it was easy to play in. Kids built sand castles on the beach, and swimmers lolled on the floating dock, which was anchored further out.

I stood in the river resisting the tug of wildness from the cool, root-beer-colored St. Croix. This was still a decade before Congress designated it wild and scenic. A blue-gill nibbled my arm. As I jerked the arm out of the water, all balance was lost, and the river's flow took over. The high arch of my foot came down on a sharp object, a stone, a shell, or something half-buried in the sand. But my feet were tough. No way was I swimming to shore to recover. Instead, I splashed into deeper water, beyond where any-one's feet touched bottom.

I inhaled the river-scented air, fresh, with a hint of fish and buried clam. Though the water appeared brownish, because it had taken on the tannins of the tree roots, especially in the deeper part, all of us in the Valley knew it was pristine. No lily-pond muck lined the bottom of the St. Croix, the way it did May's Lake. This beach gave us a clean, usually soft, sand bottom for toe-digging and exploring.

One of my first memories of St. Croix Beach was about a time my dad came with us. He loved to swim, but didn't have much free time for it. He told me his dad, my Grandpa Blomquist, had thrown him into the Mississippi River when he was a young child, expecting him to paddle back to shore. I guess he made it. My swimming lessons were more civilized than that.

That first year, having taken the beginner's course of Red Cross swimming lessons, Dad asked me to float or dog paddle out to him. When I said no, I was afraid to go out that deep, he said, "Hey, It's not deep here. See, I'm standing on the ground." When I got out to him, he laughed and showed me that he wasn't standing at all, but rather, had been treading water the whole time.

It wasn't funny to me. He had lied right to my face. I dog-paddled back to shore, and refused to talk to him the rest of the day.

Because I had continued to take the lessons every year, I was granted certain freedoms at nine. No one needed to keep a watchful eye on me. After all, how much trouble can someone get in who knows how to swim, but mostly floats and dreams instead? Anyway, swimming would mean getting my ears wet, and then feeling a hollow, echoing dizziness for days afterward. And swimming took thought. Standing or treading water out deep, while dreaming, was a whole lot better, in my opinion. I found a deep place to stand and watch the whole beach and its flurry of activity.

When Helen finished her swim, she sat down on a beach towel next to Mother. I could tell by the way they whispered to each other, that they were rehashing Valley Creek Women's Club gossip.

On the south side of the swimming beach Roxy's single leg rose into the air, as she practiced water ballet techniques we'd seen at the Minneapolis Aquatennial.

Near the dock Winky spluttered out of the water and laughed after being dunked by one of the beach regulars, the same guys who always held bikini-clad girls on their shoulders and then dropped them "accidentally" into the water.

Carol, practicing her swimming lesson homework, side-stroked back and forth for the tenth time.

And all the while I watched boats and birds and clouds from my cool vantage point in the river, singing to myself, "and the joy we share as we tarry there..."

There was a sudden movement. Out of place. Further out in deep water, where usually, only Helen swam. A dangerous place of drop-offs, and boats zipping by without warning. Just last summer someone had walked into a drop-off out there, and drowned. We knew where it was, and we knew to stay away.

My head turned towards a splashing sound. A ripple. Then nothing. Then another. A head bobbing.

Gasp. Arms grasping for something solid. Then it sank again, and I couldn't locate it. Where had it gone? No sound. No movement.

I held my breath as I watched the water surface intensely, searching for any sign of movement.

Then I saw flailing arms break the surface. I yelled, "Helen!" with all my breath.

Every person on the beach turned toward me. I froze.

"Cindy, shut up!" Roxy yelled from the other side of the beach. "They're all looking at you."

I told myself this was one of those times when feelings didn't matter, when appearances should be the last thing on my mind, and even the taunts of my sister had to be ignored. I knew to call for Helen, the strongest swimmer. "Helen, out there! Someone's drowning!" I pointed to the deep water. "Quick!"

Now, everyone looked to see arms thrashing, trying to latch on to something that wasn't there. The gawkers on the beach froze. Only Helen moved.

She catapulted across the sand and into the river, splashing as she lifted her powerful legs into the deep water. Within seconds she dove head first, surfacing yards ahead, and then furiously rotating her arms and kicking her feet, propelling her forward to the thrashing body.

After reaching the drowning swimmer, Helen draped her left arm tightly around the small body, and with great strength and determination, she swam with her other arm.

I had always thought of Helen's arms as fleshy, but now I saw them as muscle, feminine muscle, something beautiful in their strength. And that protectiveness she had always heaped on Carol, had its welcome side. She was the only person on the beach that day who responded as she did, quickly, with skill and compassion.

On the beach Helen laid the body down on the hard-packed sand and adjusted the limp body's head, chest and stomach. Nervously, we surrounded her, but not too closely, as she pressed on the lifeless back, lifting arms in a rhythm, pressing back ... breathing ... lifting arms ... breathing ... repeating over and over.

I could see now that it was a young girl, thin, with blondish hair, but that was all I knew. Press back ... breathe ... lift arms ... Finally we saw a trickle of water flow from her mouth and onto the sand. Press back ... breathe ... lift arms ... breathe.

And then, the faint sound of choking and coughing.

Helen stopped the "artificial respiration", what we had all learned in our advanced swimming classes, but had never before seen put to use. Slowly she turned the girl's frail body onto her back, and gently raised her into a sitting position.

"Ohhhh!" I said in disbelief, as I saw the girl better. "She's so white."

I wanted to say, "It's Barbara! I know her! She's Roxy's friend who lives just down the Valley from us," but I was respectful, so I just said, "Ohhh. I thought she might die. I was so scared."

As the crowd dispersed, mumbling about the lack of life guards, the carelessness of children, and their own fear of drowning, I kept repeating the phrase in my head, "We didn't let the river take her."

"We." That meant me too. I had helped.

Helen rescued Barbara, but it was I who had allowed Helen to get there in time. It was my dreamy brain that noticed the change in pattern on the surface of the water. Like searching for a four-leaf clover. Like finding a lost agate. Discovering a fawn.

No one had heard screaming. I was the one who saw it, who knew something was out of order. I had tarried, as the song says, "and the joy we share as we tarry there, none other has ever known." Yes, I was feeling joy. For once, Roxy wouldn't be sneering something nasty about my uselessness in the world. My off-in-the-clouds brain had done something important.

But on the ride home Roxy was her usual self, shoving me into the door to make room. She didn't need to remind me how different I was. I knew I hadn't been practicing water ballet or learning to swim. I had been doing what I did best. Nothing at all. Just observing.

Whoever it was, centuries ago, who discovered the lucki-ness of four-leaf clovers, probably understood that recog-nizing patterns and their alterations creates a kind of luck that aids survival.

I will remain alert to the unexpected, because it is a cer-tainty that the unexpected will come.

Back Roads

Mile after mile in varying hues
lie ditches lined in vermillions and blues,
Black-Eyed Susans, Queen Anne's Lace,
violet Vetch and Daisy's face.

I'm glad politicians do not care
if back roads look like putting-green fare
where wild pink roses wind 'round pine
and Elderberries ripen purple as wine.

The scene seems tranquil to passers-by,
but look up close at Susan's black eye,
and ablaze in the orange of Butterfly Weed
feel the heat of fire the winds seed.

chapter 6
truth telling

Dandelion
[*Taraxacum officinale*]

Each spring I loved watching out our picture window as bony and silent Adey Schuster drove his rusty plow through last year's garden, transforming a moldering field of old corn stalks and frozen tomato plants into rich, black furrows. This garden's fertile soil was due to its perfect location, the exact place where our septic system emptied into the vacant lot next door.

Adey, who had stopped calling himself Adolph after World War II, never married, and instead lived with his sister, Lillian, in their family homestead. They shared a plot of land that, aside from their garden, had little value for agricultural purposes. Its vistas of river valley and wildflowers offered them little wealth. Although they were probably in their mid-fifties when I was eight years old, they appeared to me to be in active decay.

For some reason, the two of them reminded me of the nursery rhyme about Jack Sprat and his wife. My rhyming mind repeated the ditty every time we passed their house.

Jack Sprat could eat no fat,
His wife could eat no lean.
And so between them both, you see,
They licked the platter clean.

Adey Schuster's skin hung on his bones like the already tanned leather of a starving Guernsey. Lil, as we called her, had no shape at all, a square block from head to foot, as wide as she was tall, usually covered in a dark wool sack-dress, whose color matched her mustache and spindly chin hairs. Nylon stockings clumped at her ankles, just above shapeless slipper shoes that she'd use to shuffle along the ground. As strange looking as she was to a young child, it was something else that sent shivers down my spine. Her voice.

Beneath the slurring of syllables, she emitted a kind of high-pitched nasal whine. Minnesota accents all have a kind of "embarrassed" tone to them, but hers was so much more. Everything she said sounded like a plea for help, even though Lil constantly let us know, "I can take care of myself."

———— ◦ O ◦ ————

In March 1955, I accompanied Mother to the Schuster's home to arrange for plowing of our garden. Their driveway entrance was a mile south on County Road 21, just across the road from Spike Spreeman's, a small, but beautiful house you couldn't miss, hand-built of local limestone rock. In contrast, Schuster's tar-paper shack was hidden among scrappy trees on the north side of a tall hill. Shadows allowed little light to enter their house.

Lil met us outside, just as she slammed the door of their outhouse, and she invited us into her kitchen for a cup of coffee. I felt a tight squeeze of my hand, a signal from Mother to be on my best behavior. But this squeeze was different, longer and harder, and I could feel something was off.

As I entered Lil's kitchen door, a heart-stopping, lung-choking stench overwhelmed my senses. I immediately held my breath.

In a few seconds, when I had to breathe again, I valiantly fought off the urge to retch.

Mother expected an act of hospitality from me that, it turns out, far exceeded my years. I mean, anyone would have had a hard time.

I survived by inhaling short, choppy breaths through my mouth, and managed to let only minimal air pass through my nose. The odor was worse than that of the dead field mouse in our closet wall, when we had to live with the inescapable smell of rotting flesh for a week. But this was more like a hundred rotting mice, and in my mind I visualized a mass murder scene of wild animals, stored and rotting in Lil and Adey's cellar.

Later, Mother explained in her quiet, embarrassed voice, that it had nothing to do with dead mice, rather it was the result of B.O., body odor, from germs that were not routinely washed away.

This odor followed Lil and Adey wherever they went. I was surprised when my mother actually drank a cup of coffee at her house before we left. Lil offered me a fig newton from a half-opened package. "No thanks, I'm really not hungry," I said.

It was the truth. I hated fig newtons. But I'm not sure I would have taken one anyway.

From that day on I became a self-appointed germ detective, who watched for Lil at community potlucks, and spread the word that she had brought the blueberry pie in the black pan, or the gooseberry cobbler in the scratched bucket. Then I'd make sure that Mother, or some other willing accomplice, would take Lil's offering and, little by little, throw it behind a convenient bush, so Lil thought it was being eaten. Mother and the other ladies of the Valley Creek Woman's Club were always kind to her, finding her a chair to sit on, and thanking her for her potluck item, while my friend, Judy Hancock, and I stood behind her back, holding our noses, giggling, and talking about B.O.

Adey ignored Lil as much as he could, disappearing in his rusty pickup for days at a time. He never came to community picnics, and didn't show up at church, and as far as I know, he was an atheist.

At that time, in my Valley, being an atheist was as bad as it got. My Catholic friends hadn't ever seen him at St. Francis of Assisi, and Judy confirmed that he wasn't a Methodist either.

Anyway, that forced Lil, who had never learned to drive, to fend for herself, and walk the three-mile round trip to Afton for groceries and Lutheran church activities.

But Lil seldom walked. Instead, she would stand in the middle of the road, both hands and body leaning on her cane, and stare down the next driver until he or she stopped in order not to hit her. It took ten minutes of slow-motion waddle before she then became situated in the car. And then the B.O. took over.

Well, Lil was the farthest thing from my mind that Easter as I chomped on newly received jellybeans. Easter was late this year, which gave us a chance to wear our new spring clothes. Mother made Roxy and me matching yellow organdy dresses with wide lace collars. We had spent a Saturday afternoon at Olson's Department Store in Hudson buying matching Easter bonnets and white patent leather shoes. And just the week before, Grandma Blomquist had driven out from St. Paul to bring us an Easter Lily, and give us an early holiday present, lilac perfume to touch lightly behind each ear.

On Easter Sunday, after we pinned a surprise orchid (flown from Hawaii to the Hudson Flower Shop) onto Mother's best floral dress, we were ready for church. She backed the yellow-green Studebaker out of the garage at exactly twelve minutes before nine. The air was late-April warm and moist, and the slight scent of lilac raised hopes of next month's flowers.

A mile south on the road, I could see a dark shape in the distance. As we got nearer, the shape became a huddled old woman leaning on a cane, her thumb and arm protrud-ing into the traffic lane, so that a car would have to swerve to avoid hitting her. I inhaled a loud, quick sigh of air, and held it in disbelief. It was Lil. I knew Mother was going to stop the car, open the back door, and Lil would slip into the back seat, beside me. There was no way I could avoid touching her. There was no way I could hold my breath all the way to church. I was in my Easter clothes, with lilac behind my ears, and now I would smell like B.O.

I survived the trip to church, but dashed out of the car to find my friend, Nanette, all the while taking enormous lungfuls of air. When I looked back and saw Mother es-corting Lil into the church, I panicked.

"Nanette, I gotta sit with you today. Please, ask your mother. Please, please! Otherwise I'll have to sit next to Lil, and I'll just die!"

We sat across the aisle from Lil and Mother. I watched them very closely, wondering if Mother's sense of smell had already faded with age. She never gave the slightest indication of discomfort as she shared her hymnal and sat at Lil's side. I was proud of Mother. Some day, I thought, I'd be like her, strong, principled, a real lady.

After the postlude I joined them as they shook the pas-tor's hand. To every parishioner that Easter he said, "He is risen!" and each replied, "He is risen, indeed!" But to Mother he also said, "What a thoughtful woman you are. Thank you for bringing Lillian to church this morning. Could you find it in your heart to bring her every Sunday?"

Mother replied, as if she had been thinking this answer through for some time, "Oh, I'm so sorry. You know I have three children to get ready in the morning, and it's almost impossible to arrive at church on time. I don't think she would be happy counting on us." She flashed a smile at the pastor. "You know, the Springborns' children are grown. Maybe they could bring her."

All right! She rescued me from a fate unimaginable. But I began to think about what Mother said. We were in truth a family that arrived everywhere early, except church. Mother's punctuality was renowned. We had all learned to accommodate her inner clock, so that on Sunday mornings there was never any waiting for children. We were always ready by 8:30 am and lying belly down on the living room rug reading the funny papers, until Mother would call, "Time to go." That time was at twelve minutes to nine, which got us to church just in time for the playing of the prelude.

Then it clicked. All this time Mother had been scheming to avoid Lil on the road. She must have known the Springborns left home at fifteen minutes before nine, and they would never pass by Lil. That's why we left three minutes later every Sunday, and arrived at church with no interruptions. But this Easter Sunday the Springborns were out of town, and we had been blessed with Lil.

When we drove Lil home from church, I once again held my breath until my face turned red, and then as soon as we arrived at her house, escaped out the door of the Studebaker. I ran up the closest hill I could find. At the top I sank into a meadow of furry crocuses amidst the outcroppings of rock, new life growing from the still brown grass.

That's the day I began my annual Easter trek. It's always a gamble in Minnesota to determine whether Easter Sunday will be a sunny eighty degrees, or a frigid twenty degrees with the threat of snow. Either way, I pull out my hiking boots for a hike up Schuster's Hill in search of the wild crocus, or more correctly, pasque flower, which has bloomed among the limestone outcroppings at the top of the hill since my childhood, and probably for decades before. I no longer pick the crocuses, because the land now belongs to the Belwin Outdoor Education Laboratory.

But spring's revelations are always a surprise. Only a few feet away from where I sat, dozens of fat bull snakes were sunning in a bowl-like pit at the summit of the hill. They're there every year, crawling out into the warm sunshine of spring. They don't bother me, and I am content to lie on the incline of the snake pit mound, watch the garters and bull snakes, and marvel at the fuzzy lavender blooms opening to the sky, like baby robins' beaks waiting for their mothers' digested worms.

I now know that Good Friday's hymn *"Were You There"* doesn't always lead to Handel's *"Halleluia Chorus"*. The hidden underbelly of community tolerates the poor and smelly, but only so far. We play nice, driving them to church one day, and think we have done our part. Then we gossip and laugh, dab on perfume, buy the best hat to match our new outfit, and join in the *Easter Parade*.

But, we also considered ourselves to be Easter people, so Lillian and Adolph Schuster, sister and brother, were part of a community that called them members, a community that not only helped them when needed, but also graciously asked for their help.

And just to let everyone know our hearts were in the right place, The Valley Creek Woman's Club always made sure Lillian, our Easter Lil, was sent home from church every Easter with a beautiful white lily.

Frozen

A bony child shivers
by fire circle stones,
catching sparks
on charred skate toes,
watching alone
hockey boys
chasing and whirling,
speed skaters
racing in circles,
figure skaters
defying gravity
twirling like tornadoes.

Now grown,
no longer with
protruding bones,
she pulls on her
Thinsulate gloves,
a parka of down,
laces insulated skates
over polypropylene
socks, and enters the
rink a stranger.

She traces figure-
eights cut by a
fanciful child,
learns to balance
all her weight
on a slight blade,
then races forward,

catching up with
frozen ground.

chapter 7
questioning

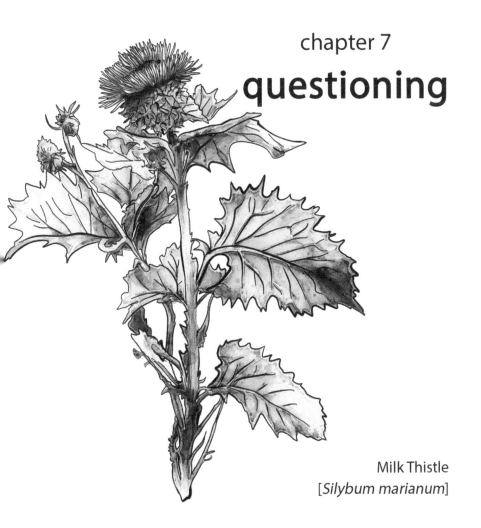

Milk Thistle
[*Silybum marianum*]

Some say the world will end in fire.
Some say in ice. – Robert Frost

O ur furnace always went *kaput* on the coldest of days. It didn't happen to everyone who heated with oil. But it happened over and over again to us, because we bought the cheap, low-viscosity heating oil, the kind that thickened as the temperature dropped, and eventually stopped its flow from our outside tank into the kitchen.

Mother would wake up first, and without complaining, pull the wool blanket from her bed, wrap it around her nightgown, and slip on her tall boots. She'd boil several pans of water on the electric stove, tramp outside, and pour them over the sluggish pipes until the oil thawed, began to flow, and heat returned. It was only then that the rest of us crawled out of bed.

Minnesota winters were hard to endure. In the 1950's, there was no polypropylene, no Goretex, and no insulated boots. My family could afford no long underwear or down jackets. We relied on wool – wool that gets wet, stays wet, and gets very cold in below-zero weather. Our hands and heads were covered with Grandma-knit wool hats and mittens, which provided some, but did not afford enough protection to fingers and ears in the bitter cold. We wore cotton socks and the new, not very warm, synthetic orlon sweaters.

I hated winter. For some reason, I got cold faster than anyone else. Roxy and Winky never complained about the cold, and they didn't understand why I could never get used to it. At school, I dawdled over lunch, so I wouldn't have to go outside for a long, cold recess. And when I did go out, instead of playing on the playground, I huddled in a wind-free corner and shivered. No matter what I did to protect myself, after recess my numb fingers would feel like they had needles stabbing through my veins. The pain only stopped after my fingers had thawed and the blood stopped rushing to them.

Roxy was embarrassed by me. She hated prissy girls, and only prissy girls disliked the cold. She said if I learned to enjoy some winter sport, I might get over this idiotic thing.

So, in December 1953, all my six-year-old desires concentrated on one thing. I decided I would learn to skate. First, I needed a pair of white leather skates with candy stripe laces. At Brownies, that was Girl Scouts for the younger kids, Jule Lind's mother taught me how to make a red yarn bob for the skate's toes out of Grandma's left-over yarn that she had given me. I cut out two cardboard donuts, and then twisted the yarn into and out of the inner hole with the colorful wool. When the circle was full of yarn, I inserted a pair of scissors and clipped the two circles apart, carefully inserting a long yarn tie between them. I pulled the tie so tight the two sides joined one another and formed a perfect yarn puff.

Now, all I needed was a pair of skates to mount my colorful bob on. My friends knew, Grandma knew, Mother knew, and everyone else knew what I wanted for Christmas. I even wrote a letter to Santa Claus that I sent to the North Pole via our rural postal service.

Downtown, the boys in Afton Park, across from Selma's Ice Cream Parlor, played hockey every day after school. When their games were done, girls, in delicate figure skates, were "allowed" to take over the rink, while the boys went into Selma's for candy and hot chocolate. But the minute the boys returned, the girls again sat on the sidelines. That prejudicial system did not rule at our rink.

At the back end of our property, a muskrat pond dried out completely in certain years, but in other years froze wide and slick, big enough for both hockey and figure skating. And this was an ice year. I followed Roxy, Chuck, and Carol's teenaged uncle David along the path, through the pines, and watched them shovel snow until they had cleared off a huge, shiny rink.

I slid on the smooth ice with my snow boots, clumsy and slow, singing the Skater's Waltz inside my head. "Da – da – da dum. Da – da – da dum." It was boring sliding in boots

I wanted to skate, even if it was just to clear the rink.

My mind wandered. "Da–da–da smart. Da–da–da smart." I had to be smart about this. I knew when I got home from the rink, no matter how hard I pleaded, Mom would give me the same answer.

"No, you can't wear tight, pointed-toe skates." She explained, "You have to wear warm boots over your toes. You know what happened to you. You're not like the others. It's too cold for you."

I'd been told the story many times, about how I'd been frost-bitten when I was young. I knew the story was true, because my toes, fingers, nose, ears, and chin always got numb before everyone else's.

It happened when I was three years old. Roxy, five at the time, and the older children of a family we were visiting on St. Mary's Point, decided to go skating on a frozen portion of the St. Croix River. I begged to go with them. Mother was skeptical, but finally said yes, and made them promise to keep a close eye on me.

The St. Croix didn't freeze over enough for walking on or skating until the coldest days of winter, and this day was no exception. It wasn't long before my hands had no feeling in them, and I wandered off, trying to find my way back to their house.

The others were too busy skating in long rope lines to notice that I was gone. It took no time at all before my fuzzy brain didn't recognize anything familiar, and I followed a deer path in the wrong direction. When my sister and the others returned home an hour later, and realized I wasn't there, the adults panicked.

They quickly organized a search party that panned out in all directions, but especially the direction of the river. They knew there was still open water on the St. Croix. They tried not to think that I might have traveled in that direction. It was December, and no one survived long in icy winter waters.

My father was relieved when, perilously close to the river, he found me hung up and dangling on a barbed wire fence I'd tried to crawl over. Barbed wire fences were a way for wealthy residents along the river to keep out unwanted visitors. I couldn't cry for help. I couldn't even cry.

My mouth had frozen shut. My mittens were stiff with ice.

One boot had fallen to the ground and was filled with snow, leaving my toes protected only by a cotton stocking.

One eyelid had closed, and the other was fighting to keep open and awake.

I'd heard this story many times over the years, and it never changed, so I know it was true.

I don't remember the journey home, stuffed inside Dad's coat, or the thawing-out process. But I know it must have been painful, because it was my first, and most severe, frostbite. I have re-experienced that knife-cutting, needle sensation of blood returning to my appendages hundreds of times over the years.

But at age six, I wanted to be like everyone else. Roxy had her skates since she was five, and my friend, Judy Hancock, two days younger than I was, had already gotten hers for her birthday. I knew I had to convince them, so I began humming the Skater's Waltz in the bathtub, while I washed dishes, as I dressed for school, and especially while I cut out pictures of skates and skaters from *Look Magazine*.

Hoping that desire could overcome the consequences of Minnesota's cold, a pair of smooth, white leather skates with red laces, pom poms, and tiny blue bells waited for me beneath the Christmas tree, enforcing my belief in Santa Claus for one more year.

Later that day, after a Christmas dinner of lutefisk, boiled potatoes, and rutabagas, limpa and butter, with molded Jello full of Mom's frozen garden raspberries, and Swedish rice pudding, I tied my long skate laces together, flung them over my shoulder, and followed my cousins, sister, and neighbors out the door.

My new skates bumped against me as I walked, one against my back, one over my heart, blue bells tinkling, as we trekked back through the pines to the frozen muskrat swamp.

Before anyone could skate, we had to clear the new snow off the rink. The older kids skated back and forth with shovels while we younger ones gathered firewood.

Even though the sun shone brightly, it didn't have enough strength that December afternoon to warm any of us. The weatherman would have called it an "arctic high" with northwest winds that blew all hope of heat into cloudless reaches of clear, blue space.

By the time the rink was cleared and the fire roaring, my fingers and toes were already as stiff as the frozen cattails still rising above the ice.

I sat on a cold granite boulder and carefully removed my mittens. It was the only way I could lace my new ice skates tight enough to keep my ankles from wobbling. But when I tried to weave the laces through the holes, my fingers moved slower and slower until they failed to respond entirely to my brain's directives. I clumsily fit them once again into my wool mittens, but it did no good.

As I know now, wool is meant to preserve a body's heat, but when the body produces little heat of its own, wool can't help. I stuck my fingers over the fire just long enough to thaw them, and I kept thawing them at intervals until I had my skates laced. Then I set out on the ice.

As my body straightened, I soon learned that balance was an acquired skill. The only way I could maneuver, on the ice or off, was to lean inward, on my ankles, more leather touching ice than blade. It was hard work, staying upright. There was no way I could twirl and spin like my sister or my older cousins Gloria and Sandy.

Suddenly Roxy grabbed my mitten. I was at the end of a long, fast whip, gliding, it seemed, a hundred miles an hour, around and around and around, laughing, my heart pounding, scared, terrified, exhilarated, and then I launched ... smashing head first into a giant snow bank at the rink's edge.

Gloria came to my rescue, helped me recover my balance, then set me off wobbling back to the granite stone beside the campfire. I unlaced my skates. I could no longer feel my toes, barely feel my fingers, and my face was paralyzed with the cold. I couldn't talk.

I scooted closer to the fire and stuck the toes of my skates over the warm coals. For a long time I sat there, listening to the melody of the Skater's Waltz floating through my brain. I was mesmerized as the others glided and twirled, and I hoped one day to be able to skate like that.

Then I smelled something strange. Something hot, something burning. I looked around, then down. To my horror the beautiful white leather toes of my skates were smoking, and had turned black.

Roxy smelled something too, and had skated over to the fire to see what was happening. "You ruined 'em, your new skates. What a dope-head!"

"Santa'll neve' bring anytin' I ask for agin," I mumbled, my mouth still too numb and stiff to speak clearly.

"Dummy, there's no Santa anyway. It's Mom and Dad'll be mad."

Disgusted, I gazed down at my skates. That moment a gust of wind shot a finger of flame out of the fire and stabbed it into my face. Strangely, I felt no heat, just a smothering sensation, then raw pain. All I could think of were the flames of hell reaching toward me because of what I had done to my precious Christmas present.

I started home, crying and shouting back at her, "You're wron' bout Santa." I hobbled up the pine path, in unlaced skates, balancing on twisted ankles.

They could hear me before I got to the door. Mother gasped when she saw the red, hive-like blotches on my face. "Quiet now, 'Tunie. All this fuss won't help."

My eyebrows and eyelashes were gone, singed by the flame, but I didn't care what my face looked like. I didn't care about the burning pain. All I could think about were my new skates, now scratched, burnt and twisted out of shape. I held back tears, but sobbed until I could catch my breath.

The fire had not warmed my fingers and toes. They were quickly diagnosed as frost-bitten. The adults discussed among themselves whether to immerse the fingers and toes first into hot or cold water. They decided that cold would be first, followed by lukewarm, and lastly hot water. It all felt the same to me. As soon as the blood began flowing into the frost-bitten flesh I felt the stabbing pain. They gently rubbed butter on my face, but nothing was gentle enough to soothe my burning face, toes, fingers... and conscience.

The skates weren't completely ruined. They were polished and sharpened. Eventually I learned to balance, but I never again loved to skate as I did before fire and ice took their toll. Even after decades, when I'm outside in the winter, my mouth freezes stiff and I am unable to talk. My full eyelashes never grew back.

Ice always seems to win the battle. My desire for winter sports still exists. I try to ski, skate, build snow-men and – women, but frost's bite is more powerful than the full burning flame of desire. Robert Frost was right to ask questions about fire and ice. But my conclusion more closely resembles T.S. Eliot's lines from "The Hollow Men":

This is the way the world ends
Not with a bang but a whimper.

A cold, frozen whimper. A giving up. Winter tasted a bite of me when I was young and tender, and kept wanting more.

Its cold keeps coming from behind, like an attacker in the dark. It leaks in beneath layers of wool. It lies hidden in the wind. First it numbs, then when the healing begins, blood flow returns with its internal knives, slashing.

I started giving up on winter that Christmas, but I didn't give up on Santa. Pastor Borg preached about the baby in the manger bringing us a new beginning. But I kept re-membering that Jesus was born in a warm place, where he wouldn't have known snow, ice, or frostbite. I understood Santa so much better. He had to wear fur-lined clothes to keep warm, and his nose looked like mine when I came in from below-zero cold. I figured that meant Santa un-derstood me too. He had to ride on the coldest night of the year in an open sleigh through snow and ice and then plunk down in a hot fireplace, boots first. I knew Santa had felt stinging needles in his toes. And I also knew they would never cause Santa to whimper.

I refused to believe what my cynical sister had told me. Sometimes it seemed that Santa was the only one who understood me, watched over me, cared for me. The song "Santa Claus is Coming to Town", written by Coots and Gillespie in 1934 reassured me:

He sees you when you're sleeping.
He knows when you're awake.

Sometimes I'd talk to him when I couldn't fall asleep. I told him he was a little stingy with the gifts last year, just paper dolls and underwear, but then, that's what I needed. And the skates this year were wonderful, until I ruined them. It wasn't his fault.

Later that night after the burned skates, when my cousins had all gone home and I was lying in my top bunk bed, I heard Roxy's sleepy breathing. My throbbing face hurt too much to sleep, my guilt keeping my brain alert, I summoned Santa once more.

"Did you know I'd mess 'em up, Santa? Was that why it took so long to get my skates? Did you know what was comin'?"

I fell asleep on the last word, never getting an answer.

"She's so sweet the honey bees
swarm around her mouth…"

– American folk song

part II
"cindy"

Crystalized

Blue-veined
skin pulled tight
over sharp bones,

corn-silk hair
clinging like
wisps of dust,

her sad eyes search
for agate and geode's
internal secret.

She'd been strong,
hearse door slamming
on her thumb,

swelling, throbbing,
holding it upright
at church, grave,

ashes to ashes,
dust to dust,
dirt on her daddy.

Her face reveals
no weathering,
but in the bloodlines,

peaks of stillness
and shadowed valleys
crystallize.

chapter 8
out-lier

Trillium
[*Trillium cernuum*]

We Valley kids hated having to take the hour-long bus ride to Stillwater Junior and Senior High Schools. Not only getting up early to catch the bus, we also had to wait at the school for the late bus to get us home around 6PM (for kids who were in clubs and sports). But the hardest thing about going to school in the big town of Stillwater, Minnesota, was that it would mean taking classes with all strangers.

As a sixth grader, I had taken tests that determined which track I would enter in seventh grade. They put me on the accelerated track, which was an honor, but I was all alone.

I became a member of a small group of students who would soon share almost all our classes throughout our high school years. It turned out they were wonderful kids, but they were mostly townies who had known each other all their lives, were used to partying together and hanging out, and I, a shy, skinny kid from rural Afton, had little chance of inclusion.

A few weeks before entering junior high, Mother had driven Roxy and me across the river to the Hudson, Wisconsin bus depot, where the two of us boarded a bus for St. Paul. She gave us enough cash for each of us to buy underwear, one pair of shoes, boots, one winter coat, and a new outfit.

We were savvy shoppers. Roxy figured out a way to skimp on underwear and boots, and use the extra money for a high quality sweater or skirt. She always bought the best clothes, I guess because she'd learned to sew in 4-H and was a seamstress herself. It didn't matter to me. I'd usually use the extra money to buy two cheaper sweaters. For shoes she'd look for the label Capezio and I'd buy PayLess.

The ride to the big city was long, but exciting, over the river, past the gravel pits and the Splinter twins' farms, then the little Catholic church on the hill overlooking the highway. After that on the left, if I strained hard, I could see the hospital where I was born, straight ahead all the railroad tracks that led into and out of the city, and finally the capitol building and cathedral off in the distance. We knew not to get off the bus until we were parked right in front of The Golden Rule Department Store.

It was still August and even our skimpy sundresses couldn't keep us from sweating as we stepped off the bus. It seemed strange that the store windows were decorated with displays of wool sweaters and skirts with matching knee-highs, corduroy jumpers, winter blouses and wool pea coats, most designed around a rich, warm color they called burgundy. (I had no idea it was named after wine.) Without shopping anywhere else, I dragged

Roxy into The Golden Rule and purchased a soft burgundy wool sweater, matching plaid skirt, and kneehighs. Later I found burgundy-colored loafers and cheap underwear. The outfit was so beautiful I knew that every time I wore it, I'd feel confident in my new school and unfamiliar surroundings.

It took awhile, but eventually Roxy purchased all she needed, plus finding a good deal on an extra pair of shoes. We were proud of our purchases. We realized we had time left, so Roxy decided to give me one of her "normal person" lessons. She led me down the street until we stood in front of the prestigious St. Paul Hotel.

"First, stand tall," Roxy pronounced. "Pretend you are a guest of this hotel."

"What? Do I look like somebody staying here?"

"No, you don't. That's why I'm telling you to stand tall."

I stuck out my chest.

"That's better. Now pretend you are … oh … how about Evelyn Grant?"

Mrs. Grant lived down the road from us, was educated, and never let us forget that her ancestors were the original pioneers in our Valley Creek community.

"Do I have to be that stuffy?" We both laughed.

"Tell them you want two chocolate éclairs to go," she whispered. Roxanne knew her way around town, but in her shyness she refused to talk to strangers. "Here's the money."

I tried to stand tall, and then walk that way into the hotel café. I saw an elderly, thin woman behind the counter, smiled at her and said, "Two chocolaty clairs, please."

"To go," Roxy whispered loudly from just inside the door. "Tell her they're 'to go'."

"To go."

I handed the woman the change Roxy had given me, and then watched as she chose two exquisite pastries and wrapped them in soft tissue.

"Remember this day," Roxy said with an air of dignity. "This is an experience worth putting in your brain scrapbook. I know you have one of those because I see it working for stupid things."

We left the hotel carrying our bags, purses and two carefully held pastries, and then wandered down the street until we found a bench in a nearby park.

"Now. Taste it."

I unwrapped the tissue, maneuvered to get the whole end of the eclair into my small mouth and then took a bite.

"Ohhhh." The custard oozed out the other end and onto my hand. "It's messy, huh?"

"Yah, but then you have some left on your fingers after it's all gone."

"Ohhh, wow." It was the most wonderful thing I had ever tasted.

"Cindy, go ask that man over there what time it is. We have to catch the bus home at two."

Even though he was seated in front of the telephone company, he didn't look like someone on lunch break. He looked more like he'd been on a prolonged lunch break throughout most of the year.

"Him? Why him? Let's go back to the hotel. I'll ask that nice lady at the counter."

"No. We don't have time."

"Then you go ask him. I'm tired of doing all the talking."

"Do you want to miss the bus or not? You go ask him, or we miss the bus. It doesn't matter to me if we sit on this park bench all night. But I bet you're chicken," Roxy said. "And ask him where we get the bus too. Got that?"

I reluctantly approached the man who looked and smelled worse up close than from far away. He didn't have a watch, but when I asked him about the time he pointed at the bank tower's clock. I wasn't sure the man could talk at all but I figured I'd ask him about the bus anyway. He pointed to the nearest intersection.

Roxy was laughing as I came back to report my findings.

"Ok. Let's go. At least we don't have to walk very far," she said.

We stood for a while on the corner and then saw not one, but three buses approaching.

"Roxy, which one do we get on?"

"I don't know, Stupid. Ask that lady."

I approached a middle-aged woman holding shopping bags and asked her which bus would take us to Hudson. (We meant Hudson, Wisconsin of course.)

"Hudson? I don't know that street," replied the woman. "Just take the Randolph Street bus. It has the longest route, so it's probably what you're looking for."

"Thanks." Neither Roxy, nor I, thought it looked right, but we boarded anyway. We stood in the aisle and read each street sign, realizing that we did not recognize any of the landmarks.

"We should be on Highway 12 by this time, heading for Wisconsin," I said.

"I know, and we're still in the city. I think we're going the wrong direction."

Finally the driver told us to get off. It was the end of the Randolph Street route. We wandered into an Embers Restaurant and called home.

Mother wasn't happy about driving into the city, finding the restaurant, and taking us home. As we drove home in silence I kept remembering the taste of that *chocolaty clair*, and wondering if I'd ever taste such a thing again. I thumbed through my shopping bags imagining what I'd look like wearing my new clothes.

A couple of weeks went by before I had a chance to wear them. Then one morning at the end of September, the temperature dropped into the forties, and my wool out-fit felt warm as I climbed into the cold school bus. I felt even warmer when Judy Hancock, who got on the bus five minutes before me, and always saved me a seat, gave me a compliment.

But when we arrived in Stillwater, and I skipped down the steps of the bus, I looked around the schoolyard and discovered I was not the only one wearing burgundy. It was everywhere, burgundy cardigans and twin sets, paisley burgundy jumpers, and sweaters just like mine.

I wanted to fit in, but I didn't want to blend in. I desperately wanted to be one of them, but I also wanted to be *me*. I should have realized that burgundy was the featured color in all the store windows. Why hadn't it occurred to me that everyone else would buy it too?

By the time I got home from school I was so sick of burgundy, I took my outfit off, threw it on the floor of my closet, and never wore it again.

For some kids fitting in wouldn't have felt so strange, but for me it meant that the rest of the year I would choose to wear my old clothes, the ones I never got compliments on, the ones with rolled up waists, the homemade sweaters, the socks with holes in the toes and heels. That was the day I realized there were lots of things other people thought I needed, but I didn't.

Even my own thoughts about what I needed were not always accurate. And strangely, there were some extra things, like access to ballet and music lessons and concerts and *chocolaty clairs*, that none of us really needed, but I had access to them, and they became some of the most important.

It's common for teenagers to want to be accepted by the group, and to have friends, but I stubbornly adhered to my own rules about what I would do to get them. My stubbornness has persisted into adulthood.

I still won't tell a lie, not even a white one.

I've gotten in trouble because I won't apologize when it's not my fault.

And I've several times convinced whole committees to do things my way, when one moment earlier they had been united in the opposite conclusion.

I always thought that characteristic came from living in the country, and being free to explore the wild world about me. My house didn't have a street number, and didn't have a sidewalk outside the door. We let our dog run loose.

When I was mad or sad or happy, I didn't seek out a friend, I ran to the creek and immersed myself in the near frozen water, or to the gravel pit to search for agates. And sometimes I followed paths further than I should have, practicing how it was to be an explorer of flowing waters, wetlands, meadows, deer paths and roads home again.

———— ∘O∘ ————

When my first child was born in 1972, I responded to a call from the University of Minnesota psychology department. They were looking for babies for their experiments. Britta was five months old. They said the experiments would in no way hurt her, and I would be present at all times.

When we arrived, the psychologists gave Britta a pacifier. She had never liked pacifiers, but when she discovered that if she sucked hard enough, a bell would ring, she responded with a mighty suck. The experiment was designed to measure how long it would take to extinguish

the "learned response," so after a few minutes the exper-
imenters no longer rang the bell, even when she sucked
her hardest. After forty minutes of sucking after the bell
was silenced, the psychologists stopped the experiment.

One of the researchers turned to me and said, "You can
pick her up now, and get her ready to go home."

"But she hasn't stopped sucking the pacifier yet. You can't
quit now. That's not accurate research," I said.

"No baby has gone longer than ten minutes after we
stopped ringing the bell. Your child has already gone
forty minutes and shows no signs of stopping."

"Yes?"

"We are removing her data from the experiment, and pretending she never came. She is what we call an out-lier."

"Out-lier?" I was a bit confused by this knowledge about
my child.

The researcher smiled and said, "You have a stubborn
child."

She was only five months old. I couldn't possibly have
taught her to be stubborn. She must have inherited it from
someone.

Ah, now I see. She got it from me.

———— ∘○∘ ————

Two short rings. The party line phone signaled for us to
answer. Before it rang again, Winky, the fastest runner

in the house, lifted the receiver, greeting the caller with a cheery, "Hel – lo."

"Mama, Mrs. Grant wants to talk to you," he shouted across two rooms.

Ordinarily I'd have continued with my project, which that day, in the summer before junior high school, was polishing my agate collection with clear fingernail polish. But not this time. My stomach turned to stone and I felt instant pressure squeeze my chest. I knew there could be only one reason Mrs. Grant would be calling my mother, and it meant trouble, my trouble.

I had only dealt with Mrs. Grant twice in my life, and I had totally botched the first time, and then yesterday, at the most important occasion of her life, it was my doing that had ruined it. I'd hoped Mother hadn't seen, but now she'd know for sure.

The first time I messed things up for Mrs. Grant was a few years earlier, during the occasion of her niece's visit. Jay and Evelyn Grant had no children of their own, so it was a special occasion to welcome one of their Eastern relatives to the Valley, especially a niece or nephew. Everyone knew Mrs. Grant was descended from the famous Lemuel Bolles, one of the first Minnesota pioneers. The real name of the creek closest to my house is Bolles Creek, next to which Jay and Evelyn Grant lived in the 1843 historic home of her famous relative.

Their home was colonial, and had a white frame with green shutters, a bare minimum of Greek revival features, over two stories and ten rooms. They had the first running water and telephone in the Valley. It was decidedly different from the Swedish and German style farmhouses almost everyone else lived in. The Grants' house looked as if it had been transplanted from New England, old and respectable.

As a child, I never thought it was that great a house, not half as pretty as the Steglich's house, the only other New England style house in the Valley, because it had old, grayed, and chipped-off paint. We joked that it looked that way because Evelyn wouldn't change anything about the house, and she must have wanted the paint to be original too.

Our house, built around the same time, had a stone foundation that could only have been built by a Swedish stonemason. Mother had a standing argument with Mrs. Grant about the age of our homes. When my parents bought our house in 1947, the deed gave the age of the house as 100 years old, and listed over 100 owners.

Evelyn insisted our house could not be that old because in 1847 the Swedish immigrants had not yet arrived in Minnesota. In my later research I found that Jacob Fahlstrom, the first Swede in Minnesota, called the "Swede Indian" had, in 1841, already settled his family of nine children into a cabin just up the Indian Trail from the site of our house. The argument never resolved, except that in the minds of our neighbors, Evelyn Grant was known as an historian, and my mother was not.

That first time when I messed up, everything happened because Mother asked the Grants' niece to babysit us while she and Dad took a rare night out. When the babysitter arrived she was wearing a lacy, white sundress, and carrying a valise full of stationery. She had no intention of entertaining three backwoods rag-a-muffins, so she calmly sat on the couch in the family room and proceeded to write letters to her friends back east. She used a fancy fountain pen, which she dipped into an ink bottle positioned on the overstuffed couch cushion next to her.

It was not my intention to upset the bottle of black ink onto the babysitter's white sundress. I had only wanted to sit on the couch and watch *Leave It to Beaver*. I was probably bopping my foot up and down too vigorously, or reaching for something, and somehow the bottle lost its balance and tipped her way. You'd have thought I'd thrown a snake on her, the way she bellowed – and kept on bellowing.

"I'll never come to this Valley again," she screamed. "You stupid, dirty little brat." Then she called my parents and insisted they drive home immediately.

Roxy and Winky thought it was wonderful, exactly what she deserved. But I hadn't meant to spill the ink, and I had ruined one of the prettiest dresses I'd ever seen.

Somehow Evelyn Grant had found it in her heart to forgive me for that, because in the summer of 1959, on the proudest occasion of her life, she chose me to hold one end of a very official ribbon, and then to be the official punch pourer at the reception. It was the culmination of years of work with the State of Minnesota and Washington County Historical Societies to have an historical marker placed near State Highway 95, just north of the village of Afton, to commemorate her forebearer, Lemuel Bolles.

That day, I wore a sleeveless flowered dress and white patent leather shoes I'd bought for elementary school graduation a few months earlier. My white-gloved hand held one end of the ceremonial ribbon, while my friend, Pat Rarig, whose family had built a home south of the Grants' on Bolles Creek, held the other end. In hindsight, I believe the only reason I was picked was because Pat insisted on it, and Pat always got what she wanted.

It was hot that August afternoon as we stood next to county commissioners, mayors, historians and important people. Evelyn Grant, dressed in a boring gray suit, looked through the bottom of her bifocals and began to read aloud the words inscribed on the marker.

"Bolles Flour Mill. About 1843, six years before Minnesota became a territory, Lemuel Bolles erected on this creek the first commercial flour mill in the Minnesota country."

She paused from her reading and looked around, trying to locate an annoying, scratching sound. I stood up straight and listened as she resumed her reading.

"Bolles salvaged wood from the shore of Lake St. Croix and carried it on his back to the mill site a mile and a half upstream. Lacking nails, he used wooden pegs in the construction of a small mill."

I found myself first hacking at the hardened dirt ground with the heel of my shoe, then digging with the toe, the shoe no longer white, but covered with beige dust. A large, red-banded agate was clearly visible beneath my feet, embedded into the hard gravel driveway. The dirt made it look brown, but I could see enough of the bands of red, orange and white beneath a coating of dried mud, to know it was a beauty. I forgot about listening to history. I had only one thought in mind, to free that agate. Then I felt the smother of collective eyes concentrating on me, and I noticed Mrs. Grant had quit reading again. I stopped digging.

"First built for grinding corn and wheat, the mill was later remodeled and was in operation as late as 1875 when Bolles died."

I had to unearth that agate before anyone else found it. Just two months earlier my cousin, Larry Kirmser from Kansas, had been visiting. As we walked through the old gravel pit he had yelled "dibs", a word entirely foreign to me, but he then explained this word's ability to claim something before someone else. He then pulled out the biggest, most beautiful banded agate I had ever seen. He took it home to Kansas with him. And then there was that stone I found in the car that Roxy had stolen from me. I'd been looking for the big one ever since. Here it was, beneath my feet. Now I could even see the light shining through its rust bands where I'd cleaned the dust off its surface with my shoe. A little heel work and it would be mine.

Pat tugged at the ribbon to get my attention, as Mrs. Grant pierced her steel eyes in my direction once more.

"The stream on which the mill was built became known as Bolles Creek."

She finished reading the inscription. The crowd clapped. The dignitaries cut the ribbon and shook hands. I pulled out the agate, plopped it into Mother's purse, and began serving punch.

No one that day mentioned my behavior, but now Mrs. Grant was on the phone asking to speak to Mother. It was serious. Mother's face wasn't smiling as she came near me.

"Evelyn has asked that you and I come to her home this afternoon at three. She didn't tell me what it was about. Do you have any idea?"

"Nope. Can't imagine." But of course I could imagine, and did imagine everything from policemen to a good bawling-out.

We walked the half-mile in silence, past Meisner's horse meadow, its long weeds waving golden with its summer yield of butter-and-eggs wildflowers, then over Valley Creek bridge (really Bolles Creek bridge), past the township hall, over the dry run, and into her yard.

Mrs. Grant met us on the creaking porch and invited us into a dark, richly furnished parlor.

"Wait here," she said.

Mother and I looked at one another, not knowing what to expect. We waited patiently until she reappeared with a large covered box. After placing it carefully on the old oak floor, she opened the lid. I gasped as my eyes focused on the contents of the treasure box.

"The stones in this rock and mineral collection come from all over the world," she said. "I either found them or bought them at their native place. In all my travels, they were my souvenirs."

She laughed. "I've gotten so old I'd almost forgotten I had them. I keep them packed away in this box and stored in the attic, but they're meant to be looked at, and loved."

She took them out, one by one, petrified wood from Wyoming, amethyst crystals from South America, black translucent Apache tear, rose quartz, fool's gold, moss agates from Montana, and black and white mica, whose layers I could peel off with my finger nail, collected at a mine in North Carolina. They were pieces of a world I wanted to know more about.

"Mrs. Grant, this is so wonderful!" I swallowed, then asked myself if I could possibly ask the next question. I decided this was my only chance, so I'd better take it.

"Can I look closer at the amethyst? Hold it up to the light maybe? It's Mom's birthstone, you know."

Her normal steel-colored eyes now appeared as soft, gray-blue wool. She replied, "It's for you. The whole collection. When I saw you yesterday, so absorbed in trying to free that agate, seeing more beauty in the bands of a dusty rock than in the inscribed words of an old historian trying to hold onto a bit of glory, I remembered what I used to be like."

She picked up an arrowhead from the collection and turned it over in her wrinkled hands. "There was a time when I came home with a torn dress because I retrieved this arrowhead from underneath the stalks of a bramble bush. Got me in a lot of trouble, but it was worth it. Put your agate beside it, and leave the collection out for everyone to see, and to touch. When it's time to pack it away, give it to some other child who will hold it dear."

Before I could think I made an audible inhaling sound as my eyes opened wide and I said, "Oh, I'll always love it!"

I grinned and said thank you, not nearly enough thanks for such a gift. In the Valley, people didn't hug or show much emotion, but I did touch every rock and mineral, showing them to Mother, and asking Mrs. Grant the names of the exotic ones. I also asked questions about the places she had visited. She promised to have me over again to continue our conversation.

On my way home with the collection, I stopped at the creek. Mother had to hurry home, but I took the time to sit on an old bucket, carefully take out and inspect each specimen, and then dip each rock and mineral into the clear, running water. I watched the colors of each band and crystal magnify in intensity. Nothing in all the world was so beautiful.

The creek babbled over its own rocks. The sky glowed a magnificent blue. The August air enfolded me like the sweet, warm heat of a cedar sauna.

Evelyn Bolles Grant, a person little known to children as anything other than a human history book, did in fact know and cherish her history, a story rooted in a community formed around a creek that bore her name. She made sure we knew why we lived in that glacial valley, and how we were interconnected to the entire world by the water running out of the limestone springs into Bolles Creek, the water that flows into the St. Croix River, into the mighty Mississippi, into the Gulf of Mexico, and finally into the great ocean. It is water that flows over rock formations and crystals thousands of miles away, water that deposits trace amounts of our Valley into folds of earth inhabited by all kinds of children.

Mrs. Grant asked me to give the collection away to another child when my life became too busy for it. I gave it to my daughter, Britta, who eventually earned her college degree in geology. She has since added many more precious stones to this collection.

Evelyn Grant never did invite me to her home again. But we always shared a smile or a wink when we saw one another at a community picnic or the grocery store. And I never lost the wonder of thinking about the outside world, wanting to go there, to touch its rocks and soil, to explore the mundane and exotic.

We shared something else too. Psychologists would probably agree that we were both out-liers, people who show a passion for something others care little about. That outlier status has remained throughout my lifetime as well. Who else owns shelves of poetry books? What adult has collections of agates and caramel rocks? Who else still locks her eyes on four-leaf clovers?

I have indeed been an out-lier my whole life. In college, I chose not to join a sorority. My reasoning was that I didn't want to divide up my friendships and live within an exclusive clique. This was the 1960's and I thought we should all be involved in breaking out of our walled silos.

At Boston University I had a strange Minnesotan accent and a regular habit of attending church each Sunday. I was chief Resident Assistant there, but the students from prominent New York or Boston Jewish families never introduced me to their parents. I suppose I understand;

I hadn't joined my roommates at dances and mixers, because I already had a fiance. And too, they still believed in cultivating friendships mainly among their own eastcoast culturally-bound tribes. My Jewish roommate for two years, Barbara, was not allowed, by her parents, to attend my Minnesota wedding, because they thought it wouldn't be "safe" for her. I've always wondered if they thought bears and wolves roamed the state, or if they were afraid of Native Americans on the warpath or something.

In Hawaii, when my husband was drafted into the military, I insisted on living off-base, and at the local church we attended, we were the only haoles (whites) – the others being Hawaiians, Japanese and immigrant Filipinos. I became the youth choir director, using my folk guitar, and Ed developed into the best basketball coach for their teen boys, who wore flip-flops as they ran against sophisticated Punahou competitors.

We moved to North Carolina for his medical fellowship, and I showed little tolerance for the discrimination in housing and social situations that I witnessed, so we moved again, this time to a tiny village in the hills of Appalachia, where I learned old-timey guitar and played with genuine Appalachian fiddlers, men who had been recorded by the Smithsonian Institute. Again, an out-lier, being the only woman musician, other than singers.

We lived in Louisiana twice, where I objected to being called a Yankee, since I wasn't a north-easterner. And I didn't appreciate the lack of, or almost non-existence of, a middle class. We, as professionals, were treated as part of the upper class there, and being from Minnesota, I detested that. I didn't want my daughter to go to "coming-out" parties, or for us to feel pressured into joining an exclusive country club. My life-long anthropology experiment has allowed me to observe other people and cultures. I am still an out-lier, as I now live in a blazing red state, and can't hide my cornflower blue heart.

I talk about where my daughter (and her daughter) got their single-mindedness, but how about me? Where did I get this tendency of being an out-lier?

My mom called herself "a horse trader", someone who can adjust to any situation. I have some of that, but looking back at my dad's personality, and his unique behavior, I am convinced that he needed to be "his own person" no matter the consequences. On the surface he was an out-lier as a non-drinking musician, a city kid living in rural Minnesota, married to a farmer's daughter. But I have way more to add to that list. Get ready!

Dialysis

Century-old oak once again
time-determined dialysis drains, weakens;
your sinking sap recalls memories of torture.

In fall, flushed with color,
your warm, sweet sap now steals and stores
its verdant shade underground.

No longer soft, plump, your condition
exposes wind-writhing naked beauty,
acutely skeletal, but upward.

Now the owl
sleeps lightly,
yet remains in faith

Until the blizzard passes
the grasses
return
and new life rises.

chapter 9

courage

Iris
[*Iris latifolia*]

Ollie, ollie, oxen free. Git outta that biffy, Winky. I know you're hiding there! If you don't git out, it's gonna git tipped!" It didn't take long before little Winky, holding his nose and laughing, ran out into the yard.

"Biffy" was the polite term we used for the rickety, hold-your-nose stinky outhouse in the Andersons' yard. It was next to their falling-down, grayish-red, see-through-the-slats barn at the side of their lot, and was a remnant from the last half of the 19th century. It was a favorite hiding place, frequented during our games of hide and seek.

The Andersons lived in a rented, 80-year-old, two-story wooden house, just south of our place. It was owned by Roy Johnson, who would later sell the adjoining property to Charles Bell, chairman of the board of General Mills, who turned it into what is now known as the Belwin Outdoor Learning Center.

We often recruited Chuck, Mark and Brent for baseball, football, Simon Says, or on hot days, water games under the bridge. Winky spent hours throwing a baseball back and forth with Brent. Roxy took every opportunity to talk about teenage matters with Chuck, who was a year older than she was. But other than being on a baseball or football team with Mark, who was my age, and had a feisty streak in him, we had little to do with one another.

Just south of their house, past the creek, on the west side of the road, stood what I thought was the most beautiful structure in the Valley, the Steglich home. A replica of a New England manor, like Evelyn Grant's home, but much larger, it was white with green awnings and trimmed with a wrap-around porch. Hiding it from the road were enormous blue spruce trees, planted one hundred or more years earlier by the original Valley pioneers.

David Steglich was the most grown up of our gang. Already in high school, when we were still in elementary school, he probably wouldn't have had anything to do with us, except he was Carol's uncle, and a friend of Chuck's. There was another reason too. David had been out of school, due to an illness, for most of the 1956 school year. By that summer, he still fatigued easily, but he was ready to do something other than lie in bed. Unfortunately, his strict mother kept him home. She was overly protective of David because she'd already lost one son, and she was not well herself, suffering from heart problems.

So the neighborhood came to David.

His disease, *nephritis*, had killed his only brother. Doctors call it the *Finn Disease*, because it was (and is) common in people of Finnish descent. David's mother, Irja, had immigrated to the U.S. from Finland, and his father, Eric, from Denmark, after the First World War.

None of us could pronounce *nephritis*, so we called it *Goliath*. We all knew the story of the giant and the king-to-be. The name seemed appropriate to us because David was our fearless leader, organizer and entertainer. We never imagined how truly gargantuan this disease, this *Goliath*, would become.

Though limited to home for long months at a time, David's life was exciting. He owned a chemistry set and performed smoky and stinky experiments for his curious onlookers. If we asked politely, Irja would even sometimes allow us to tiptoe into the attic, and listen to David talk to voices from around the world on his shortwave radio. And for unknown reasons I was most attracted to David's pet birds, dogs, rabbits, horse, lizards, frogs, and especially snakes. He showed us how the hog-nose snake used temper tantrums to protect itself, and how the bull and garter snakes, which eat rodents, are really our friends. He even got me to hold these snakes. Now that, to me, was a genuine act of faith.

David wouldn't lie to me, even if my intuition screamed at me to run. He taught me I didn't have to act like a girl. I didn't need to be afraid of snakes and mice.

And I could take off my shirt and run around in shorts, just like the Anderson boys. Roxy said it was okay for me, because I was only nine years old, but she was too mature and would never be able to go shirtless again.

David, who wasn't allowed to go anywhere, was like a big brother we all loved, and we made it our duty to get him to laugh. One day as we were joking around, pretending to be characters from fairy tales, I said, "Why not? Let's put on a play."

Roxy piped in, "I'll do it if I get to be gussied up like a queen."

Chuck said, "I'll be the prince," and eyed his queen. David nodded his head and quickly started organizing. That day a lot of us my age and younger wanted to be in the play, so David decided Snow White and the Seven Dwarfs would be the best. How special it was for a gang of kids whose ages ran a gamut of ten years, to all be included.

Snow White would be my beautiful eleven-year-old sister, with her snow white skin and auburn hair, and Prince Charming would be played by Chuck. He was tall for his twelve years, and when I look back on it, actually good looking, and he definitely saw himself as charming and prince-like. But the star of the production was Scout, David's pinto pony. At the end of the play Scout came on stage carrying Roxy, sitting side-saddle on his back, led by Prince Charming.

I still chuckle as I remember being the Queen and looking into the mirror saying, "Mirror, mirror, on the wall, who is the fairest of them all?" And of course it was easy to play, because my sister was so beautiful, and I was just a rag-a-muffin who wanted to be beautiful, just like the Queen.

I enjoyed poisoning the apple and fooling the dwarfs. The dwarfs were Winky, Carol, Mark and Brent Anderson, and the three Olson kids, Mark, Charlotte and Peter. They were told to just act goofy, as they were all naturals at it, and to sing, *"Heigh ho, heigh ho, it's off to work we go..."* They spent whole afternoons giggling other lyrics, such as: *Heigh ho, heigh ho, it's off to school we go. We learn some junk and then we flunk, heigh ho, heigh ho.* Until director David brought us back to task.

Part of the fun was making the costumes. Snow White had a lace blouse and a long billowing skirt, which we borrowed from Mother, because it had to flow over the side of Scout. All the dwarfs put on shorts and vests and fake beards. And I, as the Queen, got to wear an old formal from Carol's dress-up clothes, safety-pinned to fit me. We fashioned a crown for the prince, and we made him wear his tall leather boots.

The performance was on a perfect summer afternoon on Steglich's immense green lawn. We had picked flowers for Snow White to wear in her hair, and made a circle of clover for Scout's neck. At the end we all came out to take a bow, followed by our director, David, who received many shouted *Bravos* from the audience of our parents and neighbors.

We celebrated our success by arranging a camp-out in Steglich's back hundred acres. Each of us carried a bedroll, attached with twine to our backs, and delegated food. We formed a line behind director David, Prince Charming, Snow White, and the wicked Queen, followed by the seven dwarfs arranged according to height. Heigh ho, heigh ho ...

David first led us through a dry-run ravine, then south up a steep hill planted with rows of future Christmas trees of Scotch and Norway Pine. Finally we came to a summer blooming meadow at the hilltop, purple with vetch and spotted with buttercups and daisies. We arranged our bedrolls in a semi-circle around a rock-enclosed fire pit that marked the center of the clearing, where it was obvious that David had camped before. Since the climb had been hot and strenuous, the boys, Carol, and I shed our shirts, and then scattered to gather firewood for the evening.

I smelled it first, then my sister, then everyone.

"It's a skunk! Peeewww!" Carol shouted.

David commanded, "Everyone around the fire pit. Quick! It could be rabid. Skunks only act friendly if they've got rabies. Get in your bed-rolls and don't move."

He rustled through his belongings and brought out a slingshot. The skunk peeked its head through the tangled vetch.

I gasped.

At least the skunk wasn't foaming at the mouth like the one that had come to our back door just a week earlier. We all knew that even if a skunk didn't have rabies, it could wreak havoc with our noses. When our dog had been sprayed, even a tomato juice bath couldn't get the putrid smell out.

David lifted the slingshot to his eye, pulled the elastic, aimed. BINGO! It was a good enough shot to send the skunk racing to Timbuktu. We'll never know why it didn't spray us first, but I guess it must have sensed whom it was up against.

The moon rose late that night. We all saw it because we were still awake listening to stories of ghosts, murderers, and flying saucers. David had memorized every book he'd read in those long, bed-ridden months, and he entertained us until our eyelids closed. When he thought the dwarves were asleep, he, Chuck, and Roxy took turns whispering dirty jokes to one another. I absorbed every word, with eyes closed, laughing into my pillow at what I understood, and storing away words I didn't know, to ask my sister sometime when she was in a good mood.

When we marched home the next day, we asked our parents if we could stay one more night in the woods. It was Irja who said, "No." The mercury had dropped too low. She was sure David hadn't had enough sleep, and one night's strain was enough.

After that summer David considered himself too old to hang around the Valley urchins. I didn't see him again until I attended his wedding. He had finished a couple of years at the University of Minnesota, met his fiancée, Audrey, and decided to marry and move to Oklahoma to work as an x-ray technician.

But Goliath found him there. David's kidneys failed again, and he and Audrey moved back to Valley Creek. His father made room for them in his house. Eric was happy to have them because Irja had recently died of another heart attack.

Once situated in the Valley, David trekked into the Twin Cities for dialysis treatments. Doctors told him dialysis wasn't a permanent solution, and his only chance for survival was an experimental procedure, called a kidney transplant. In the mid-1960's few doctors had performed kidney transplants, and they knew virtually nothing about tissue typing. David had no relative who could donate a kidney for him, and the future looked bleak. Hospitals demanded thousands of dollars, which he didn't have, for a transplant that probably wouldn't work.

After exhausting every resource, David put down his slingshot and waited to die.

Late one night the phone rang. It was one of those dreaded calls when you know someone is dying or has been in an accident. The voice was from Hennepin County Hospital in Minneapolis. Eric knew it was bad news. The doctor on the other end told him there had been a car accident. But it was no one known to the Steglichs. A man had died and his relatives decided to release his one good kidney.

It was unbelievably good news! Did David want it? They had chosen David as the best candidate for the kidney because of his young age. They told him not to worry about the expense. Just hurry.

Doctors called it a cadaver kidney, meaning it came from a dead body, not a relative, not even one that had been tissue typed to match David. He would essentially be a guinea pig. It was a very long shot with his slingshot, but David said "yes" and aimed.

His body accepted the kidney, with the help of hundreds of drugs that stripped him of his strength, his stomach, his bone mass, and caused numerous other side effects. Doctors told him if he lived he'd never be able to father children. Yet, five years later he and Audrey had not one child, but two. Ten years later he braved another kidney transplant with all its additional side effects. It lengthened his life long enough to see his children graduate from high school, and to see them also marry.

At his fiftieth birthday, it was apparent David's second transplanted kidney had succumbed to the same disease. Doctors advised a third transplant. David responded, "The Bible says there's a time to be born, and a time to die."

Standing eye to eye with his old foe, Goliath, David acknowledged the strength of his unworthy opponent. The slingshot had worked twice, but his aging hands refused to pull it again. He died within the year, a few days after celebrating the birth of his first grandchild.

I vividly recall director David boosting Snow White onto the back of Scout, showing her how to ride sidesaddle in her long princess skirt. And I remember with joy, following him up the hill into an adventure, where he rescued us with his good aim. I am so proud of him, my neighbor and friend, fighting for his life as a pioneer in the field of transplantation, and fighting, too, for the lives of millions of transplant patients who have and will benefit from David and his courage.

David taught me something else too. That night while we were camping, he let me try his slingshot. David stood behind me, took hold of both the slingshot and my hands, and guided it into a taut position. "Are you ready to let go? Do you see where you're aiming?" he said, my hands already tired from the stretch.

"Yah, I see it. Yah, I'm ready." He let go, allowing me to fire, right on target.

Trail to an Inner Lake: Voyageurs National Park

I am not wanted here. Deer flies' nasty bites
invite me to return to trailhead, their tornado flight

In precision around my crumpled hat
rivals the decibel level of air-force fighters.

I follow wild blueberry droppings
of bear and buck — but unluckily

They've already scoured the bushes
and left none for my collecting.

Through the thicket thunders hoarse blowing
of a she-bear, warning: I am not wanted here.

As I reach the lake and dig my toes into cool water,
a near-by mother otter chatter-scolds me, as loons

whistle warnings to their frightened chicks. Alert osprey
fly from their pine perch to hide in tall birch branches.

I only wanted to know what we had left behind, but like
the dolphin who rejected life on land, and lost its feet,

My manufactured shoes slipped on the granite sheath
and got trapped in the trail's muddy sloughs.

Still I continue exploring, ignoring the "I am not
wanted here" signs (poison ivy, nettles) to glimpse

the untamed, the unnamed, the unsettled, the domain
of the stinging insect, which I have entered with no repellant.

chapter 10
boundaries

Tiger Lily
[*Lilium superbum*]

A mobster has confessed to the killing of Chicago gangster, Tony DeVito," announced Dave Moore, the anchor on the six o'clock news. He then went on to give a brief history of the mob in Minnesota and the particulars of the case, and then looking straight at the camera stated, "And the informer has disclosed that the body is buried somewhere on the outskirts of the metropolitan Twin Cities."

Roxy cocked her eye, then slowly moved her gaze toward me. We knew it was up to us to find the body.

Each day Dave Moore announced new clues: at the junction of two creeks, near a rocky ledge, where an old barn was falling down. We matched each clue to our terrain, and became more and more convinced that Tony DeVito had come to his final resting place in our valley.

To recruit help we turned to our reluctant new neighbors, Kathy and Nancy Alexander. Their father was an appointee of the governor of Minnesota, and we figured if we found the body, we'd have the full authority of the state behind us, important because we also knew we might run into the full authority of the mob.

"Ya can't be sissies now," Roxy announced, as if she was tough enough for this assignment, but wasn't sure about the rest of us.

"Ya. I heard Dad talkin' about gangsters." Turning to Kathy and Nancy, I added, "They come into the nightclub where he's playin', and demand free food and drinks all the time, and if they don't git it, or don't git somethin' else they want, the whole kit'n-ka-boodle'll be in ashes by mornin'."

"For once, she's right," Roxy said. "Dad's driven us by the black, burned out remains of more than one of 'em. He said the club owners probably wouldn't pay the mobsters their protection money, or wouldn't pay 'em enough, or on time. He knows their names and faces, mostly the Twin Cities mobsters, but he's seen the Chicago ones too. You know, one thing about those gangsters is they love good food. That's why they eat at the St. Paul House, 'cause of their popovers and steaks." Then in her know-it-all voice she added, "And of course they love the jazz, best band anywhere."

"Yeah, Dad doesn't paint a pretty picture of 'em."

What I didn't know then was that mobsters used these clubs to launder their illegal money. The practice started in New Orleans with immigrant Italian club owners, and continued into the big cities and Las Vegas. Jazz clubs couldn't make enough money without special help, and mobsters loved listening to jazz, so they scratched each others' backs.

In the end we decided to tough it out, not tell Dad, or anyone, what we were up to. Instead we armed ourselves with a Swiss army knife, a miniature Indian tomahawk, and large club-like walking sticks. We knew we could never sweet talk gangsters, who caressed their machine guns with more care than they did their wives (according to the films we had seen).

"Sorry, girl," I said to our German short-hair, Freckles, as I chained her to a tree. "Can't follow us today. Know you could sniff out a dead body, but you're too noisy."

"And we'll be walkin' close to Old Sourpuss' property," Roxy added. "We've all heard the stories about how he hates kids and dogs. Heck, he'd downright shoot us too if he knew we were there."

It made me shiver to think of Old Sourpuss. I'd seen old John Sauers riding in a car, and once at his mailbox, about half a mile north of our house. He mostly stayed to himself, with his two sons, at his place, set back from the road and hidden by huge pines. He never came to a Fourth of July picnic or a potluck, or to visit anybody for any reason. He was only known to others in the Valley by his complaints about their dogs, cars and kids. I had seen his youngest adult son several times at Beno's when we got gasoline. He was missing one of his hands. Mom told me he'd had an accident that cut off his hand. I imagined it was either from a lawnmower, or maybe he had disobeyed his dad really badly and Old Sourpuss had chopped it off himself!

I shut off my thoughts about the old man, and concentrated on the search. We started with our first clue, which was easy to find. The oldest barn around (at least it seemed to be the oldest with its chipping paint and sky clearly visible through the timbers) stood behind the Andersons' house. From there we followed deer paths between the rows of planted pines, through the heaps and valleys of the gravel pit, and over sand hills, avoiding rampant patches of sand burrs and poison ivy.

We knew enough to wear long pants and socks. Country kids never let wood ticks and snakes keep us inside, and we had learned to identify "leaves of three, let them be" as soon as we could walk. City kids called everything with three leaves poison ivy, but we could identify wild strawberry, box elder, blackberry, and the look-alike Virginia creeper vine. We stayed away from whitish-green berries on a small woody stalk, and never dug into the sand under a cliff if it had roots in it. Twice neighbors had been hospitalized with poison ivy. Irja Steglich had mistakenly harvested its beautiful green berries and arranged them into a May basket. I doubt she had seen that kind of ivy in her native Finland. And a few years later her son, David, got a terrible case from the juice of its poisonous roots. He had spent an afternoon engineering roads and tunnels in a sandy ravine filled with woody roots that were connected to the poisonous three leaf plants just a few feet away. We knew enough to let the poison ivy be.

The deer trails we followed led us around numerous woodland potholes and sloughs, and finally to an open meadow with round spots of tamped down grass.

"There it is," Nancy shouted.

We all ran toward the meadow, falling into the grassy bed.

"Somethin's been here, that's for sure," I said.

"Ya, somethin', but not a gangster," Roxy said in her authoritative voice. "This is where deer slept last night. If you're quiet you might see 'em."

We needed a rest. We laid down in the long grass and watched for any animal movement, waiting for our own racing hearts to slow.

"We need a con-frence," Roxy announced. "Whaddya think this grave'll look like?"

None of us had ever seen a grave other than in a cemetery where a grave was just a big mowed lawn with a marble marker. We never buried our dogs. They had always just disappeared.

"Do ya think they put 'em in a pine box, like in the cowboy shows?" I asked.

"No, Stupid! How ya gonna carry a pine box out here?" my sister replied. "It'd be just his body, but I'm sure they dug it into the ground so ravens and coyotes wouldn't eat 'em."

"You mean, we might be lookin' for ... bones?" asked Nancy. She was the youngest of the four of us, and we probably shouldn't have taken her with us to do this adult job.

"Of course we're lookin' for bones," Kathy replied. "He's been dead a long time, and they don't do funeral home stuff to murdered bodies. So let's start lookin' for surface bones or a lump with a suspicious marker on it, like a pile of rocks or somethin'."

Inside my brain I started singing *Dem bones, dem bones, dem dry bones …*

Nancy and I were quiet for a long time, neither of us sure we should continue this search. But we kept following the two older girls across the sand hill road, up Haslund's hill, around the newly planted pine seedlings, and finally under a barbed wire fence marked with a sign, *TRESPASSERS WILL BE PROSECUTED.* We knew we were entering the well-patrolled domain of John Sauers, the infamous Old Sourpuss.

He owned acres of beautiful land. We proceeded quietly. As we checked out the vista from a high hill overlooking a hidden lake, my sister pointed and whispered, "There's a rocky ledge. We're gittin' close. We need to find where the two creeks meet."

"Ya, that's the next clue."

"I can see one of the creeks from here," she said, "flowin' out of the lake."

"There's the other creek," I said, pointing to the north.

"That's not a creek," replied Kathy. "It's a cattail swamp. Cattails like standin' water, not a clean, cold stream. But let's go check it out anyway. Come on!"

As I made my way down the hill I began asking myself, "What'll happen if we find the body? Who'll touch it? How'll we know if it's Tony DeVito's, or just some old pioneer?" And then the big question popped into my head. "What if mobsters are patrolling the area?"

I walked slower and slower, dropping further behind the other girls, until they were out of sight. I spied a branch of fat, juicy blackcaps in a thicket just to the left of where the others had disappeared. My stomach growled. We'd forgotten to bring snacks or drinks with us, and we'd been walking up and down hills for a couple of hours already. I popped one berry into my mouth, then another. After I finished off the first bush, whose berries were large and luscious that year due to a rainy spring, I spied more berries further into the thicket. I pulled apart the bushes to grab another handful, but never got a chance to taste them.

"Aaaaahhh!!!"

I don't know where the volume came from, but I know it could have been heard in Chicago. I continued screaming.

Roxy followed the yelling and ran to me in a flash, shoving her hand over my mouth.

"Shut up! You want Sourpuss to know we're here? Shut up!"

After I calmed down, she released her hand. "You see a cougar or somethin'?"

By that time Nancy and Kathy had also arrived to see what I was shouting about. My shaky hand pointed to an opening beneath the blackcap thorns. All three of them gasped simultaneously as we stared at a pile of bones."

After the stunned silence Kathy said, "Bones, we said we might find bones, but I never thought we would!"

"What we gonna do?" I whispered.

"We need the authorities," my sister replied.

"But ... What about the sign? We can't be on this property." I said. "We're trespassers. They'll put us in jail if we get the authorities."

Silence again. I was sure they could all hear my heart pounding.

"Maybe," said Nancy in her little girl voice, "we ought to tell our moms."

"Yeahhh ..." I said, and noticed the others nodding their heads.

We tied a red bandana marker onto a tree and found our way home, this time the fast way, via Valley Creek Road, with stories of gangsters, bones, and jail on our minds.

I started thinking and questioning myself. "By wanting so much to find the remains of Tony DeVito, had I somehow contacted his criminal soul that was leading me down into a dark, unknown path? Why had I stopped at those bushes? Why hadn't I just collected a few berries close to me, and moved on? It was my fault we'd found the bones, and now I was getting everyone else in trouble too!"

When we arrived home, thirsty, tired and all chattering at once, Mother stopped us and said, "Roxanne, you tell me."

"The bones, Mom! We found the bones in a bush at Sauer's."

"You found his body?" Mother asked. "Tony DeVito's body?"

"Ya," I said, "but we can't go there. We'd be trespassing."

"God help us," she whispered under her breath. "When your father comes home we'll all go together and look." She'd heard the news reports. She knew the mobster was out there somewhere. I could tell she feared and dreaded this onerous task as much as we did.

Kathy and Nancy went home debating between themselves whether to tell their parents at all. They didn't. That left Mother, Father, Roxy and me to retrace our steps, following the deer paths until we came to the barbed wire fence and the *TRESPASSERS WILL BE PROSECUTED* sign.

I looked at Dad. He winked and lifted the fence so we could all crawl under it. "What's he going to do to us anyway," Father laughed, "feed us arsenic?"

I didn't understand the joke, but Mother did.

We finally located the red bandana and the blackcap bushes. When I pulled back the branch, Mother gasped.

"Well, I'll be!" said Father. He leaned down and looked closer. "This isn't Tony DeVito. These are dog bones."

He reached into the bush and pulled out a dog collar. Poking around with a stick he discovered three skulls and enough bones to have belonged to our lost dog, Cinders, the Andersons' Toby, and Applebys' disappeared dog, Princess.

Dad threw dirt on top of the remains and said, "We've missed you, but you're in a better place now."

We stood silent a moment.

Everyone knew Old Sourpuss hated dogs, but until now it was only conjecture that he'd poisoned them with arsenic when he caught them on his property. They had tres-passed, and they'd been prosecuted. There was nothing anyone could do.

Soon after that, we brought our new golden lab puppy to Cynthia Bend, who lived at the top of Sand Hill Road, a driveway sized dirt path that bordered our property on the north. She was known as the best animal trainer in the valley. She taught "Goldie" to stay in our yard. I think I was named after Cynthia Bend. Mom and Dad would have met the Bends shortly before my birth. When I've asked about my name, Mother only says, "I liked the name." Fortunately, taking her name didn't influence my wan-dering. Leaving home has always suited me well.

In our country there exists a crisis of boundaries, perhaps more than ever. No one seems to know where to draw the line between safety and freedom, freedom and responsi-bility, between the rights of community and individual-ity. Large countries are breaking into smaller, ethnically bound states, while New Age peaceniks proclaim Space-ship Earth, where all humans and animals ride together, sharing the same home.

That first questioning of boundaries, when I accepted a gangster's challenge to explore the valleys and thickets beyond my own backyard, led me to a dark reality. Now I think twice before I listen to the challenges of others.

Back then I had no idea that in the real world, in my own family's world, boundaries had already been crossed, in-volving real flesh and bones.

The body of Tony DeVito has never been found.

First Language

Perched on the living room rug
I banged brass pots and pans,
playing percussion to Dad's records,
a mellow beat to Goodman's jazz,
muffled timpani for the Pines of Rome,
and a tinny tap of the spoon for mules
as they happily trod on the trail
of Grofé's Grand Canyon Suite.

I treasured sitting by my dad
on his organ bench, on sweet nights
at the elegant St. Paul House, watching
his stocking feet reach for the bass pedals,
and his hands play the two registers
on his beloved Hammond organ,
at the same time conducting his band
of 'bone and sax, keyboard and drum.

Afternoons at home our radio hummed out
the Lone Ranger's French horn rills
that signaled galloping horses,
and quietly on Sundays the Mormon
Tabernacle Choir's community of voices,
and when the music filled my Dad
his whole body sighed, and sometimes,
when it was so beautiful, the hairs
of his arms would rise in salute.

He chose the horn for my beautiful sister,
but I chose trombone for myself,
and sat with the boys, blowing the best notes
in Stars and Stripes Forever,
not the piccolo solo, or trumpet fanfare,
but the bombastic counter melody,
by John Phillip Sousa, grandfather of the band leader
my dad had played with and arranged for,
before the war sent him home.

Later, when we couldn't afford
to buy a good instrument for me,
I gave up trombone for a folk guitar
I redeemed with S and H Green Stamps,
good enough for strumming
the three chords required for
Ain't Gonna Study War No More.
In college I bought my koa wood guitar,
made by a company called Harmony,

and hung it around my neck
with the same blue strap I still use,
covered with white, woven peace signs.
It made a muffled, but sweet sound,
when I sang for my babies, when my students
picked it up and strummed, This Land Is Your Land,
when I wrote a song as my lover lay almost dying,
as I sang it to him lying there,
as he squeezed my hand,

when I play my son's bluegrass mass,
to celebrate our lives,
when I join my granddaughter
in singing, Take me ridin' in the car, car.
Music has been my native language,
even before I crawled out Mom's window,
a young girl, with Mary Travers hair,
onto that Valley Creek rooftop
and sang Blowin' in the Wind
to the century old maples.

chapter 11

more **secrets**

Daisy
[*Bellis perennis*]

B est friends have a way of entering the breath we breathe, so that nothing inside us is secret, and no matter what we do, it changes us. Best friends don't need to be "soul mates," in fact, we've found that the most successful best friends are different from us, different in ways that make us richer, deeper, more compassionate. Merrill Nelson and my dad diverged in many ways, but they shared one love — jazz.

My dad wasn't used to having a best friend. Always the first one invited to parties, he was convinced it was because he'd provide hours of free, cool jazz piano. That way he didn't need to talk to anyone, and he could spend time playing the expensive pianos of other people. And Dad had grown up poor — dirt poor — so, I can only imagine it felt like he was different, an outsider. But he loved to entertain.

He spent most of his waking hours picking out the melodies of the big band hits he heard on the radio, but also composing his own variations. He told me his fingers weren't long enough for the difficult chording of classical pieces, but what he lacked in reach, he made up for in dexterity. Jazz suited both his personality and his body well.

Jazz came up the Mississippi, from Memphis and New Orleans. Even though the river was essential to St. Paul, the primordial goo that created a loose, laid-back jazz didn't happen there. But by the 1920's and 30's it had jived up-river, using its rhythms to shake loose even stiff Scandinavian souls. Every once in a while jazz was played on popular WCCO radio, but mostly on hot summer evenings, Johnny heard its melodies and chords wafting into his part of St. Paul from local West Side bars.

He lived close enough to the river's high bluffs to be able to see the dirt paths leading to limestone caves on the opposite side, notoriously used for decades by both Chicago and local gangsters for illegal and illicit activities.

I've been in those caves, some used now to grow mushrooms, others used by geologists, one is a cavern/restaurant where I attended a wedding. But there is still mystery there, where a teenage suicide cult met not long ago, and pledged their deaths.

———— ▫O▫ ————

All Minnesota children learn that the Mississippi's waters come from Lake Itasca in northern Minnesota, and then flow all the way to the Gulf of Mexico. But Johnny had no interest in the river. In those days the Mississippi ran muddy and polluted. He knew how to swim, because there was that story of him telling me that his dad threw him into the river, with no instructions, and told him to swim back to shore. He somehow showed enough strength to counteract the river's muddy flow, but not easily. From then on he tried to avoid the Mississippi.

Until he heard the jazz of New Orleans and St. Louis, Johnny's music had none of the river in it.

He loved the classical European music he studied, first from his mother, and then, because of his exceptional talent, from a Hamline University professor who took him on as a student. In the Hamline Cathedral the pipe organ was king, and Johnny forgot time as he sat at the console, using both his hands and feet to pump out music. Scandinavian culture, with its history of suffering, had perfected ways to keep its citizens from expressing great joy or sorrow.

Sacred music was the one avenue still allowed.

Growing up between two World Wars, and almost starving during the days of the Great Depression, taxed his ability to display the stoicism he was modeled.

Don't cry. Don't complain. Don't bring attention on oneself. Keep your head down and soldier on.

Dad often told the story about the day during the Great Depression, when his mother brought home an egg for him. They were so pleased, and she fried it and set it on a plate for him. But all he could manage to think was that if he ate it, it would be gone. My dad stared at the plate until the egg was inedible. He never ate it. That was poverty, but even more, it showed the stoicism Scandinavian culture developed to survive it.

He began questioning the old-country cultural norms. It seemed as though they led to dead ends. I could see that when he listened to jazz, or better yet, attempted to play it, he felt alive, renewed, and his inhibitions disappeared.

He didn't fit the typical profile of a musician. After his tonsils were removed at age twelve, Dad told me he started gaining weight. I think his poverty also reflected a poor diet.

His round face grew rounder, and his chin, even at a young age, doubled when he nodded. With age, his Swedish blond hair darkened, and because his gray-blue eyes were neither dark nor light, he didn't really appear Scandinavian, even though he was a full-blooded Swede. But when Johnny Blomquist smiled, the cracks and valleys of his face revealed a wry sense of humor and intelligence, and his eyes an emotional intimacy. According to his younger sister, Jeune, the precocious boy was irresistible to women. She believed his charm got him asked to all the parties, not just his musical ability.

(Did I tell you my mother's only advice to me before I got married? "Never marry a musician.")

At sixteen Johnny heard about a citywide harmonica competition. He borrowed the instrument from a friend, sat on his porch all weekend experimenting with sounds and melodies, and the next weekend won first prize, or so he said. About the same time he landed a job on weekends, improvising the running background for silent movies, on the Orpheum Theater's house organ. It suited his itch to experiment, and he soon began to compose as he played, and to toss in jazz phrasing and complex chords as the movie's climax approached.

At seventeen, he put together his own jazz band, a dance orchestra called *The Seven Shades of Blue*. Each musician sported a slightly different color of blue tie. I imagine Dad's as azure, the color of an unclouded sky. I learned about the band and this phase of my dad's life from a newspaper article written by his brother-in-law. I found the yellowed paper in dad's early-years scrapbook, probably all collected and put together by Grandma Blomquist.

My dad was the director and keys man (piano player). He recruited two saxophonists from his Humboldt High School senior class, both the drummer and second trumpet belonged to his Methodist youth group, and the first trumpet worked days at the neighborhood drug store, where he would also concoct a variety of fizzy drinks he'd try out on band members.

Johnny needed a good, solid trombone player, someone who could stand in front of the band and make the girls swoon with flashy glissandos, with a personality like Tommy Dorsey. After his weekly pipe-organ lesson uptown at the college, Johnny headed to the Student Center to get a drink. He glanced at the bulletin board to see if there were any good bands playing on campus that weekend. But instead, he found a scribbled, hand-written note, pinned into the middle of the board.

Just arrived at Hamline, studying education. My first love is jazz. Play t-bone. Am looking for band. Contact me at frosh men's dorm. Any time.
– Merrill Nelson

That note changed everything.

For his first rehearsal, Merrill skipped lunch and used the change he had saved to ride the streetcar across town to Johnny's parents' tiny house in a run-down neighborhood on St. Paul's West Side, the only home in the group with a piano. Merrill walked in, tall, thin, strawberry blond and dimple-faced, and took out his horn.

"Let's get started," was his only comment, setting his books down on a free table. He'd study during breaks.

After a couple of months, Merrill convinced Johnny they had enough arrangements to fill a whole dance program. The timing couldn't have been better, since just that day, Johnny had heard on the street that the Sons of Herman, a German-American fraternal organization on Congress Street, was planning a dance.

My dad, whose given name was John Gustave Adolph Blomquist, Swedish-American and named after the king, that day decided to take on a more German sounding name. I picture my young father trying on different names, maybe Meyer, Bach ... no, that was too classical ... or Goodman, after the fabulous clarinetist Benny.

He finally settled on Johnny Brant, and used it to secure the dance gig for the *Seven Shades of Blue.* They opened that night with Dad's arrangement of Duke Ellington's

"Mood Indigo", featuring a sultry blues duet for keys and t-bone.

By the time high school graduation came around, Johnny had planned a future for himself different from what his dad had in mind.

"Congratulations, Son. Been saving all my life for Hamline. That college was good for Ethel. It'll be good for you too. You know this damn stiff, half-finger?" He shook his head. "Not gonna happen to you. By God's grace you'll never use the sweat of your brow to earn a living."

"I know, Dad. Chemistry is the future."

"Ya, chemistry. You do the thinking. Let someone else do the sweat."

Dad's father, Gustave "Gus" Blomquist, was a freemason who had spent a lifetime laboring with his hands, working on the railroad, and later tool and die making. Despite having permanently injured his fingers at work, in his spare time he carved imaginative figures of people and animals out of wood – my favorite being a bow-legged, guitar-playing cowboy that I now affectionately call Ragtime Cowboy Joe. Grandpa also carved an ornate canopy bed, desk, cabinet and matching mirror for Grandma after he saw them in a magazine article about 17th century furniture in French castles.

Every once in a while, he'd carve a wooden die and then cast brass figures from it. That's how he made my wonderful shiny open-mouthed, fish ashtray, that still somehow smells of cigarettes 50 years after the last one was discarded there, and a seven-light brass candelabra that I now have on my dining room table in Oklahoma.

Every time I think of Grandpa's masterpieces, I wonder who this man really was. He fought constantly with my Dad, a man I thought was mostly level-headed (except about rock and roll), so it was hard to know the truth.

Grandpa once told Roxy and me that he listened every afternoon to Dick Clark's rock and roll show on television. We were astounded! More than once he argued with my mother that we should be allowed to watch it too, despite my father's protests. I had the feeling he was trying to teach my parents to be less strict than he had been, that maybe he had learned something valuable he was trying to pass on.

Aunt Jeune, Dad's half-sister, recalls a story about when my Grandpa Gus was five years old, toward the end of the nineteenth century. As Grandpa had told Jeune, he and his mother were living with Mrs. Palmer, a Swedish immigrant, on St. Paul's West Side. Grandpa's father, Lars, had abandoned them and sailed back to Sweden to be with a mysterious mistress, with whom he stayed for a year before returning. Of course, this is all from Grandpa's recollection, so who knows what the real story was. But I can imagine Lars, my great-grandfather, the Swedish mason who had grown up an orphan, and become a rough railroad man. His philandering doesn't surprise me, given what I've recently found out about my own dad.

Anyway, little Gus was mostly on his own all day, and wandered through the St. Paul streets. As he told Jeune, one day he found a playground where young children were forming a line. He joined in and followed them into the school building. Despite the fact that Grandpa couldn't speak a word of English, and the teacher didn't understand Swedish, she did not send him to the principal, or make him return to the street. Instead she gave him string and beads and allowed him to stay all afternoon, working on an art project. Her kindness and understanding were so extraordinary to his life that he kept the beaded ornament he had made that day. (It is still in the family.)

But somehow the bead artist and woodcarver in Grandpa wasn't able to reach out to the musician in my dad. Years later, with what I know now, I think it had everything to do with my dad being that ladies man his sister described – ladies man that too closely resembled Grandpa's own father.

Grandpa Gus's parents immigrated to America from Stockholm, Sweden. Lars Blomquist came first, and his wife, Annie Ringman, followed him. She survived the brutal sea voyage, endless train ride to Chicago, and then north to Minnesota. Two years later she gave birth to Gus in the train depot of a tiny town called Dassel while in the process of moving to that railroad hub. He would be their only child. She had already given birth to another child, out of wedlock, in Sweden, also named Gustave, but he had died as a toddler.

I have a photo of Great-Grandfather Lars, unbelievably handsome with his long mustache and tall stature, but I have no image of my great-grandmother born in the tiny town of Nykoping, Sweden. I think of her with pity, having been dragged along to the new world at the wrong time with the wrong person. She had to have been tough as granite to survive her husband's neglect, and later alcoholism.

I know Lars lived with my grandfather and his family until he died in 1923. I remember my father telling me horror stories about living with his grandfather. But I do not know if his grandmother, Annie, also lived with them. Maybe she had thrown him out of her house. That's only speculation. Never a word was spoken about her.

In my research I found that Annie lived to be 95 years old, dying in 1950, right there in St. Paul. She was my father's grandmother, but I never saw her, or heard about her. I could have met her at age three, or at least heard about her dying. This is another secret, why both Dad and Grandpa never talked about her, but it's too late now to find an answer.

"But you know, Dad," Johnny Brant, grandson of Lars, son of Gus, said, "I won't be a tool and die maker. I won't injure my hands, because I need my hands to play piano."

"Ya, music," Gus said in his slight Swedish accent. "The pipe organ at Hamline Church. We'll come listen. But you remember, study the chemistry too. Ya?"

It was useless for Dad to say more. Grandpa didn't listen to him. He couldn't figure out if his dad didn't want to listen, or just didn't know how. I'm not sure my dad understood how hard Gus and Lars had labored, and that they saw him as wasting his life on useless music and women.

That fall Johnny enrolled at Hamline University, but instead of attending chemistry labs, he rehearsed with a campus jazz group Merrill had organized. According to his sister, he signed his papers "Johnny Brant", and every sentence from his mouth somehow led back to Benny Goodman or Lionel Hampton or rhythm or a new arrangement. He put in his time, but did so poorly in his classes, that one day he finally announced he'd be leaving school to join a band in Rochester.

When he told his dad about quitting college Gus shouted, "Oh, Johnny! No! Get your degree. How much food you put in your mouth from music? And such music!" He raised his voice beyond comfort and in exasperation said, "I tried to tell you for years. Music will get you nowhere. But you wouldn't quit, so I figured I'd buy you the best lessons I could, at the university, hoping you'd play cathedral organ, not the dance music."

Gus's face was red hot, and he choked over his words. "I want my son respected, not embarrassing me by playing in bars, for drinking folks who slobber over each other."

"Dammit Dad, I am choosing to live in a different world than you do. I need more than church music."

"Shame on you. I say, shame on you. You've had every chance, and you just don't care about Ethel and me any more."

"It doesn't have anything to do with you or Mother." Dad pulled his left lip up in a sneer and said, "You're such an S.O.B." and added, "I can't study chemistry or play hymns when my brain is buzzing with jazz."

As Johnny walked out of the room Grandpa tried to ignore him, but finished the conversation with these words, as my Aunt Jeune told them to me, "Well then, don't expect your mother and me to ever come hear you play the devil's music. Ya, we taught you right, but something else has taken over."

It was years before Johnny fully understood why his parents had disapproved of him being a musician. During the Second World War he had discovered that Ethel was not his birth mother. In fact, his dad had not married Ethel until 5 years after his first wife died, when my dad was 6 years old. Later, Leonard Olson, an engineer at the munitions plant where Dad was working during the war, approached Johnny and told him that he, Leonard, was his real uncle. Johnny learned about his birth mother's musical background, and a music obsession that matched his own. It gave him probable cause, but not acceptance of their behavior.

I remember my dad telling me that when he confronted Grandpa with the information about his mother, Grandpa said, "You're lucky you never knew her." I was deeply shocked, but Dad never said another word about it. There's something secret here. I knew Dad's mother had died "from the milk," which probably in 1913 meant tuberculosis, since they weren't pasteurizing milk yet. But what anger was behind this message is lost forever.

"You're lucky you never knew her."

———— ∘O∘ ————

Luck, it's a strange thing.

Dad's friend Merrill didn't rely on luck. He continued at Hamline, determined to earn his teacher's degree, despite Johnny's continual, annoying letters, trying to coax him to join whatever band he was presently part of. Although they banded together each summer, come September, Johnny would moan when Merrill returned to school.

My dad wanted more than Minnesota life and fame. He hadn't grown up in a small, unchanging town like Sleepy Eye, where Merrill came from. Dad was a river-city kid, street-smart, open-eyed, ready to hitch a ride downstream.

By 1936, Johnny had already played keyboard for bands in Rochester, Austin, St. Paul, and Minneapolis. He was busy arranging and writing new material, though all the while waiting for his friend. So just days after Merrill Nelson graduated with his bachelor's degree in education, and had happily found a position teaching school, my dad wrote to every big band agent in America asking for possible openings for keys and t-bone.

I have a copy of that letter.

——— ◦O◦ ———

Merrill and Johnny toured the country together from Boston to Charleston to New Orleans to Chicago, and played in all the small dance halls in between. They finished their touring years as part of the John Philip

Sousa III Band. On the circuit Merrill Nelson became known as the Professor, since his college degree was a rarity.

They shared wild experiences, but none as scary as the night in August of 1940 when a deadly hurricane blew in. Dad never tired of telling us this story. It obviously meant a lot to him.

They were entertaining on a tour boat off the North Carolina coast when violent winds came up and waves crashed over the dance floor. The captain managed to sail the boat back to a protruding levee and everyone was told to abandon ship. Most couldn't run very far, and so they held onto small trees that grew on the edges of the rocky embankment. Johnny and Merrill crawled down to the lea side and clung to the biggest boulders they could find, and then watched in horror as one after another of the flimsy trees above them, and the frightened people holding onto them, were uprooted and tossed out to sea by the wild winds.

Fifty people died that night, and the next day, both Dad and Merrill were reported dead in the newspaper. Johnny was ten days short of his 28th birthday.

I wondered if Merrill told that story to his kids the way Dad did to us? Dad always ended it with, "... and what did I learn? Don't ever cling to puny trees growing on rocks. Remember that. They won't hold. Grab on to the old ones, the ones that have sent their roots down deep, or to the tall green palms that know how to bend in the wind. Don't cling to small trees, Child, remember that." And then he'd stare for a moment into nowhere.

———— ∘O∘ ————

I first met Professor Merrill in 1953. For a six-year-old, the trip to Sleepy Eye seemed forever far. When we arrived, the house and town did indeed appear sleepy to my eyes. But I remember almost every moment of that trip, because there was nothing ordinary about my father's friend.

Though slim, Merrill's presence filled the room, making him seem much larger than his frame. His light gold Scandinavian skin and wavy hair reminded me of caramel rocks I found in the gravel pit behind our house. The rocks were really called chert, another kind of chalcedony, different from agate and jasper. I liked my name for the rocks better because they were golden brown and smooth as caramel, and disguised their inner strength in the same way as caramel apples. He didn't wear glasses with plastic black frames like other men. I knew his were wire-rimmed. I could see his glowing, sweet eyes, which led me to conclude that he more closely matched the characteristics of caramel than of chert.

He bent over to my height, with great gentleness took my hand, and in a voice as soft as a lullaby said, "My dear, sweet child. It is with the greatest of joy that you have entered my home this day in the hamlet of Sleepy Eye. I will be at your service. Please let me know of all your needs, no matter how small."

That day too he took out his trombone and jammed with my father, playing the piano, all afternoon. Music was a secret language the two of them shared. I heard it, but its complexity and interconnections overwhelmed me, at the same time creating great joy.

Both my dad and Merrill would die at a young age, less than a year apart. I guess that was the consequence of hard living. Since I only saw Merrill Nelson one other time in my life, that day stayed cemented in my mind.

Usually I only heard Dad play once a year, on my birthday, when Mother would bring me to the nightclub where he played. I'd order anything I wanted off the menu, usually frog legs and popovers. After I finished my birthday cake I'd walk up to Dad's bench, sit beside him and listen as he played "Happy Birthday" to me. Then I'd request "Danny Boy", my mom's favorite song.

It was the very definition of special to sit on the bench with my father, leader of the band, and request whatever I wanted. I felt the vibration of the organ against my legs, and the energy of everyone's smiles concentrating on this grand birthday girl. And it was the only place to observe how my dad's dextrous feet swept over the foot pedals silently, in his stockings.

But that day, at Merrill's house in Sleepy Eye, I heard the two musicians playing only for themselves. I thought the trombone must have been wrought in heaven and handed down by angels, such sweet and glossy music poured out of that bell.

———— ∘O∘ ————

On Sunday mornings we'd park next to the church cemetery on top of Afton's high bluff, stare down at the blue ribbon river, and walk toward the small, white wooden church we knew as Memorial Lutheran.

Although my dad worked late on Saturday night, his band playing until one in the morning, he almost always rose for church. I doubt if his musician friends knew that when he was younger, he had wanted to be a Methodist minister. He had been raised Methodist because his parents were tee-totalers, and the denomination's message of pietism suited them.

He told me it was our secret, not to be shared with anyone. I think he recognized a kind of spirituality in me that the others didn't share, and wanted me to know how much he valued it. But just as true, it had to be a secret because it didn't fit the worldly image he portrayed to others.

What I loved best about church was sitting next to him as he sang the Lutheran liturgy and hymns in a powerful bass. On the other hand, I always finagled to sit at least four bodies away from Mother, who sang just as loud in a noxious, swoopy soprano. She loved to sing, but her voice didn't come out like Dad's.

I could sing the liturgy by heart before I turned three, and by nine I had begged the organist to let me sing with the adult choir, which I occasionally did if Mom could get me to midweek practices.

My big break came near my tenth birthday when Pastor asked me to sing a solo at Sunday Family Night. Those nights were less formal than morning church.

They started with prayer, but after that, anything could happen. No one played Bingo or cards, or drank alcohol, or told bawdy jokes, but we did have sing-a-longs and concerts by family groups and children's choirs, and at Christmas, Santa Claus might come, or Santa Lucia might appear with Swedish buns and krumkakor.

The choir director decided I would sing the first verse of a popular tune that started, "Mommy told me something that every girl should know." It went on to tell how if you let the devil into your room he'd never leave you alone. It declared, "Smilers never lose, and frowners never win, so let the sun shine in."

It made sense to me. Living in Minnesota gave me a real appreciation for sunlight. In December, because of the state's far northern latitude, we had only eight hours of sunshine per day. Those who got to school or work before eight in the morning and came home after four didn't see the sun at all. Imagine all those people who worked in a building without windows. They had to imagine sunshine. They had to hold it in their heart until the weekend, and hope that Saturday and Sunday would not be overcast.

What was really strange to me, was that in winter on the coldest of days the sun shone brightly, but contained no warmth at all, except of course the sunshine that made its way inside, through the slits in our window's lacy drapes, and formed concentrated pools of light and heat on the floor. I called them "sun puddles," my favorite winter place to sit in the kitchen, after I had chased away our cat.

The night of my solo I wore a yellow popcorn stitch sweater Grandma Knoblauch had knit for me, bright as sunshine itself. My stomach felt a slight ache, an uneasiness, until Mrs. Rosenquist called my name. Then I walked proudly to the front of the church. As I sang the song about keeping the devil away and letting the sun shine in, I felt as if I were talking to my friends and family about something I knew was true.

Dad's transparent skin glowed red as I sang. In hindsight I know it must have been the moment when he thought of his great plan. He would ask his friend, Merrill, to come for our Sunday Family Night and entertain us with his Musical Hall Tree. (He had something else in mind too.)

My mother and dad felt personally responsible for the church, because they considered the pastor incompetent. At least, that's what I heard around the house. This minister was new, replacing a long loved pastor.

Fresh out of seminary, he smoked cigarettes, which in it-self would not have been condemned by my parents, but he smoked them in the church basement! It seemed to many of the parishioners that the only reason he had gone into ministry was not that he had been called by God, as ministers are supposed to be, but that he had survived po-lio, and could do nothing else.

They confused me. No Christian I knew would judge a man by a physical disability, especially polio, which everyone feared. I think the problem was that he wouldn't tell us about his calling to the ministry. If he wouldn't talk about it, they assumed it had never happened. Parishioners ex-pected him to tell them about an intimate experience with

God, that none of the Swedish, Norwegian and German Lutheran congregants, in a lifetime as long as Abraham's, would ever talk about themselves.

I actually liked Pastor Carlson. I figured his reasoning was right. He couldn't be a farmer like many in our congregation, or a carpenter. And he had to have talent to be a musician, so what else? And after all, he'd asked me to sing a solo.

Everyone waited for his next move. The church needed an organ. Lutherans can sing to a piano for just so long. He needed to appoint an organ committee and oversee its work. Then the congregation would see what kind of a minister he really was.

My dad, who had played the organ for decades, stood ready to be appointed to that committee.

———— ∘O∘ ————

On a sunny afternoon one month later, Roxy practiced reaching high notes on her French horn. Two years earlier she had passed the music test Mr. George Regis, our band director at the high school, had devised, and so was allowed to choose an instrument to study. She had wanted to play flute, as did all her girlfriends, but Dad decided that some parental intervention was needed. After all, how much did a ten-year-old girl know about music, or the sounds of instruments, or especially about musical careers?

My sister told me she felt super-special that night at the school. All the instruments were on display, when Dad took her aside, stooped down to her level, and told her frankly, "You will play French horn. It is not something children understand, but someday you'll thank me for this."

No one argued with my father, and Roxy actually loved it, being the only one who lifted the curved brass instrument onto her lap, stuck her small hand inside the bell and blew harder and harder into the mouthpiece until a faint sound appeared. The exotic sounding instrument would be hers, and hers alone.

She perfected the muted lonesome sounds of the horn, and although at first timid, she later performed her solos *par excellence* in concert pieces. It gave my sister a kind of elevated snob appeal that suited her well.

But that day she was still learning, and we were trying to concentrate on something other than her screeching broken notes, when an unfamiliar car drove up. Professor Merrill emerged carrying his trombone case. I knew he would be coming. His special concert had been advertised at church and all week on WAVN, the local radio station. He'd be the star of Sunday Family Night. But I hadn't realized he'd play for us, because he'd be performing all evening.

I ran and opened the door for him as Roxy put away her instrument and Mother put on a pot of coffee.

"Welcome, Little One," he said to me as he doffed a white Panama hat. "You've grown so since I've seen you last. I hope what I brought will fit you well."

Why would he be bringing me clothes?

He walked into our living room and laid the trombone case on our faded green couch. The elongated case was orange-brown, with no nicks or scratches, and when he opened it, its soft orange velvet lining brightened the room. Against the velvet lay three separate pieces, a brass slide, bell, and a large silver-colored mouthpiece. It took only moments to slip the three together. He held it to his mouth and played the melody of "Panus Angelicus". Its slow high mourn sounded absolutely as if it had come straight from the angels.

"Oh, please play more," I begged.

"No. I want you to play." He handed me the trombone, placing my fingers in the right slots and positions, guiding my hand to softly slide the brass up and down until I got a feel for the instrument. As I put my mouth to the huge mouthpiece I suddenly withdrew it. My brain hinted at something so wonderful I was scared to ask about it.

Timidly I looked up at Merrill. "Is it ... for me? Is this my trombone?"

I looked at his twinkling eyes. I saw my dad grin. Mother nodded yes.

I couldn't talk. My heart beat so fast all I could do was turn a cartwheel in the middle of the living room. (Thinking back on it, it's uncanny that my granddaughter, Svea, does the same thing, cartwheel after cartwheel every time she gets excited.) Everyone laughed.

When I regained my composure, I closed my sweaty hands around the cold, brass bars. I had just passed the music test, and my parents knew I didn't want a flute, or a French horn. For four years, ever since I'd heard Merrill Nelson play his trombone that day in Sleepy Eye, it was the only instrument I would ever consider. And here it was in my hands.

"But you're a girl," Winky sneered, and then added, "Everyone's gonna laugh at you."

The Professor answered, "Oh, far from the truth, young man. She will be admired. Music will give her courage."

———— ₀O₀ ————

As members and guests of Memorial Lutheran Church filed into the sanctuary that night, they witnessed a strange sight. Instead of a choir or minister in long robes standing before them, an embellished hall tree – the kind folks usually use in their front hall for coats and sweaters and rainwear – stood covered with instruments, sticks, glasses, and assorted junk. Leaning on it was a familiar looking man in bow tie and professor suit, black graduation hat, and granny glasses, answering to the name of Professor Merrill Nelson and his Musical Hall Tree.

For two hours he found music in ordinary things you might have in any kitchen, pots and pans, glasses full of water, or spoons. But he also played the trumpet, trombone (sliding the slide with his foot while he beat a drum with his hand), harmonica, juice harp, clarinet, and saxophone. And through it all, he talked to us in his Professor voice, making the ordinary extraordinary, and the complicated funny. We laughed so hard at times we couldn't hear the music.

Afterwards, in the cozy church basement, we enjoyed coffee, a potluck assortment of cookies, and Kool-aid. Pastor Carlson walked over to where our family gathered at one of the tables, but he did not sit down. He directed a question to both my dad and Merrill. "How do the two of you know each other?"

The Professor answered, "We're like brothers, been playing together for a long time. He drew me out of little Sleepy Eye long enough to see the world, and he keeps the sleep out of my eyes still."

"But," asked the pastor, "you don't play in bars, do you? Aren't you a teacher?"

"Yes, I am a teacher, but I miss playing with my colleagues in a band."

"Is there a problem, sir?" Dad asked, his face reddening, as he rose to confront spindly Pastor Carlson.

"Not a problem, really," he replied, "just an unfortunate circumstance, I guess. Because you play in clubs, don't you? Clubs where liquor is served?"

I stopped eating my cookie and ignored everything else in the room. Suddenly there were only two men in front of me, their voices rising, their bodies stiffening. Everyone knew my dad's jovial side, but only those of us in the family knew his temper. His thundering voice could come out of nowhere, like the tornado the summer before that hit just down the road, the deadly storm following an absolute stillness of eerie green light.

"Yes. My band plays nightly at the St. Paul House in Shakopee." He picked up his cup of grape *Kool-Aid* and held it within inches of the pastor's face. "This is as close to alcohol as I get, and as a matter of fact, I never accept any drinks at all from the patrons. It's a respectable supper club."

The pastor backed up. I don't know if he had already made his decision, or if Dad's intimidating behavior forced the pastor's actions, but at that moment Pastor Carlson cleared his voice and said. "I know you've been expecting to become chairman of the organ committee, but I have decided to put someone else in that position." The pastor moved further away from the table as he continued, "and we will not be needing your services at all."

————— ₒOₒ —————

Our family never went back. We drifted for a while, then joined Bethlehem Lutheran Church in Bayport, ten miles north, up the river. (My husband and I later got married in that church.)

Bayport had a bowling alley and bar, two Protestant stone churches, a café, bank, drug store, school, fire department, Sathre's filling station, and the White Pine Inn, which was an enormous brick hotel and restaurant that sat at an angle to the main street and flaunted its importance through two-story white pillars at its entrance. The Inn didn't fit the size or the tenor of the village, and as a small child I didn't understand why it was there. Later I learned that Bayport was a company town, built by and for the mammoth Andersen Window Corporation. Its owners and executives lived out on The Point, an isolated peninsula thrust into the St. Croix River, and they conducted their important business at the White Pine Inn.

It wasn't long before my dad developed a connection to the town. He brought his band to play nightly at the new Bayport Yacht Club, a complex of docks, boats and an elegant restaurant south of the main village, designed for Andersen executives and rich city folk who wanted to spend an afternoon or weekend on the St. Croix River.

My mother worked there too, as a waitress. Often I saw Mom and Dad dance together, while the sax player, Tommy Bauer, took over the band. I remember getting a glimpse of what it must have been like for them before us, before complications, when romance was real. Despite my mother's terrible singing voice, she danced smoothly, in his arms, her curly hair flinging from side to side, her hips following the subtleties of his movements.

Their love of Bayport meant nothing to me. I still felt like an outsider at church, and my family didn't seem to care. I had to take the bus to Bayport on Wednesday afternoons after school for confirmation class. The Bayport kids recognized that I wasn't a regular on the bus and no one talked to me or offered a seat. Even at church, where I knew my classmates, I still wasn't one of them. They'd all gone through Bayport Elementary School together, and wondered why I suddenly showed up at their church.

But Dad loved Bethlehem Lutheran. On Sunday mornings he would close his eyes and hum the bass part along with their great choir. He worked with them on an arrangement of the Seven-fold Amen he had heard in the Methodist church of his youth.

They later sang it at his funeral.

Grandpa Blomquist didn't attend his son's funeral on October 3, 1960, an already cold day amid the falling leaves at Bayport Cemetery. I was surprised Grandpa wasn't there, because we had a second service at the graveside performed by the Masonic Lodge.

Dad was the one who never found enough time to attend the lodge meetings, but Grandpa was a higher-level mason, and devoted to the brotherhood. I now think he couldn't get himself to attend the funeral for other personal reasons, which I discovered decades later.

I don't remember anything about the funeral, except that the church was filled beyond capacity with faces I did not recognize. Most of them went home after the service, but my neighbor, and lifetime friend Judy Hancock, was there at the graveside. Her face registered the sadness that mine couldn't.

I do remember the masonic service. Maybe it was because I finally saw a familiar face. Maybe it was because the actions of the masons seemed so strange to me. Maybe it was because my body was upright and allowed blood to once again reach my brain. The leader threw dirt on the casket as it was being lowered down into the hole, and said, "Ashes to ashes, dust to dust." That concrete image was like concrete itself, heavy and permanent, my father forever gone.

Grandma told us that Grandpa didn't come to the funeral because he wasn't ready to let his son go. Seemed to me he'd never latched on. He had kept his word, never listening to my father play his jazz. Grandpa mourned over Dad's death for three months, and then finally drove out to Bayport to see the grave of John Gustave Adolph Blomquist.

As he knelt alone on the cemetery's December frozen ground, feeling the ache of unresolved sorrow, a stab of pain assaulted his arm.

Panicking from loss of breath and pain, he drove alone all the way back into St. Paul, straight to the hospital. And died.

A few months later we received a letter from Sleepy Eye. Professor Merrill Nelson's heart had also failed.

———— ○ ————

I wondered about those lines I had sung bravely in church, "smilers never lose and frowners never win." It wasn't true. I'd never seen Professor Merrill frown. He was a pro at making people laugh.

I knew that sometimes my dad actually displayed some of those seven, sad, jazzy shades of blue, but I'd seen his wide grin so many more times. He was the one who often had our whole dinner table laughing with his silly language.

He was the one who made my mother smile as she danced to *Mood Indigo*.

The song was all wrong. The biggest smilers in my life lost. Something felt as if it would never be whole again. The song's words haunted me. "The devil will never ever leave you if your heart is filled with gloom."

I felt as Dad and Merrill must have felt, long ago, on the night of the hurricane, huddled close to the embankment. This time it was people I loved who were uprooted by hurricane gusts and hurled into the wind, never to be seen again. I was having a hard time finding strong rooted trees to cling to. I prayed that my own roots would hold me upright.

I remembered Dad's words to me, "Don't cling onto small trees."

After awhile, when the gloom wouldn't go away, I decided to make my own sunshine, hang pots and pans and drums and glasses on the hall tree in our entryway, and speak Professor language to everyone I knew (at least to the ones who could understand). Each time I felt the gloom coming on, I'd raise the shades and windows of my room. And even though I could never make it sound the way Professor Merrill did, I'd lift high my glossy brass trombone, hold it to my lips, and blow into it the sweetest song I knew, *Panus Angelicus*, the melody pouring from my horn, powered with the breath of angels.

All my life, my friends have loved the sounds of violins and cellos. My son plays all the stringed instruments. My granddaughter is learning the piano. But to me, there is nothing more beautiful than the high mourning sound of a trombone, or the military pomposity of a trombone section blaring out a John Philip Sousa march.

Just as my father showed me when he listened to a majestic pipe-organ playing Bach, the hairs on my arm also rise. I love Bach, and pipe organs, but for me the hairs rise when I am overwhelmed by the high mellow, the marching bellow of brass, and the celebrating glissandos of the trombone.

Opening Doors

When my grandma with the college degree,
whose white hair rolled tightly at her neck,
served me Fig Newtons instead of real cookies,
and strawberry jam on ice cream,
I decided I didn't like her desserts,
and I especially didn't like figs,
so later, when I lived in a house with
an old prolific fig tree in the yard,
I knew we would never eat them all.
A motherly woman at the store
suggested cooking the figs together
with strawberry jello to make jam.
I was a skeptic, but went home
and brewed up a batch
and spread it on my just-baked bread
and couldn't believe the sweet berry flavor
and consistency, just like the preserves
I'd made as a child from wild strawberries
I'd found in our back acres
and carefully picked, cleaned
and cooked into jars and jars of jam
that we gave as presents for Christmas,
but when I gave this fig-version away,
my friend called it white-trash jam
and laughed and laughed,
and I laughed too, knowing
it wasn't real. But hadn't I rescued
the figs that would have rotted
on the ground, hadn't I transformed
them from mere brown fruit
to something they may have aspired to,
opened doors to new flavor,
found grace in the act of mixing?

chapter 12

grace

Lilac
[*Syringa vulgaris*]

T here she stood, in the entryway of Mother's house, shaking the snow off her coat, and looking lost. The pupils in her oddly familiar, dilated, slate-blue eyes focused on me. Sheepishly she said, "Then... I'm your sister."

The room fell silent.

That particular Christmas day we had just finished our main meal and were happily eating dessert, Swedish rice pudding, a combination of rice, cream, almond extract, raisins and sugar that left us feeling full and sweet. My niece, Dayna, had discovered the hidden almond in her portion. Our Swedish tradition was that the finder of the almond in their pudding would get another Christmas present, as well as a year full of good luck. The other grandchildren groaned, "Grandma, she always gets the prize," as Mother handed Dayna the gift, this year a box of caramels. I had noticed earlier that Heather, the oldest grandchild, made sure to put the pudding that contained the nut in front of Dayna, the youngest and, according to Heather, the sweetest of the lot.

The kids were still shouting about the inequality when Wink noticed a car pulling into Mom's driveway.

"Are you expecting anyone else, Ma?" he said in a flat droll voice. He's the only one in the family who would use that name for Mother. Roxy and I thought of it as too country.

At age eighteen Winky had told everyone to drop the y in his name, and call him Wink. At twenty-one his then-fiancee, Susan, decided that he should be called by his given name, John. We had never called him that because it was too confusing while my dad, John, was living. And to make it more confusing, Wink had actually been called Leigh, his middle name, by his teachers at school. But I still call him Wink, which is irritating to Susan, but he's my brother, so I figure I have the right.

"So Wink, who does it look like?" I asked, and got one of those, you-know-what-you're-supposed-to-becalling-him looks from the other side of the table.

Wink, clearly annoyed that someone would just drop in on Christmas, watched as the car door opened. "Who in the world would intrude like this?" He looked closer. "I don't have the slightest. A woman. Late 40's. Alone. Somebody from church, maybe?"

"On Christmas?" Roxanne said.

Christmas 1986. We were in Valley Creek for the holidays that year, one of the few times Roxanne, Wink, and I, no-mads that we are, all lived in the state of Minnesota. The various members of our extended family sat in the dining room around Mother's enormous antique oak table, found at one of the numerous auctions she'd attend on many a Saturday morning. It's the way her house in later years became full of antiques. In contrast to when I grew up, our table, as well as everything else in the house was, to use my husband's phrase, motel modern.

My dad had built the dining room over the garage in 1950. I remember him crouched on the floor, the sound of hammering interrupted every few minutes with shouted expletives. But when he finished, Mom and Dad were both pleased with its unique look, wood slats punctuated by dark pegs to give it that old-timey feel, as if they had been attached the old way, by peg, and not by nails. The walls were thick knotty pine. A two-part barn door always had its top half-open to the living room. An old Christmas cactus and several enormous ferns obscured both the windows and Mother's generous lace curtains. Other than the kitchen, this was where the family always gathered.

When the room was new, and we didn't yet own a dining table, it became our family room for watching television or doing homework. Full of old stuffed chairs and a couch, the floor was covered by a colorful, handmade braided rug that mother had fashioned from our old wool coats.

The day we brought home the first television in Valley Creek, we inaugurated the room. Mom decided to position the Setchell-Carlson on the south wall, while Dad, portly and not always graceful, climbed onto the roof to attach the antenna. Half our neighbors, watching Dad climb onto the roof, came to help. They all then crowded into our new room as Mom turned on the switch, and located WCCO, channel 4, on the dial. The chattering stopped as Jackie Gleason, aka Ralph Cramden, crazy-danced his way into the room of his NY apartment, and at the same time entered our house and Valley. It was in that room where I soon watched Miss Francis teach me the alphabet, and where I watched Queen For A Day, and dreamed of making my mother a queen. But my favorite in those pre-school years was the Wedding Show, featuring one nuptial ceremony a day, always someone beautiful, happy and loved.

I walked to the edge of this room, now for dining, and peered out the front door window. The unknown woman, slowly progressing up the icy stairs, scared away a pair of skittish woodpeckers feeding at the front feeder. They abandoned their feast of bacon suet and flew to a nearby oak. Unafraid, the little chickadees, juncos, and dressed-for-Christmas cardinals continued their sunflower seed dinner.

I pulled the door open before the stranger could knock. "Merry Christmas. Can I help you?" I said with a broad smile, concerned that the others might not be as friendly.

She stared at me for a moment, swallowed, then politely asked, "Is this the home of John Blomquist? There was no name on the mailbox."

I didn't know how to answer. Dad had died 26 years previously, in 1960. Mother had remarried. But this was the home Dad had lived in for thirteen years. Wink, of course, lived next door, though only a few people called him John. "John senior or junior?" I asked.

"I must be in the right place." She glanced around the room. "I'm looking for a John Blomquist who would be in his late 70's or so I would guess." She walked further into the room and quickly surveyed the faces.

I could see by her expression that she was disappointed there was no old man in the room. Her heart must have been beating out of control.

"Maybe I'm in the wrong place. Sorry to disturb you at dinner. I should go."

"No, no. Tell us what you're looking for. He used to live here," I said.

So much of both Mother and Dad's lives had been kept secret from us that I was burning to find out whatever this might lead to. "He's been gone a long time now. Died in 1960. I'm his daughter. Is there something I can help you with?"

———— ∘O∘ ————

Grace. My half-sister. I was forty years old and didn't even know she existed. But finding it out that day explained a lot.

Grace was raised in the part of St. Paul where street-lights are perched on ornate metal poles, their light shining softly through leaded glass, a place of sidewalks and manicured grass. Pretty different from the Valley, where whatever grew, grew.

I caught an orange bus each day, nearly an hour to a consolidated public school. She walked with her friends a few blocks to a small Catholic prep school.

She was a pampered only child, raised by a single mother who owned and ran a prosperous business. I was raised by a widowed single mother, who, try as she might, could barely eke out a living.

Grace's mother forbade her to ever ask her father's name.

She didn't know her dad was a musician, or a Swede, or that he could be scary one moment and make us laugh the next.

She never giggled until her stomach hurt as he kidded at the dinner table saying, "Please pass a bress a peed ….

"No! I mean, please rass a press a beed ….

"No! I mean, pass a piece of bread, please ….

… Oh my!"

She couldn't have known how he struggled to keep his weight down, or how he sprinkled sugar on tomatoes and piled salt on everything else.

She wouldn't have heard the precious egg story (about him not eating the egg on his plate during the Depression) we had all heard dozens of times.

Her mother wouldn't have told her how he grew up in a tarpaper shack, the size of a garage, on a cliff overlooking the rail-yards and river.

Grace would have never heard his broad mellow bass voice singing *The Sevenfold Amen*.

She had no way to know that she has Dad's eyes, and that same high Blomquist nose-bridge as Roxy and I have.

When the emotional explosion began to resolve, my brain asked so many questions I could not get them out. I knew

Roxanne and Wink had to be thinking and feeling the same sort of chaos as I was.

Did Dad have another life he kept secret from us? From Mother?

The silence broke with the swish of heads simultaneously turning toward Mom. How much of this did she know? Or was it even true?

Mother sat on a high backed chair on the opposite side of the table. The glass in her prized cherry china cabinet reflected the sparse hair on the back of her head. Years earlier she had found the cabinet from an ad an old woman had placed in the *Stillwater Gazette*. She had papers to prove it had been owned by the wealthy Tozer family, the lumber barons along the St. Croix River in the 1800's. She had it filled with her collection of antique hand-cut glass.

I expected Mom to be outraged. I watched for tightness in her neck, slitting of her eyes. I expected her to come up with some story about the other John Blomquist in the city, the realtor, whose mail we often received.

I certainly never expected to see a grin sweep over Mother's mouth. I was shocked as she rose, extended her hand, and said, "Grace, I'm Dorothy, and I've always wanted to meet you."

"Mother!" Roxanne shouted. "You even know her name?"

"Grace Jorissen," the guest replied hesitantly as she returned Mother's handshake.

"Jorissen, Jorgenson. Seems we have similar names." Mother, who had married Jim Jorgenson in 1969, clearly found the circumstances fascinating.

The rest of us were not as pleased. I could see Roxanne's face turning red. Wink stood by the window shaking his head.

"You don't think having a half-sister is something we'd want to know about?" I asked Mother angrily, then turned to Grace and blurted out, "Are you older than us? When were you born?"

"Who is your mother?" Wink asked.

Even Heather, the teenager, who, judging by her smirk, was clearly finding the whole event amusing, joined in. "When did you find out about us?"

"Mother! This is unbelievable. Outrageous! The children are here," Roxanne said. "An illegitimate child? Maybe this isn't the place to talk."

Grace's shoulders tightened. Her breathing became labored. I could see how much courage it must have taken to come that day.

I held up my hand. "Let's all calm down here. We have a guest," I said. The barrage of questions stopped.

Mother replied, "There's nothing here we can't say in front of the kids. Grace is the child of your dad's first marriage. Welcome to my home, Grace. I hope we can be a little more civil from now on."

After a beat, I took Grace's coat and hung it on an entryway hook. "What did you come to tell us?"

Wink, who was clearly annoyed that this was happening on Christmas Day, managed to find a spare kitchen chair and gestured for her to join us around the dining room table. We all made room for her by scrunching together.

Around the circle, Mother introduced Grace to all the family members, and then to her husband, Jim, a giant, friendly man, who had come in from the living room and was now calmly seated at the head of the table.

Grace nodded to each and smiled at the children. "I have four of my own. I hope you'll meet them."

She continued, "My mother isn't well, and I figured if I wanted to know something about my dad ...your dad... I'd have to ask my mother now."

"She never told you anything?" Roxanne asked.

"No. Nothing. I was forbidden to ever bring up the subject, but I always wanted to know.

"So, last week when I finally got the courage to ask, all she told me was his name. I went to the Ramsey County Courthouse in St. Paul and traced the name to this address."

"You live here? In Minnesota? The Cities?"

"Yes. Not far from here actually."

"And you didn't even know he'd been dead all these years?"

"No," she whispered.

"All I have is a name, and I didn't even have that until a few days ago. I grew up with my mother's last name."

I was dumbstruck. It was not the first, and it would not be the last family secret I was to uncover in the years ahead.

Wasn't I normal? I had a lovely family. I practically ran the church I belonged to. I worked at a legitimate job and earned a graduate degree. I'd lived twenty miles from St. Paul, and been there hundreds of times for concerts, museums, shopping, sports events, parades, and it turns out, I'd had a sister there all that time.

I wondered if I'd ever sat next to her at the ballet, or cheered against her basketball team at a state conference meet.

Had I tried on a pair of Capezios in the chair next to hers at The Golden Rule Department Store? Would I have recognized her Blomquist nose?

Had I ever checked out a book from the Ramsey County Library that she had read just before me? My mind scanned all of my city experiences and came up empty. I would never know.

"Let me get you some coffee, Grace. Cream or sugar?" Mother asked.

"Sugar. Thanks."

I wondered if she'd ever been to that little coffee shop on Grand where I gave my first poetry reading.

"You probably got that sugar habit from Dad," I said. "He put lots of sugar in it … in anything."

Mother walked up a step into the kitchen to get the coffee pot, her ear tilted toward us so she wouldn't miss any of the conversation. I could always tell when Mom was nervous because she'd push her coffee away. She'd had a terrible digestive problem all the years I knew her, and for her, coffee was deadly.

But, somehow, today nothing seemed to be bothering her. In fact, she appeared to be enjoying this new-found relative. Years of being a beautician in her own shop in the basement of our house had honed her social skills to a fine point. She was at her best with company and large family groups, and add to that a little controversy, and she glowed.

In contrast, my brother, Wink, hated controversy, hated large groups of anything, and judging by his eye twitch, I think he stayed that day only because he could think of no polite way to leave.

"Then, you probably don't know he was a musician," Wink said.

That was an interesting comment from Wink, of course, since he was the least musical in the family. He had often let us know what little interest he had in our kind of music, and Roxy and I countered with our constant derogation of every sport Wink thought was important. His athletic interests had been developed despite our lack of family support. When he was in college Wink actually tried out for the Minnesota Twins. He was a natural. I didn't appreciate his abilities until I met my own husband, and learned to value the world of sports through him.

Roxanne watched Grace through a tightened slit in her eyes while unconsciously drumming her fingers on the table. "Yah," she butted in. "He played in the big bands of the 30's and 40's."

"Ended up in John Philip Sousa III's band," I added. "Not the one who wrote the marches. Sousa's grandson's band."

I wondered if she'd ever been standing along Wabasha Street during St. Paul's icy Winter Carnival Parade. Could she have seen the Stillwater High School band marching past her, with me in the front row, blowing furiously into a cold trombone mouthpiece the brassy refrains of a John Philip Sousa march?

"A musician? I'm a musician. What did he play?" Grace asked.

"Jazz. Piano and organ. He was fabulous. When we were kids we'd go to the nightclubs on our birthday to hear him. Had his own band by then."

"Piano? But I play piano! I'm a piano teacher."

My skin formed goose bumps.

Mother handed Grace a tall mug of coffee. Grace took it by placing both her hands around the mug as if she needed it to warm her body. "Got my Master's Degree in Piano Performance at St. Thomas."

"Oh my gosh!" I said. "Another musician, and without knowing. Can't be!"

Mom again, "Anyone else want coffee refills?"

"Sure, Mom, why not just bring the pot to the table?"

"Now it makes sense why Mother never wanted me to spend so much time at the piano," said Grace. "Every-one else's parents couldn't get them to practice, and mine got upset when I did."

It felt as though I was working on a thousand piece jigsaw puzzle, each jagged piece fitting neatly into a slot I didn't even know existed.

"Grace, we need to talk." It was finally Mother's turn.

"Your story sounds just like Johnny's. His mother taught him piano, but then he became obsessed with it. That's all he wanted to do. His dad kept telling him to spend more time studying, like his sister Jeune, study chemistry, use his brain instead of his hands, but all he could think about was jazz."

"Stop." Roxanne lifted her stiffened fingers to the edge of her face. "Wait a minute. This story is going way too fast. There are important questions to ask."

She dropped her hands, looked to the far window, fidgeted with her lip, and then proceeded slowly. "First, I want to know, was Dad actually married to her mother," Roxanne asked Mom in a low tone, "and then divorced, or is there something else we need to know?"

I relaxed as Mother started telling the story. "John married Grace's mother when he was only 21 years old. He left for long periods of time to play in big bands all over the country. But when World War II started, he called it quits, and came home again."

"So when did I come into the picture?" Grace asked.

"Well, you were born shortly after he came home."

"Nine months after, probably," Wink sneered.

"John was disowned by his parents for marrying a Catholic. But when Gracie was born they welcomed him back."

Mother looked at Grace and said, "You know your mother owned a business in St. Paul. They supplied goods for the war effort. But what you probably didn't know was that she needed John's help.

"He thought working there would be temporary, and then he'd get back to his music. But she never intended it that way. At least that's what he told me.

"So, eventually, he felt he had to leave her."

Immediately an image popped into my brain: 13 years old again, at my Grandmother's house. "Oh my Gosh! I can't believe this!" I interrupted. "I remember... isn't it funny what you remember?... Listen!"

I talked in a rush of memory, information surfacing so fast I couldn't believe it had been buried for decades. "I was 13, and we were at Grandma Blomquist's house after Dad's funeral and she took out this scrapbook she had put together with all kinds of stuff about Dad in it."

I shook my head clear, and remembered that Mother had been there too, right next to me. "Do you remember, Mom? We were all sitting on the side of the canopy bed, that gorgeous one Grandpa carved for Grandma. You were looking at old photographs and I had the scrapbook all to myself. It was full of old flyers and dance programs from all over the country at places he'd played. It had photos of him with famous musicians and beautiful women leaning against old fancy cars and in front of famous dance halls."

"I do remember that scrapbook vaguely," Mother said. "I wonder what ever happened to it."

"I sure don't know," I answered, "but what I do know is that among the photos, I found a musty yellowed page of newspaper, folded neatly. When I unfolded it, I couldn't believe it was a headline from the social section of the St.

Paul Pioneer Press, that said ... It really did ... I remember it now! ... HENPECKED MUSICIAN CALLS IT QUITS."

"No way!" Wink said.

"Yah, I remember that word, 'henpecked' because I thought, 'my dad? I don't think so' but it WAS about him, on the society page.

"I snickered and passed the scrapbook to you, Mom, shouting something like, 'Henpecked? Of all people!' but you never saw it, because Grandma grabbed it out of my hands faster than I'd ever seen her move. She slammed the scrapbook shut, and announced it was time for Fig Newtons and coffee in the kitchen."

"I really would like to know where that scrapbook is," Mother said.

"I guess it registered in my brain because I wasn't supposed to see it, so I never let that headline go."

It was astonishing to me recently, when my son actually found the articles from the St. Paul Pioneer Press, about my "henpecked" dad.

It turns out, my father had a gift for branding. He had labeled himself the "henpecked husband", and used the words "stifled" and "gigolo" to further convince judges (and the media) that he had been wronged by his wife.

I'm not sure what I think about this, knowing what I know now. I am starting to see that I have only been able to see part of the picture.

Here are the newsworthy headlines that were actually printed:

Henpecked, Claim.

John G. Blomquist, 32, sued for divorce in St. Paul because, he said, he is "henpecked." He said his wife, Ann, 35, 1750 Kenard Street, made him give up his career as a pianist, made him go to work in a hardware store of which she is an executive, and made him hand his monthly paychecks over to her.

She paid $14,000 income tax last year, he paid $500, he said.

Pianist Gets Divorce on "Henpecked" Plea.

John G. Blomquist, 32, 806 Case Avenue, St. Paul, a self-styled "henpecked husband," Thursday was awarded a divorce in Ramsey district court from the woman he claimed had "stifled" his professional aspirations as a pianist.

In his complaint, Blomquist alleged his wife, Ann, 35, 1750 Kenard Street, had forced him to quit playing in a band to work at a company where she was an executive and that she made him appear a gigolo in the eyes of other employees.

District Judge Carlton F. McNally awarded Blomquist $1,500 from the sale of their $7,700 home and ruled that the wife should receive no alimony or support for their 9-year-old child.

———— ∘O∘ ————

"I can't believe you remembered that, but you're right," Mother said. "Your dad gave up a wife, money, society, and the hardest of all, you," and pointed to Grace, "to be able to play his jazz, his first love."

"Except I don't see the romance in that, Mom. That's disgusting," I said, and wondered how close we might have been to being given up as well.

"Even to her dying day," replied Grace, swallowing, and then breathing deeply, "Mother wouldn't tell me why she hated him so much, but I knew she did, because of that wilted look she got every time I asked about him."

Grace hesitated for a moment, recreating her mother's face in her mind.

"You know, maybe it wasn't hate. Maybe pain.

"I don't know, but she refused to ever say his name."

"Banana bread's gone," cried Dayna, Wink's youngest child, from across the wide table. "Grandma, is there more?"

"Dayna, don't bother Grandma right now," replied her mother. "You can get some in the kitchen."

Once Dayna excused herself from the table, Grace asked, "Why? I don't understand why he couldn't have stayed in touch?"

"John didn't have a choice," Mother explained. "Your mother was Catholic, and especially in the 1940's, divorces were tough to come by. In the end, she and the whole Blomquist family had hurt one another beyond repair.

"She insisted that he not see you again. Ever.

"And, I don't know if you knew, but the judge had ruled that he would not pay child support either."

"Oh ... How I've blamed him all these years," she whispered softly, "and it was my mother who kept us apart."

Grace, who had come to our door with an expectation of meeting her father, now bent her head and trembled. She had learned that he was long gone, but even worse, that her mother might have been the cause of his lifelong absence.

I'm always amazed at what parents keep from their children in the name of what's right, when there's nothing right about it.

Of course, my dad was no better at disclosure than his ex-wife had been. All of us were hurt by not knowing, all of us betrayed.

My legs sent out a slight twinge, a marker I'd realized over the years that invariably signaled a migraine headache coming on. I sat quietly waiting for Mother to begin her defense of my dad once again.

"But John kept a close eye on you anyway. You didn't know it, but his sister, Jeune Kirmser, a social worker for the schools, called you into her office every year and asked how you were doing. She never told you who she was. It was terribly hard on both of them."

"I remember that! They'd call me into the office, and I always knew I'd done nothing wrong (except once, but they didn't catch me). Anyway ... that must have been her, my aunt. I remember this lady with a really different voice ... more like a cello than a violin ... with resonance."

We laughed and said, "That's her."

"Aunt Jeune did that?" Wink asked. "That's hard to believe."

None of us had much of a relationship with our aunt Jeune, my father's only sibling and half-sister who lived half a year each year in Manhattan, Kansas, and the other half in London.

But up until her death a few years ago, I always received a birthday and Christmas letter from her, written as though it could be included in a journal of scholarly letters. In her own way, she made sure to let us know that each of us were loved and important to her.

While all of John's kids were really important to Aunt Jeune, she thought of my mother as an uneducated farm girl. And my mother thought of Jeune as an arrogant intellectual, who didn't know anything about people's feelings. They were both partially right, and unfortunately, neither ever tried to bridge the gap. Mother had intelligence and charm that Jeune never knew, and Jeune had the fire to be a successful social worker, poet, and community activist.

Heather brought out a plate of *krumkake* and *sandbakkels*, two varieties of Scandinavian cookies our family makes every Christmas, both made from the same ingredients, flour, sugar, eggs and butter, but fashioned into different shapes.

"Aunt Grace," said Heather, "you might as well start learning how to be a good Swede. You didn't even know you were half-Swedish, did you? Yup, butter cookies. That'll do it."

Everyone laughed and gladly took their share of sugar to lighten the atmosphere. But it didn't take the edge off our feelings of betrayal.

"Mother! I want to know why you never told us." Roxanne asked. She pulled her chair slightly away from the table and crossed her legs.

"Hell! Dad was married before, had a kid, and got divorced. Come on, what is it with these secrets? What else don't we know?"

Roxanne's dry attitude had developed with age. I could see Mother stiffening.

Only recently, nearly 40 years after this visit by Grace to Valley Creek, and a decade since Mother's passing, did I learn more of the story.

Dad not only left his first wife because he didn't like working at her company, or that he wanted to play jazz … but also because of my mother.

In a rare visit to see my aging Aunt Jeune before her own death, she told me that my mother had also worked for Dad's first wife's company, as a photographer's assistant to my dad.

The boss found out about my mom and dad's affair, and she gave him an ultimatum.

Johnny chose Mom, and he chose the baby (my sister, Roxanne) who would be arriving within months.

They moved out of the city, bought acreage in Valley Creek, and started the mink farm together.

———— ∘O∘ ————

"Mom, since we're talking about secrets, why don't you tell Grace how Dad found out about his *own* family."

"Oh great! More emotional crap!" Wink chimed in and shook his head. The light was starting to fade outside the windows, as we sat around the table, our strange new family.

"At the start of World War II, Johnny registered for the draft. When he went to the courthouse to get a copy of his birth certificate, he glanced at his mother's name, but ..."

She shook her finger in the air as she said, "It wasn't his mother's name at all, so he took it back to the clerk and asked her to correct it. The clerk assured him the name was in order, and suggested ..."

Mother cleared her voice and continued, "...that he might want to ask his father about it."

Grace took a bite of *krumkake*, which crumbled in her hands.

"It's okay," Heather said as she handed Grace a napkin, "It's supposed to crumble. *Krumkake* means crumb cake."

Mother didn't allow herself to be interrupted. "John drove straight home and confronted his dad, who only said, 'Oh, that was your mother. She died when you were a year old, from bad milk. But forget about her. You're lucky you never knew her. Ethel is your real mother.'"

"Can you believe it?" I said. "Lucky he never knew her?"

"No one would tell him anything about this 'Emma Olson,' the name on the birth certificate, until one day toward the end of the war. Johnny was working on the line at the ammunition plant, when he was approached by an older man who introduced himself as Leonard Olson, John's uncle, his birth mother's brother."

On the other side of the dining room the two smallest boys were not only finishing off the cookies, but were starting to elbow the girls. "Kent and Peter," Wink suggested nicely in his calm, authoritative tone, "I think it's time to find your snowmobile suits. I bet if you asked Grandpa Jim nicely, he'd take you for a ride on Oscar."

Jim Jorgenson had won a bonanza at the Prairie Island Casino and invested it in "Oscar", what he soon christened the four-wheeler. He loved to take his grandchildren on fast and curvy rides across the back acres.

Jim was a former farmer who worked at the Minnesota State Prison, but still had a farmer's mindset. He had a gigantic garden in summer, and used the rest of the back acreage to raise prairie grasses. He surrounded the garden with a tall fence to keep out the deer, but he also let the acres of tall grass grow around the garden, so that he could shoot them during hunting season, with both bow and gun.

"Yahhhh! Grandpa, can we go?"

"Sure, I'll gas 'er up. Don't forget your boots," Jim replied with a grin.

Peter tore out the door, and headed for his house next door to find the appropriate winter-wear for both himself and Kent.

Mother continued, "Uncle Leonard told John that his mother, Emma, had been a concert pianist in Europe. Played the major concert halls before she emigrated from Sweden to the U.S. He said she knew Jussi Bjorling, the famous Swedish tenor."

"And see, Grandpa didn't want my dad to take after her, just like your mom not wanting you to play the piano. But it didn't work," I said. "Dad was 18 before he even knew his birth mother existed, let alone that she was a pianist. Can you believe it? And now you too! In the genes!"

"Another thing you need to know, Grace. Emma's grandparents met while they sang in the king of Sweden's choir." Roxanne liked that part of the story, probably because she had sung in her school choir, played French horn in the concert band, and began college as a music major herself.

We spent the rest of that afternoon eating leftovers, watching the boys sliding down the hill, and filling Grace in on what we Blomquists felt was important history—our history— now that she would be one of us.

Now we were also part of her. We have been changed by Grace, opened to a new understanding of ourselves and our history.

Eventually Grace became my son Kent's piano teacher. Due to both genes and wonderful teaching, he is now the next in line: accomplished musician, with his PhD in Musical Composition.

Amazing grace, how sweet the sound.

Sometimes in the middle of confusion, grace appears. A mensch from a sleepy little town … a yellowed article in an old scrapbook … un-asked-for help … an ill-timed mink bite … an unexpected win at the casino … a northern Minnesota agate carried south in the ice of a glacier … jewelweed among the stinging nettles.

I wish I could say that was the last of all the family secrets.

Grace was a shock, but a good one. We adapted, and we expanded our family to include hers. We'd heard about Dad's crazy family before and now this was a great story to add on to it.

But that's just the beginning.

Hidden

Artists say white space is as important as painted,
as if surrounding air holds the image up.

That's how her avoidance felt, as if
the silence held the story in place.

I waited days, talked of children and food,
until the two of us were alone.

Mom, can I take some lilies? Happy to be
busy, she found garden shoes and trowel.

We worked together digging, as I said,
You know, Wink told me the secret ...

I figured, she said, looking down.
... Not surprising, I stated.

She lifted her watery brown eyes.
No, not surprising, she answered.

Stunned that something hidden
for decades could be so easily dismissed,

her faint smile returned as she
arranged lily-of-the-valley slips

into an empty ice cream bucket,
sugar and cream and ice gone.

chapter 13
judge not

Lily-of-the-valley
[*Convallaria majalis*]

I thought I'd take this to the grave with me," Mother confessed to my brother, Wink, just before she died. "But now I think you'd better know."

"Know what, Ma?"

"You might have some ..." she coughed and laid her head back, "some other brother or sister who might claim this house, and any other inheritance."
"Well gee, Ma," Wink replied in his carefree, matter of fact tone, trying not to rile Mother up further. "What's this all about?"

"After Johnny died, I went to the federal building in the Cities to apply for social security – you know those monthly checks you got through college – the lady there had me prove I was Johnny's wife."
She coughed again, and continued slowly. "Because there had been another woman there already, who claimed she was his wife, and had a kid, or maybe kids, I don't remember, Johnny's dependents, and she claimed the social security money was hers."

"This wasn't Grace's mother was it? Somebody else? Do you know who it was, Ma?"

"No, not Grace's mother. She had nothing to do with Johnny. I don't know. Lady wouldn't say ... and I didn't want to know."

"And that's it? Did she say where they lived?"

"Don't know. Don't want to know."

"Do you even have a clue?"

"No ... but it was my fault."

"Ma, that's crazy."

"I didn't want any more kids."

"But that's your right. You'd already had three, and for God's sake, he'd already had four, counting Grace."

"He wanted more."

"He was a jerk, Ma. Didn't respect you." He sighed, "And you've known this for how long? That was 48 years ago, and you never thought about telling us, or looking into it?"

"You can do something if you want to, but don't tell me. I just want to rest now."

————— ∘O∘ —————

My father had rejected St. Paul society and all its rules. Shortly after being granted his annulment from Grace's mother, he married Dorothy, a beautiful farm girl who had recently left home to study at Rasmussen Business School in Minneapolis, and then worked as his assistant.

As I wrote earlier, they bought acreage in remote Valley Creek, twenty miles east of St. Paul, and planned to raise mink for the luxury fur business.

But when one of the mink bit Mother, Dad decided he had none of the instincts he needed to be a farmer.

They continued to live in the old farmhouse on the sand hill, but instead of mink farming, the family planted 100 penny-a-piece pine trees every year until they covered the entire farm, and Dad made a living playing music, delivering newspapers, and for a short while, as an insurance agent. We grew up as country kids, despite the fact that our city-smart dad commuted nightly into the city to play with his band.

One night at the club, a man offered to buy Dad a drink during his break, and pulled up a chair at the table where he sat resting. Dad must have mentioned something about his migraine headache, something he'd been plagued with for years, because the man stood up, put his hands around Dad's neck and without a word, abruptly rotated it until there was a loud CLICK.

Dad's headache disappeared, and in fact, over the next couple weeks and months, did not come back. Incredibly enthused by the success of that adjustment, Dad later contacted the man, a chiropractor, and decided he was ready to become a student again.

I was in first grade when my father enrolled in chiropractic school in Minneapolis by day, (he actually composed their school song that ended with the words *Northwestern College of Chiropractic, hail oh hail to thee*) and played piano in a club by night.

In contrast to his unsuccessful college career, this time he got all A's. Four years later he earned his doctoral degree in Chiropractics (D.C.). But even after graduation, as he worked in a successful chiropractic practice in St. Paul, and then later in Stillwater, he continued to play organ and conduct his band full time, six nights a week.

This all seemed to fit into his unique worldview. Remember Rule No.1? Don't give up what you love.

He'd learned his lesson early with Grace, and he wouldn't give up his passion again. He decided to practice both chiropractic and music, even though the rigor of it, plus other dietary and social choices, would eventually kill him at a young age.

But there's more behind this rule, and I didn't learn about it until my 7th decade of life. It has to do with family secrets. Sometimes the only way to follow your own "rule" is to do it in the shadows.

Dad learned early that his family approved of secrets, as in never telling him about his own mother. He used the same technique with us, when he didn't tell us about his first marriage, or our half-sister Grace.

That coping mechanism worked well with his first wife, since she didn't appear to know about Johnny's philandering during his band tours, or with my mother.

And so it should have been no surprise at all to my mother, that he continued his secretive ways, his "don't give up what you love" rule, not adapting it even for her, or for his children.

———— ∘O∘ ————

Wink called and told me, with his consistent and calm tone, what Mother had said about some other family.

The next day, checking for genealogical data online, I discovered the birth certificates of two boys and a girl, born in the early 1950's. They had lived in the outskirts of the Twin Cities, and their listed father was someone by the name of John Adolph Blomquist.

Adolph was my father's second middle name, one that he never used around us. Nevertheless, I knew immediately that he had registered for this other family using that second middle name, to confuse anyone who might check the records.

It feels like a sick joke he left behind, waiting all of these years to come out of the shadows and surprise his offspring.

Another secret I had already known from Minnesota state records, was that Johnny had lost a brother to pneumonia when he was very young. That brother's name was Bruce. And one of the children listed as fathered by John Adolph Blomquist is named Bruce. It made sense.

Obviously there was another woman that my father loved, and with whom he had children.

He wouldn't give those kids up. Or was it the three of us that he wouldn't give up? Was that the root of his deception? Love for us kids?

———— ∘O∘ ————

As I have watched my children and grandchildren grow up, and seen the world for what it is – I have been rethinking my father's marriages and his philandering, and even his behavior earlier as he traveled the country with a big band, and flaunted his popularity with all kinds of women.

Johnny had managed to jump through all the hoops the Catholic Church demanded of him to divorce his first wife, and to marry my mother. But the consequences were dire. In the terms of that divorce, my dad was never again to see his first child, Grace, from that marriage. How painful that must have been, and continued to be throughout his life.

I didn't learn about Grace until we were both middle-aged. At the time, I was angry that such a grave secret had been kept from both of us. But what I learned, as my mother lay dying, about Dad marrying yet another woman, without divorcing my mother, or even letting her know about it, made me furious.

How had this man I knew as so lovable ... conducted this kind of life? He was home very seldom, but was intimate and kind when there (except for rare outbursts of anger).

I recently came upon his Humboldt High School yearbook from St. Paul. In it he had recorded a phrase below his name – a phrase that was to identify his personhood or philosophy.

The yearbook read, "I am sure care is an enemy of life."

I read that over and over. Who would say that?

What kind of hole did Johnny have inside to feel that he should not care for or be cared for by another?

At first I thought he had felt suffocated by the care of his step-mother Ethel, and his father who wanted him to be a scientist, not a musician. But now I see it differently.

His biological mother had died when he was around a year old, and I do not know who cared for him before Grandpa married Ethel, five years later. We now know what a crucial time those years are within a child's life, towards developing trust and intimacy. I also know they were very poor, and had little food.

As a therapist myself, many years later, and the spouse of a developmental pediatrician, I now believe that my dad may have had an attachment disorder, so that it was difficult to be intimate in any lasting way with any one person.

Dad never got along with his parents, and if we visited, it was always for a short time.

He also told us he did not like his only sister, Jeune, even though she told me she loved him dearly, and told me that he had watched out for her when they were growing up.

I remember my dad telling me the only reason he got asked to parties as a teenager was because he played the piano.

Looking at his yearbook, it doesn't seem that way. He was involved in all kinds of activities, and even served as an officer for some of them. But even if it wasn't completely true, it was clear Johnny believed he was only liked for what he could do, and not for who he really was.

I find it interesting that at his funeral there were so many people they couldn't all fit into the church. He was loved by hundreds of people, but I'm not sure he knew it. I'm not sure he felt it.

I guess it's fitting, then, that his grave stands by itself in Bayport, Minnesota.

My mother is buried in Afton, with her second husband, Jim, beside her there. Dad's first wife is buried in St. Paul. And his third wife, Irene, also in some suburb of the Cities.

Grandpa and Grandma are buried in Acacia Park Cemetery in Mendota Heights. His half-sister, Jeune, who adored him, but was disregarded and ignored, is buried with her husband, Phil, in Manhattan, Kansas.

Speaking of death, I imagine that he never got over the death of his mother. He told us he didn't remember it, but I'm sure that deep inside, he felt abandoned.

Despite people who loved him, he never felt cared for, never felt he belonged anywhere. And now he resides in a community graveyard, around people who did not know him.

I just learned a few months ago that his daughter by his third wife, I'll call her JB, goes to his grave every Memorial Day to decorate it with flowers. I also stop by every time I visit Minnesota.

In this human world we are part of, one person's pain often invades others … in this case, my mother.

My dad's actions in life, as much as he might have tried to justify or fix things (no one knows what he was going through), were not harmless.

After he died we had nothing, except mortgage payments due on our house. Not only was Mother left with three children and a mortgage, this double whammy of death and betrayal dropped her into a hole so dark, that she quit her job as receptionist where Dad had worked.

Mother refused to be in the presence of people who praised my dad, because they did not know the whole story.

On that dark day in September 1960, we three children lost not only a dad, but also the mother we knew.

I took over the cooking.

No one did the cleaning.

Our old house needed to be painted, but we had no money for it, so Roxy, age 15, and I, at 13, climbed the tall ladders, following Mother's instructions, and painted the entire outside of our wooden home.

Roxy got us all on the school bus on time, and we became feral children, not that different from Grandpa Gus and his mother, abandoned by his Dad who went back to Sweden, a little like Great-Grandpa Lars who we found out recently had been an orphan and had to take on the yoke of adulthood far too early.

We became hardscrabble kids, as tough as our ancestors had been.

It took a year before Roxy and I went to the city and bought Mother a new outfit, colored brightly, with shoes to match, and told her it was time to move on.

That new dress we bought her did wake her up. She began thinking about a career, becoming a hairdresser.

It wasn't easy. She took the money from our Social Security checks to pay for tuition at the Ritter Beauty College in St. Paul. Our neighbors easily added her to their commuter schedule, and she started a new phase of her life, as a student, just like the three of us.

———— ▫O▫ ————

Family secrets were the norm. I knew lots of juicy gossip about my neighbors that I would never tell anyone, because if I did, they'd tell our own secrets.

Citizens needed to hold their heads high and call themselves good Christians. The past was altered to be remembered the way they wished it had been. Secrets were the lockboxes that assured community solidarity.

No wonder my family was drawn to this sandy, glacial Valley, which functioned mostly in isolation. Close to the city, but not urban. Close to farms, but not agrarian. Close to the suburbs, but not under their rules of uniformity. People could live their own free lives here.

Thinking back, it's clear that Pastor Carlson, as he had rejected Dad for the organ committee – a new pastor, new to our area — did not understand the first rule of our Valley, *judge not, and ye shall not be judged.*

Churchy people might have called him a "pietist," a person who believes in strict godly living as a Christian requirement. Although, in hindsight, I don't know how his cigarette smoking got past those standards.

Not all Lutherans are pietists, or to use Garrison Keillor's term, *Gloomy Lutherans.* However, with the German and Scandinavian heritage of Minnesota, we did have our fair share.

My dad was seldom gloomy. Maybe that's why it seemed to me that everyone loved him. Though he could not be described as Santa Claus–like, he did have a middle much like a bowl full of jelly, his eyes did twinkle, and his cheeks were rosy, covered with Swedish–skin spider veins.

I could tell when Dad was at his most relaxed, because he'd sit with only his toes touching the floor and his knees, pointed sideways, bouncing lightly up and down.

John's abstinence from alcohol had nothing to do with the concept of sin, but rather because he had endured a child's pain living with an alcoholic grandfather. He'd also bailed drunken musician friends out of jail, covered for them when they couldn't perform, and watched their families fall apart. The pastor hadn't thought to ask about that, and instead had ruled my dad guilty by association.

Speaking of pietists, Grandma and Grandpa Blomquist were a good example of that kind of religion, it seems to me. Though Grandpa was 100% Swedish, and brought up Lutheran, he had decided he preferred the Methodists because they used grape juice for communion, and abstained entirely from alcohol. Every year at Christmas, Grandpa's Jewish employer, Mr. Kaplan, gave him an expensive bottle of fine wine. And every year I remember my mother complaining about what a terrible waste it was, as Grandma poured it down the drain.

Alcohol was not my grandparent's only prohibition. We'd laugh about the times they drove out unexpectedly from St. Paul. One of us would notice them turning into the driveway and shout, "Get rid of the cards. Hide the pennies," and giggle as we all shouted, "Stop the sinning!"

Then we'd madly snatch up the game of Poker or War or Double Solitaire sprawled on the living room rug, rush into the bedroom, pull out the coloring books and crayons, and drop them onto the floor.

By the time Grandma and Grandpa made it up the steps and knocked loudly on the front door, we'd be placidly coloring within the lines.

More often, it would have been just me playing Solitaire on the floor. My brother and sister always seemed to be moving, walking, throwing a ball, involved in something. But I loved to lounge on the braided rug, examining its lumps and bumps and array of colors while I played cards all by myself.

I was fascinated with the distorted pictures of kings and queens, the waxy way the cards felt in my hands, and I loved to shuffle them as one of Mother's Bridge-playing friends did it, first forward, then backwards, each card finding a new place, hiding, readjusting, starting over.

And if no one would take the time to play cards with me, I loved the idea of being able to play a game with just myself, at the race-car rate I learned to sling the cards.

One steadfast rule I imposed on myself was never to cheat, because a win doesn't have that "aah" moment if there's been fudging of cards.

Dad learned all the rules in his childhood, but somewhere along the way he also learned it was in his best interest to hide his behaviors, and not judge himself.

My other grandmother, Grandma Knoblauch, was just as pious. She didn't allow alcohol either, but there was one exception, although she pretended not to know it. Every Christmas, while Grandma finished the last touches of dinner, my mom, uncles and Grandpa gathered in the ante-room, amid muddy boots, tools of all shapes and sizes, and hooks full of winter overcoats, to sneak a bottle of Christmas wine.

Mother alluded once that her German neighbors in Miesville, friends of Grandpa, lived on the proceeds of their hooch stills during the years of Prohibition. I could never get her to tell me anything else about it, but my cousin Leona knows their names. I wouldn't doubt that Mom's two brothers, Russell and Wilmer, had more than just a passing knowledge of the illegal operations.

I seldom hear children any more calling their grandparents by their last names, but that is how we referred to ours. I was fifteen before I knew what their first names were: Gustave, Frank, Ethel, and Anne. Knowing their names would have humanized them for me.

But our relationships were formal, and the use of last names reflected that formality. It also meant not touching, unless they indicated they wanted a perfunctory hello or goodbye kiss on the cheek.

These grandparents weren't babysitters, or mentors, or even storytellers. They were elders to be respected (from their perspective), and elders to be mostly dismissed (from ours).

None of them knew the styles of the day, or the popular music, or even the books we read.

I had no understanding that their generation had a right to their own styles, way of thinking, and rules, and that they had survived by living that way.

I learned two sets of rules, a strict set from grandparents, and another, more relative one from my home and Valley neighbors.

My dad and neighbors smoked cigarettes. Most of them had no qualms about drinking beer, wine, or even hard liquor. But I don't remember ever seeing alcohol misused.

The neighbors were Catholic, Baptist, Unitarian, Methodist and nothing-in-particular, and everyone seemed to be pretty independent, having his/her own ideas about how to live.

None of them seemed evil. They all worked hard, minded their own business, and did what needed to be done.

I remember one day, Mr. Pothan, the owner of one of the grocery stores in Afton, drove into our driveway. He had never been to our home, but we knew him well because

Roxy worked part time in the store. As I answered the door he said, "Is your mother home, and Winky?"

"Ya, sure. I'll get'em."

"I'd like to talk to them alone if I could," he continued.

Oh-oh. I knew Winky was in trouble then.

I could guess what it was about too. Recently I'd noticed my brother had red licorice sticks hanging out of his pockets, and I'd wondered where they came from, since candy wasn't something we had money for.

They banished me to the living room while they talked in the kitchen, but I had good ears and could hear my mother's voice rise when she said my brother's name. We never talked about it, yet it wasn't much of a leap to figure out he had stolen the candy.

Later, I informed Roxy, as if I had heard the whole thing.

Nobody called the police, which would have been the Washington County Sheriff's Department. Winky just quietly swept floors and dusted shelves at Pothan's Grocery Store until the candy had been paid off. And no one was told. No need for it.

In order to live the Valley way, its residents followed a set of unstated rules, learned early and often.

Live and let live.

Accept everyone unless proven untrustworthy.

Don't complain, and always do what needs to be done.

Judge not.

And finally, God helps those who help themselves.

We lived and died by those precepts. However, if a neighbor got in trouble, and put forth effort, then Valley residents would help just enough to get them on their feet again, just enough so no one was beholden to anyone else.

When Dad died, there were so many donated casseroles, jellos and roasts that the multitudes gathered couldn't have eaten them in a week. And just as fast, they stopped coming when it was time for us to get along on our own.

The stoic residents of the Valley understood the rules, and the necessity of secrets. We resided in a Valley named after two fast flowing creeks that looked serene, but were secretly frigid, fast-flowing and turbulent, just like us.

Every once in a while, hidden debris bobbed to the surface, some sticky gossip, often eroding the creek's sandy banks, sometimes even altering the course of the stream.

But eventually it all flowed downstream, never returning.

"Moons and Junes and ferris wheels.
The dizzy dancing way you feel..."

– From "Both Sides Now" by Joni Mitchell

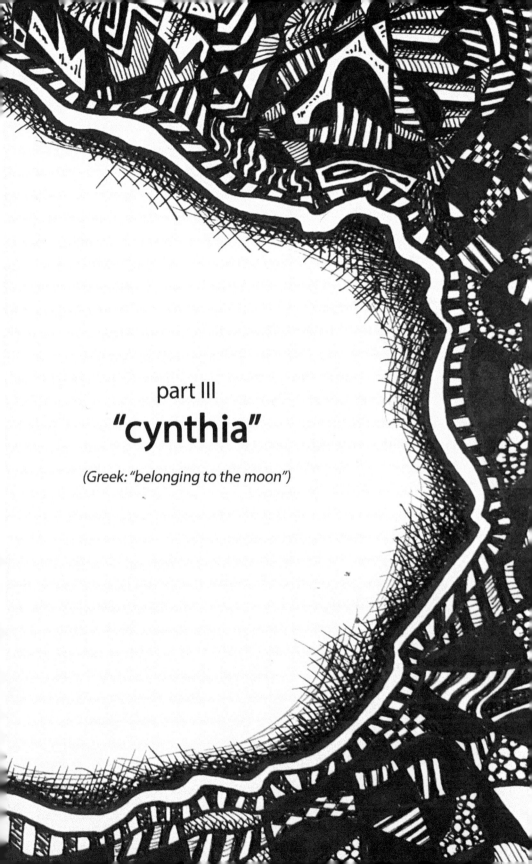

part III
"cynthia"

(Greek: "belonging to the moon")

Wounded

When she asked what I'd wear, I said, paisley,
dark, wiggly fabric draped over my tight shoulders,

the familiar dress massaging flesh and something else
deeply wounded in my thirteen-year-old frame.

I love shapes of paisley as they whirl and twist,
colors blending into the last light of sunset,

the almost-dark time when shades of purple spread
across sky, creep into air and take over my breath.

I chose the paisley dress for father's funeral,
its dim light all that was left of day.

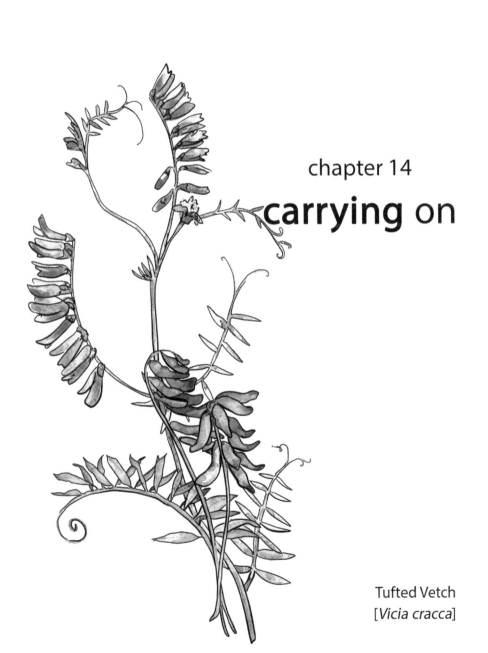

chapter 14

carrying on

Tufted Vetch
[*Vicia cracca*]

I am the middle child. Not first. Not last.
Not first girl. Not the expected boy.
Not the aggressive older one. Not the lovable baby.
Not the attention–seeker. Not the helpless one.

Middle child.

Recent research has shown their vulnerability, finding that middle children have the least education, do the least well financially, and have the hardest time leaving home.

My husband, a developmental pediatrician, tells me it may be dangerous for a middle child to be born with a mellow disposition. Their needs may be too easily overlooked.

Mother tried to meet my needs, but I didn't scream or shout them out, didn't tell her when I was hungry, didn't cry when I was wet.

But she knew enough to ask the right question. One day she bundled me in my snowsuit, put me safely in the arms of my sister in the back seat of the car, and drove to see Dr. Jensen, in Stillwater.

"She doesn't cry, Doctor. What does that mean?" Mother tried to explain the seriousness of this situation, but he only laughed.

"Good," he said. "She won't get spoiled." This was pre–Dr. Spock mentality, when the prevailing philosophy of child-rearing was to pay as little attention to them as possible.

At one year of age, I was not yet twelve pounds. I had not even doubled my birth weight.

Father never figured out what to do with me either. He tickled Roxy and Winky until they laughed so hard tears rolled down their cheeks.

I hated this tickling. He'd come near me and I'd run outside.

"No," I'd yell. "It doesn't tickle. It hurts."

He'd catch me, confident in his ability to make me laugh, his hands digging into all the tickle zones of my body, but I never laughed. Tears rolled silently down my cheeks as I wished over and over that instead of trying to make me laugh, he would plop me into his big lap, and we would listen to his hi-fi records, together humming Benny Goodman and The Four Freshmen melodies.

I desperately wanted him to notice the 'me' hidden inside, the one who loved his music, the one who heard music in everything, like the soft tones of the morning when I had not quite awakened, and the mourning doves cooing on the wires above my bedroom.

The evening also held magic, its silence broken only by the call of whip-poor-wills serving as backdrop for the wild dreams I conjured, dreams where the band was at my back, and I sang on one professional stage after another, the audience listening with intent, bursting into applause at the end of my renditions.

It's all I ever wanted, to be a jazz or pop singer.

Mother saved precious cash for Roxy and me to take tap and ballet lessons. Since my sister was older than I was, she made her wishes known louder and stronger. She was an exquisite dancer. She needed to take those lessons.

But I was miserable. The dance instructor let me know I was not as graceful as my sister, and couldn't I try a little harder?

One time I got up enough nerve to ask Mother, "Can't I please take voice lessons?"

She replied, "But you're already taking dance. Isn't that enough?"

She didn't know I'd gone through all of Dad's sheet music and learned the lyrics to every song, and on those special occasions, when she took the whole family to the night-club to hear Dad's band, I was ready to sing along with any of his tunes.

When I was bored at school I'd always have a melody pulsing through my consciousness. Through church sermons, parent's lectures, long car rides, baseball games, my brain was full of melodies and lyrics.

At age four she found me plunking out tunes at the piano.

"Would you like to learn to play that right?"

"Oh, yah," I replied. "I want to play songs."

The next week we drove the pea-green Studebaker north on Valley Creek Road over the two miles of winding asphalt leading to the interstate highway, turned east, away from the big city, and made our way across the wide river bridge to Wisconsin. I'd seen the St. Croix River before, when we'd gone to Hudson shopping. And I'd been swimming at its beaches in Lakeland and St. Croix Beach every summer.

Gloria Haslund, Afton historian and neighbor, remembers when I said my first word. It was at the beach while looking out over the wide lake. I pointed to a boat whizzing past and said "Peed Boat." It doesn't surprise me that my first word was in response to a percussive sound.

That day, as we stopped at the tollbooth to pay our quarter, I could hear the restless howl of the wind, the waves lapping at cement barrier legs, and the powerful rush of water beneath us as it joyously journeyed southward. I imagined all the levies, dams, ditches and powerful bridges that would try to control its spirit, and knew the river would have its way.

We drove through Hudson to a tall, two-story home north of downtown. Its lace-covered windows marked the home of our minister and his wife. Pastor Borg, much loved and respected by all his parishioners, was charged with the care of both the Afton and Hudson Lutheran churches, but the parsonage stood in Hudson. (He was the uncle of Marcus Borg, who would become famous in the 1990's as a Jesus Seminar scholar and author). But we weren't there to see the pastor. We came that day to meet with Mrs. Borg, our church organist, and potential piano teacher.

I didn't get it. Why wouldn't Daddy teach me? He loved music. I tried to tell Mother, "I want to play like Daddy. Mrs. Borg's music's awful. You go to church and she plays so slow. Sounds like somebody died."

"Your father says he doesn't know how to teach children, and Mrs. Borg is very good. She's giving us a discount, and I expect you'll be respectful."

I tried to be respectful, but in my four-year-old mind it was boring, and had no connection to the tunes I had fallen in love with. I couldn't make myself practice, and I quit before I learned much of anything about the piano. The one thing I remembered was middle C.

Middle C. Not a high note. Not a low note.

Not a sharp or a flat or a minor or anything interesting.

Just plain old middle C. Easy to find. Quietly waiting there in the middle.

That's where I found myself on the afternoon of my father's funeral. Thirteen years old, sitting at the bench of his Hammond organ, striking middle C over and over again.

Dad's band members had rented a trailer and brought His Hammond D3 Organ home to us from the nightclub, and placed it in the room Dad had built.

As I sat there, I remembered all the times I had crawled onto that bench while Dad played and sang "Happy Birthday" to me. Now the instrument seemed enormous with its layers of keys, switches, and foot pedals.

An uncontrolled craving grew inside me.

I was the mellow one, the one who knew how to put up with anything. I knew I could live without talking to him, without sitting on his lap or laughing at his jokes. I'd hate the loneliness of it, but I could do it.

I knew our family could survive. We had an enormous garden. I could gather wild berries and asparagus. Winky would happily fish in our surrounding lakes and streams. We'd make it.

But I wasn't sure what I'd do without the music.

I still had Dad's records, his sheet music, the memory of tunes sung with him. I still played trombone in the band, but it would never be the same.

I hated that I lacked the power, and the natural ease, to exchange the pumping of feet and the dexterity of my hands to produce not just notes, but music, from that organ.

I wanted so much to play "Jesu, Joy of Man's Desiring", fortissimo, on that organ. It would have filled empty spaces. But each time my hands touched its keys, the sounds came out dissonant, and when my thumb, wrapped in gauze and tape, from smashing it in the car door at the funeral, struck the keyboard, the excruciating pain I experienced earlier in the day reappeared.

———— ∘O∘ ————

That morning Roxy had asked, "What are you wearing to the funeral? It's supposed to be black, you know. Got anything close to black?"

"No. You know what I have. I like color."

"Well, something kind of dark then?"

"Dark. I don't like dark. I don't like funerals. Dad would've liked red."

"You're right." Roxy replied. "I'm wearing my navy suit, with a red bow in my hair."

I thought for awhile, opened the door of my closet and thumbed through the dresses. "My purple paisley is dark, but it's lively. That's what I'll wear."

I took my time to get ready, curling my hair, and putting on the garter belt and nylons I had just bought for my thirteenth birthday. I found a clean slip, pulled the dress over my head, and put on my Sunday shoes.

I rode silently with the rest of the family to the funeral home.

Everybody was there except Grandpa Blomquist, who said he couldn't say good-bye yet. Even a child understands that parents are supposed to die before their children. I've since understood other issues between them, but that day I just knew Grandpa wasn't there.

We entered long, black limousines that took us to the church. Still no one spoke. That was not unusual for our family. They seldom talked about bad feelings. I recalled the almost daily advice given by Mother, "If you don't have something good to say, don't say it."

There was definitely nothing good to say.

The limousine parked in front of our church, Bethlehem Lutheran, in Bayport. The undertaker got out of his seat, walked slowly around the front of the long black car, and opened the door for our family to exit. First Mother walked out, dignified and sure of step, followed by Roxy, and then Winky.

As I steadied myself from the imbalance of my new mini-heels, I clutched the door-jamb for support. Winky, without thought, slammed the door shut.

The heavy hearse door crushed my thumb.

My exhaled breath exploded into a whine. It was several seconds of pain before I inhaled again. I shoved my flattened, already purple thumb, into my mouth for comfort, thinking the cool wet of my tongue could relieve the unbearable throbbing.

Why did this have to happen at my father's funeral, a time to celebrate his life? The one thing I knew, even during the pain, was that I was not going to disrupt Dad's service by crying or complaining.

This day was for him, not me.

One of the undertakers rushed me to the downstairs bathroom of the church, where in less than two minutes my finger was washed and wrapped with wet paper towels. I was told to hold it still during the service, keeping my thumb in an upright position. No matter how much throbbing or pain I felt, I would not allow myself to cry.

I joined my family in the front pew of the church, and watched the painted face and body of my father not responding to the rhythm or the lyrics of hymns and organ preludes. My finger created a rhythm unlike any other, but I remained as still as he was.

——— ·O· ———

Later at home, sitting hopelessly at the organ, I again felt the throbbing pain. I kept striking middle C. No one had noticed I arrived late for the after-the-funeral reception. My uncle was happy to take me to the doctor's office to get an x-ray and have my finger set. He didn't want to be at the reception either.

"Middle C." A man's voice. I looked up.

"I see you know something about music." I recognized Irv Trestman, the sax player from Dad's band. He later sold me (at a discounted price) my first guitar, a koa wood Harmony, during the folk music craze of the late 60's.

I couldn't talk. Tears formed in my eyes and fell down my cheeks when I blinked.

"The music isn't gone."

He put his hand on my shoulder. "You'll find yours. It may not be piano or organ, but you'll find your music."

"I play trombone, you know, but it's not the same. You can't play it by itself. I want the whole sound, all the parts together. Make it fill this place." I shook my head and looked down.

"Your dad could sure do that." He paused.

"You must know that middle C is the note that organizes all others," he said. "How could anyone find the chord they want without knowing where C is on the keyboard? Listen carefully to its pure tone. Listen to it until it tells you how to move on."

I struck the note again. I listened.

And I listened, until I heard my dad's voice. It was nothing mysterious. It was a repeating of the last words he'd spoken to me before his heart attack.

I had asked permission to go somewhere I knew he didn't want me to go, but he had said instead, "Yes, because I trust you."

"I trust you."

I struck middle C again.

"I trust you."

I rose from the seat of the organ, and started organizing the dozens of casseroles, pies and salads deposited on our kitchen counter. I set out paper plates, napkins, silverware, started the coffee, and then excused myself to my room.

There I wrote a poem for Mother, something that matched my thirteen-year-old understanding, about the heavenly choir needing an organist.

It didn't matter what the content was, as I wrote I felt as if something inside me burst free.

Exploded.

I heard not only words, but notes and melodies entering my brain, not death marches, not pop melodies, but jazz. I ran outside and dragged my feet through piles of red maple leaves, dead but still brilliant in their falling, and sang, "Oh When the Saints Go Marching In".
Roxy ran out of the house and shouted, "Shut up. What's the matter with you. Are you crazy?"

"Oh no. You can't be crazy when people count on you. You just keep marchin'."

"Well," she said. "Do it a little quieter then, so people won't hear you."

I lifted my gauze-and-taped thumb, high as a drum major's wand, and said, "Don't worry. I'm the middle child."

That's how I began my teen-aged years, with little money, no father, and a strong concept of carrying on. I had dreams, and I knew I had to, and could, rely on myself to achieve them.

I still played trombone, but little by little I began to rely more on the music of poetry, the words of Carl Sandburg, the Swede from Chicago, who wrote without rhyme, but described my Midwestern life in melodic language.

And the words of Yevgeny Yevtushenko, whose poetry was smuggled out of Russia and read by young poets everywhere. He was Russian at a time I was not supposed to listen to Russians, but in his poem "Lies," he said,

Telling lies to the young is wrong.
Proving to them that lies are true is wrong.
Telling them that God's in his heaven
and all's right with the world is wrong.

By that time the Vietnam War was raging and I knew all was not right in the world. I loved to believe that God was in some heaven somewhere making everything okay, but at the same time I came from a single parent home, and struggled with poverty and isolation.

Yevgeny Yevtushenko later escaped from Russia when his life was in danger. He had nowhere to go, and the University of Tulsa offered him a job and a home. As an adult poet I met him here, both of us working on the same international literary journal. He died a few years ago, but I am still inspired by his spirit and words. *Don't Die Before You're Dead*, he named his autobiography, a book that inspired my husband to survive a near-death experience of his own.

I came to understand that Middle C is more like the eternal note that underlies everything. When I play it, or hear it played, it is as though my dad is with me.

This joy can come and go, but "C" is there to bring back balance, self, focus, structure, meaning – maybe even the "God" that Yevtushenko says is elusive.

Patience of the Cross Timbers *

Hundreds of years growing on a steep hill, desolate, aging
despite scarce nourishment, they wait for history to recognize them.

Crooked cedars, centuries old, twist in the shifting light of seasons,
and cling to a long forgotten hill shared by three-hundred-year-old

post oaks, every head cut off by lightning, every stump holding out
side limbs, like wires on ragged and weathered clothes-line poles.

Recorded history is revealed in the cross timbers' rings, some narrow
as a spider's thread, examined not by eye, but magnified to count each

period of drought, season of rain, each scarring fire, tornado, flood,
times of settlement and grazing. Washington Irving slept here

among the timbers, now a century older, and proclaimed them
beautiful. They have waited these years to hear it once again.

I wait. Transition is permanent. I understand these trees that grow
around rock and moss, trees which stretch limbs in crooked lines

seeking elusive light, trying to catch run-away water, clinging to life
long enough to leave a legacy on the land before becoming

firewood. Their endurance, spiritual patience, their mandala
of encyclopedic rings. What they have is what I want.

---

*The Cross Timbers are the only remaining old-growth forest in the American
Southwest, made up of post oak and red cedar, aged 300 to 1000 years old, discovered in 1999 in Oklahoma.

chapter 15

my land

Black-eyed Susan
[*Rudbeckia hirta*]

Poems are made by fools like me,
But only God can make a tree. – Joyce Kilmer

T he bottoms of my feet were so tough from running barefoot my entire childhood, I couldn't feel the needles of a sand burr even if I stepped on one. Active welts from mosquito, spider and black fly bites covered my exposed summer skin, and my knees had no normal patches at all, only a mismatched map of scars and leftover road rash from bike wipe-outs on stony tar roads.

Spending more time outdoors than indoors on the long, sunny days of Minnesota summers resulted in a body covered with freckles and sunburn, but no tan.

During the summer of 1965, after my high school graduation, I worked days at Northwestern Bell Telephone Company in St. Paul, dressing in my school clothes, and acting like a real employee doing drafting of telephone lines. But on the way home, at night, I stopped at my house first,

changed into comfy camping clothes, and followed a secret trail into the backwoods.

There, my longtime friend and neighbor, Carol Appleby,
and I lived a wild summer's dream in our own tent, which
we had pitched in a small woodland opening. Surrounded
by jack pine, raspberry bushes, and wild roses, the air always smelled like Christmas candy, and the path around
the tent was soft as kid gloves, formed from decades of
browned pine needle droppings.

We ate and read by Coleman stove and lantern, and kept
our own hours and visitors. We discovered all kinds of
new friends, mostly male, and mostly private school
types.

Carol and I joked about how, when we lived in our everyday houses we were considered boring. Then put the two
of us in a simple tent, and suddenly we were irresistible.

It wasn't about sex. It was about long, intimate hours
talking by candlelight about life's meaning, reciting Yevtushenko and Ferlinghetti, and pondering our future.

We spent that last summer of our childhood camped out
in the woods, knowing that the future would require some
kind of domestication from us.

We also knew the future would have us following different
roads. At the end of that summer I left for college, and she
left for South Africa as an exchange student.

I started in the fall at Gustavus Adolphus College, but later
transferred to Boston University. It was at B.U. where my
street-smart New York City roommate suddenly laughed

at me as I lay in bed studying. It wasn't unusual, her making fun of me.

Gerri was sexy, lewd, and profane-mouthed, and divided up her diet pills, selling them to her druggy friends. She felt stuck with a goody-two-shoes Midwestern roommate, and the only thing that kept our talk civil was the fact that I was engaged to a Harvard Medical School student.

"What's so funny?" I asked, wondering what faux-pas I had stepped into this time.

"Your feet," she replied, and kept laughing.

"What about my feet?" I started to be nervous.

"The bottoms are black, even though your skin is lily white. How in the world did you get fucking black feet?"

"Oh," I replied, and looked. "I guess they are. Aren't yours?"

"No! Not even Blacks have black bottomed feet. Not that color!"

"Never thought about it. Guess it's from years of goin' barefoot on blacktop. When it's hot, tar melts, and presto! Black feet. Can't get it off. Calluses just form over it."

She always made me feel as though I was trash, and I knew this explanation wouldn't change that.

I remember her turning away and saying, "Man, you really are country!"

She was the same person who later remarked that my wool clothes stank, quipping as if it was funny, and didn't we have dry cleaners in Minnesota?

She once commented that our drinking water must be awfully good.

I said, "Sure," but I knew something stupid was coming. "But why do *you* think so?"

"Coming off the mountains the way it does out there."

I had to tell her that we had no mountains in Minnesota, and not anywhere near. And we had great water because we were the land of 10,000 lakes.

"Whatever," I said. She made me look at the Valley as an outsider might see it, defend my home, and it made me feel closer to it.

I realized I was rooted in the land. Not any land. That land. The place where creeks flow into valleys, where the internal organs of sand hills are powered by agates, quartz, jasper, and granite, carried from a distant northern plain by a centuries-ago glacier.

I was rooted, not only because I had camped out in a tent for a summer, sleeping in the heat and cool, listening to raindrops on canvas and wind howling in the treetops, and waking to welcoming calls of morning birds. It was not only because I tried to converse while competing with loud, insistent evening whip-poor-wills. And not only because my feet had been callused and stained black by the Valley's tar roads.

My connection ran deeper than that.

———— ∘O∘ ————

I first heard the words of the poem 'Trees' recited by Miss Kilkelly, my second grade teacher.

Since we were in a new school building and had no playground equipment yet, during recess we played tag on the sandy, barren lot outside the new Afton-Lakeland grade school, a sprawling one-story brick building.

One day a huge truck, loaded full of pine seedlings, drove past us onto the back of the school lot. Instead of explaining to us that the older children and parent volunteers would plant these trees as a windbreak and natural fence around the property, my teacher got a faraway look in her eyes and began to speak, as if inspired by a higher power:

> *I think that I shall never see*
> *A poem lovely as a tree.*

Somehow these words seemed just right at that moment. Not even the boys giggled.

That Sunday I told Grandma Blomquist about the poem. She'd been to college, a math major at Hamline University, and I'd heard her talk about Shakespeare and other poets. She knew the poem immediately and recited it to the whole family gathered at her house. It surprised me because she recited it with such grace and ease. At the end we all clapped.

For Christmas that year, Grandma gave me a leather-bound book of poetry. On page 39 was printed:

> *"Trees" by Sergeant Joyce Kilmer, 165th Infantry (69th New York), A.E.F. (Born December 6, 1886; killed in action near Ourcy, July 30, 1918.)*

An oval picture of Kilmer, dressed in military uniform, was set alongside the poem. His dark determined eyes peered out from under a helmet, and he seemed to be looking directly at me.

I wondered if he knew his words would last longer than his frail body. I wanted to know if he had written about trees while confined to a foxhole, imagining their life-giving beauty.

Or had he found a lone tree standing on a barren field full of dead soldiers, the only vestige of life?

I dreamed about that picture, those dark eyes, the haunting words, *killed in action*.

My grandfathers did not fight in that "great" war, and we had a history of not going to war ... My great-grandfather had left Germany in the 19th century to avoid the Kaiser's draft.

My father did not fight in World War II, nor did my uncles.

My brother did not fight in Vietnam.

My husband served after being drafted, but he didn't fight, he took care of babies on an Army base in Hawaii during that war.

Just like all the other secrets, I didn't know that I had come from this long line of pacifists until the controversies of the Vietnam War began, and I asked Mother about my dad. She showed me a letter he had written which explained how he had obtained a physical deferment for a rupture, but that he had planned on being a conscientious objector. He never told her why, but she thought he just objected to war in general.

Most of my other relatives were farmers, and they were needed at home, to sustain life, not take it.

When I read Father's letter, the picture of Sergeant Joyce Kilmer floated into my mind again, the soldier who wrote poetry, the man who looked for redemption within the green trees and valleys of battlegrounds. How would my father, the musician, have fared in the face of not only death, but in the direct killing of another man?

Would his music have taken different overtones?

Would there have been music at all in his life after this?

My dad didn't like the poem 'Trees'. He told us he thought it was too flowery. Although he was a sensitive musician, he was more of a male Scandinavian stoic. Memories of the 1930's Dust Bowl in the Midwest probably aided in the poem's popularity. By then we all knew the importance of trees and long grasses in preventing erosion and dust.

'Trees' left its mark on me. I discovered poetry that year, and with it, I began seeing with a poet's eyes. Joyce Kilmer had made me take a second look at the trees on our own property.

He had declared they were more beautiful than a poem. How could that be? What had I been missing?

I started looking at trees in a new way. I began climbing trees to discover what was at the top. On the way up I peeked into bird nests. At the top I found vistas.

I used the fragrant pine needle floors beneath huge blue spruces for secret places in which to dream. As I began looking up, I saw stratus and darkening cumulonimbus clouds and hawks and variations of sky.

Little by little I came to recognize the difference between the pines; two needle clusters of long, dark green signified Red Pine (Norway Pine), five needle clusters of medium long, white-backed needles were the White Pine, two short needles in a cluster belonged to the scrappy Jack. Next I learned the deciduous trees and identification not only by leaf, but also by silhouette in the winter woods.

Nature and poetry became united. And ever since, they have intertwined and continue to serve as my lifetime spiritual map.

———— ∘O∘ ————

The Sommerdorfs were our oldest family friends, people who were not relatives, but had all the same privileges. They could drop by without calling, hug us, and even make something into a joke when you did something really stupid. They were Winky's godparents.

But the Sommerdorfs were different from anyone else I knew. They had no beer stored in their refrigerator for Sunday football watching. They didn't go to movies on Friday night, not even Ol' Yeller. Rose Sommerdorf wore no lipstick or perfume. Being pretty wasn't important.

"God loves you the way you came out of the womb," Rose would say. "Don't need any fancies."

And when it came to Sunday morning, the Sommerdorfs spent long hours at the Church of the Nazarene, a church where members were expected, as Rose frequently reminded us, to live "as Jesus did."

When I tried to explain why a boy at school and I fought over marbles, Mother just said, "What would the Sommerdorfs do?"

I knew I had lost. "They'd turn their other cheek," I said in defeat.

"That's right," said Mother. "Remember it."

When I didn't want to share my Halloween candy with Winky, Mother let me know that the Sommerdorfs would "offer up their fish for the 10,000." It wasn't in Sunday school I learned about the Sermon on the Mount or the Prodigal Son. The Sommerdorfs took the prodigal *anything* into their fold.

They lived in a small house in the city. One Sunday afternoon on the way to their house I asked my parents why we were such good friends with people who lived so far away from us. She started to say they had been neighbors when they both lived near Lake Vadnais, shortly after Mom and Dad were married, but Father spoke up.

"I want you to know how hard it is to get work as a musician. Your grandpa warned me against it. But I had to do what my heart told me. Your mother was pregnant with Roxanne at the time, and I was out of work. I heard a country club in St. Paul needed an organist, so I went there to see about the job."

He shook his head and chuckled as he remembered. "They said I could start that weekend, but there was a hitch. The club had no organ. I was supposed to supply my own. That meant I still didn't have a job."

As he drove into their driveway he stopped, turned his face to the back seat and directed his story to us children. "We saw Rose and Joyce Sommerdorf that afternoon as they were playing with their kids on the lawn, and told them our sad story. They wanted to know how much an organ would cost. I told them if I had enough to buy an organ, it would be a Hammond B3, and that meant big bucks."

He scrunched his lips together so his mustache barely tickled his lower lip, lifted his eyebrows and said, "Two days later they were at our door with the cash to buy an organ. I hadn't asked. I hadn't even imagined.

They had small children and were living off Joyce's barely adequate salary. They took every cent they had saved and gave it to me, and they wouldn't even let me write them an I-owe-you."

We all marched to the door as Dad finished the story. "That's who the Sommerdorfs are. We're their friends not because they helped me, but because I need to be around people like that, people who don't think twice about giving the shirt off their back even in below-zero weather."

Blessed by God. Extraordinary people. Not only church-goers, but doers.

A child's faith doesn't comprehend the complexities or ambiguities of the real world. That's why I didn't understand how several years later, after twenty years of work at an East St. Paul company, Joyce could be permanently laid off. Everyone was outraged. Was this his reward for diligence?

Rose and Joyce moved their family out of St. Paul and into our Valley. By that time my father was no longer living, but he would have loved the old farmhouse they bought, with its property bordering Bolles Creek. The big house had room enough for the hundreds of foster children that would eventually make their home at the Sommerdorfs'.

(When they retired from foster parenting, Rose and Joyce, then in their late 60's, decided to adopt the last five foster children still in their care. At the same time the governor of Minnesota awarded them a Recognition of Merit for their extraordinary service as foster parents at a ceremony in the capitol building.)

For a while after they moved to the Valley, Joyce sold real estate for Clemens Realty. It provided him with a good excuse to explore its hills and valleys. He also spent long hours in his garden, pampering flowers, raspberries, strawberries and every kind of vegetable imaginable.

Around this time, two significant people entered Joyce's life, one a small child, and the other a multi-millionaire.

I was at the Sommerdorf house the day a social worker from the city dropped by. She pleaded with them to take "just one more child," a two-year-old, into their home. It would be a long-term placement.

She was a Native American child, from the Santee Sioux tribe, who had been abandoned by her mother, and was too old (they thought) to be adopted. In those days being Native American created another strike against her. But the Sommerdorfs never rejected a child in need, even though they already had a full house of children with special medical needs.

Hers were the blackest eyes I'd ever seen, partially hidden through scraggly black hair, their gaze never leaving her feet. She said nothing, but slowly slid into the space beneath the kitchen table. Someone noticed her slow motion, and nicknamed her Pokey.

I felt a weight on my shoe. When I peeked under the tablecloth I saw the little girl lying on the floor, with her head gently resting on my foot as a pillow.

I had never thought much about children before. I hated playing dolls as a child, and figured kids were just as boring. I put my hand under the table. She drew it to her cheek, then slowly glided out and upward onto my lap. Even though she didn't understand English (her mother had spoken her native tongue), I whispered into her ear, "My name is Cindy. I'm your friend."

The nickname Pokey stuck with everyone but Joyce, who called her by her given name, Lillian. He wanted her to know who she was, so he took her for walks down well-worn paths, along beaver trails, to where ginseng grew and bittersweet intertwined among century-old burr oaks.

As they walked, Joyce would say, "Your name is Lillian, and you are a real American." He'd point out where deer had slept and lady-slippers bloomed. They learned the land together, slowly, one foot at a time.

When Joyce, after all his wandering and studying, finally knew every inch of his land, he received an unexpected telephone call. A multi-millionaire, Charlie Bell, chairman of the board of Minneapolis-based General Mills, was interested in his land, as well as the Steglichs', Grants', Rarigs', Johnsons', Spreemans', Schusters', and even our land – as much as he could get.

To everyone's surprise, Bell's intentions were far different from those of a land developer. His dream was education, teaching children from the city about prairies and wild-flowers. He would eventually buy enough land to create an outdoor classroom, an entire ecosystem to explore and study.

The Sommerdorfs kept the farmhouse, but sold their land to this man with whom they shared a dream. Charlie Bell hired Joyce to develop the miles of trails in what is still known as the Belwin Outdoor Education Laboratory. It was on those trails that I, and many others, first saw a Canada Goose, wild turkey, and beavers. I learned to cross-country ski there, as well as exploring all day on paths of pine chips.

Two years later Pokey was about to blow out the candles on her fifth birthday cake, when the Sommerdorfs' telephone rang. The social worker had good news. She'd found an adoptive family for Pokey, a minister and his wife who had no children of their own. Despite living in rural southern Minnesota, they promised to continue teaching her about her Native American heritage.

Of course it was good news, but we had all assumed she would never be adopted, and would live out her childhood at the Sommerdorf home. And Rose and Joyce knew what it was like to say goodbye to a child they loved, to hold in their sadness until the child was gone, so she could become someone better.

But I was young and didn't understand. My mother had taught me not to cry, but the tears welled in my eyes anyway. I picked her up and hugged her as hard as I could, then said, "I'll never forget you, Pokey. Never."

Her black, saucer eyes stared into mine as she said, "My name is Lillian. I love you too." She held tightly onto my hand for a long while and then skipped into the next room.

As I watched her leave, I couldn't speak.

When I finally swallowed, and was able to talk, I called to her, "And my name is Cynthia."

This whole complex name game was hard to understand. I had three pet dogs during my childhood, that were given to us, all named Cindy. I knew what Pokey must have felt when called by her demeaning nickname. She wasn't slow. She wasn't any old Pocahontas. And neither was I. Two of us learning to stand up for ourselves.

Joyce stood at the far end of the kitchen, smiling and nodding, knowing he had taught her well.

She was probably too young to ever remember me. Adoption agencies would also make sure she never remembered the name of Rose or Joyce Sommerdorf. But what will always remain in her bones are memories of trails and animals, of flowers and trees, of love and pride given to her those many years ago.

It's taken a long time for "fools like me" to feel that I am a creature of this land, alongside its other inhabitants. A few years ago, I first visited a beautiful park in North Carolina called the Joyce Kilmer Forest. He would be proud his name is associated with the beautiful trees there, and how they inspire thousands to rethink forests, and find joy in poetry.

I also now live in Oklahoma, land of the Cherokee and many other nations, many of whose original homelands, in North Carolina, I have also walked upon. I now counsel Native American children who live at a residential facility in Oaks, Oklahoma, and who need a little extra support from a social worker like me.

I see Lillian in every one of their faces.

A long time ago two Joyces, the foster-father and the soldier-poet, tried to teach us about the sacredness of creation.

In the face of advancing climate change, I think of this, and I do my very small part.

I plant a tree.

Tending

I come from a do-what-you-have-to-do home.
Mother's advice, Don't marry a musician.
Never understood leisure, found it easier to work.

Grandma added, time to sleep when you're dead.
Both spouses laid to rest early.
I don't write about love.

I pen poems about zinnias and hollyhocks
planted near her house, her shed,
and when she'd cultivated all her own space

she put in rose bushes and peonies next door,
where her lifelong friend, who died,
used to plant petunias.

Her friend's husband mended Grandma's fence,
mowed her grass, kept clear her path for thirty years,
and when Mr. McKeg died,

Grandma, not knowing how to cry,
stopped eating, called her family to her side,
said it was time to sleep,
and instructed us to care for her garden.

I don't write romance.
I pen poems about tending roses,
attending to one another.

chapter 16
the shadow

Wild Rose
[*Rosa canina*]

T he Valley was a great place to be in love.

Trout streams bubbled through hills reminiscent of West Yellowstone, and sunrises and sunsets peeked over lily-pond lakes and between mounds of enormous tree-covered moraines, birthed through centuries of transient glaciers.

Blue "sewing needles," otherwise known as damselflies, mated while flying through the air attached to one another. Canada Geese were finding their mates for life.

In this magical place, a few struggling farmers decided to cut their losses by selling their sandy, barren, but picturesque, land to city slickers. They, in turn, built spacious lake homes, country hide-a-ways, and converted smelly farms into gentleman ranches.

My dad, newly in love, needed a hide-a-way to escape St. Paul society gossip columns. And Mom didn't like cities. So even after their mink farm failed, it made sense that they would stay here in Valley Creek.

Dad tried selling insurance for a while, and rediscovered what he already knew, that he wasn't a salesman. So music had to pay the bills, even though it meant long and tedious commutes to nightclubs, in the Twin Cities, the far suburb of Shakopee, and even to Northern Wisconsin bars in tourist towns.

We thought after he became a chiropractor, he'd settle down and be at home more, but his first practice was on West 7th St. in St. Paul, and developing a practice took long hours. Later our Valley location was perfect for when he moved his practice to Stillwater. But he still never gave up the long commutes, because he refused to give up the music.

When he died in 1960, we remained in the Valley, this time for its comfort, cradling us between its pine-dressed sand hills.

The cabin owners (mostly summer-only residents) and gentlemen farmers (those who worked day-jobs besides keeping the clean, model farms) kept ties to the city. Within a two mile radius of my Washington County house lived a Ramsey County judge, a successful inventor, a millionaire lumberman, a dairy businessman and an owner of major downtown St. Paul real estate. Many of them, as well as their adult children, eventually came to live full time in their country homes. We'd meet them in grocery stores, gas stations, on walks along the road, and we would exchange greetings about the weather, or the condition of Valley Creek Road, or about new residents, but never about the details of each other's lives.

We knew some of the families had children our age, but they weren't part of our neighborhood gang. They didn't attend our birthday parties, and we didn't call them, even if we needed more players for baseball. And they didn't come to the annual Fourth of July celebration. They had their own.

When it came to July Fourth, the Valley women knew how to put on a great show. We all wanted fireworks, but they were expensive, so the Valley Creek Women's Club applied for the Minnesota state permit, while the wealthier inhabitants of the valley contributed most of the funds to purchase the fireworks. We shared the explosions in the sky, heard the ooh's and aah's from their properties, but never saw one another, except distantly, by the light of flaming rockets high above May's Lake. We sat on one shore, while they shot off the fireworks from the other shore. On our side of the small lake we held a potluck supper, three-legged races, and an egg toss. I imagined they must have had a catered dinner with wine.

Sometimes I'd sneak away from the games early, run out to the sloping hill overlooking the lake, and strain my eyes to get a glimpse of them. They looked just like my friends as they laughed and pushed each other into the water.

There was one difference they all had. They weren't curious about us. We knew their names and faces, but that was all. Even consolidation of schools didn't get them to attend the brand new Afton-Lakeland Elementary School or Stillwater High School. Instead, their parents car-pooled them into St. Paul, the boys to St. Paul Academy, and the girls to Summit School.

Every once in a while one of them would fail or get kicked out for bad behavior, attend our school for a semester or a year, and then return again to private school. One of the families tried public school for a few years, hoping their children would become part of the local community, but they too eventually returned to their private schools.

I squinted to see the features on their faces as I listened to their words floating easily across the water.

No *"ain't"s, "I seen"s,* or *"sherbert"s,* only words shouted to one another in an accent a little more British than their counterparts on this side of the lake, who were still busy chewing crackers in order to be the first to whistle *"Home On The Range"* and win a first prize balloon.

In other words … we were worlds apart.

I waited until I was sixteen to get a close-up look at their world. The judge's family hired me as a summer maid, with great pay. I washed their floors by hand, and cleaned their many toilets, things I'd never even done at home. I learned fast, all the while watching for cues in speech, in habits, and in style.

I especially watched their son, my age, who acted as if I didn't exist, even when I was in the same room. He had a thick, squat wrestler's stature, all muscle, usually clad in khaki, his hair cut clean with slanted, sandy bangs over his eyes. He knew he was privileged.

No one at Stillwater High School had that assurance. His agenda didn't include a gangly, country girl who cleaned homes.

The boys at my high school didn't include me either, but for a different reason. They called me *"scholar"*, and said I was too smart for my own good. That was in the era before women's liberation, when we were supposed to be pretty, sexy, and above all − "help-mates".

I had a few dates, and was even asked to the Junior Prom by Roy "Pinky" Herschleb, the most popular boy in our class. He played drums in Band, but more importantly, he was the drummer of the *More-Tishens*, a rock band that traveled around the Twin Cities in an old hearse. I attended some of their gigs as a rock band groupie, every once in a while wondering how it must have been for my mom as she watched my dad play his jazz.

I had to lie to Mom, and tell her I was somewhere else when I went to see Pinky and the *More-Tishens*. There was still an unalterable rule, set up by Dad before he died. It wasn't about staying out too late. It was about not listening to rock and roll (what Dad called *noise*), let alone allowing myself to come under its spell.

After the prom Pinky ignored me again. Several observers saw him rip up our formal prom picture. I remember him complimenting me when he came to my house on Prom night, so it had to be about something other than how I looked that night. It no doubt was his response to the next day's activities (and my use of the word *"no"*).

At our twentieth high school reunion, Pinky, who by that time was working on a fishing boat in Alaska, had forgotten most of his school memories. He came over to me and said, "I hear we went to the Prom together. Greg reminded me, 'cause I don't remember much from back then."

"Yes," I answered, "It was a wonderful night, and we even got a photo from the Prom in the yearbook. We doubled with Mark Campbell and Pat Rarig." He was still handsome, but somehow he seemed sweeter that night, and I loved that he had chosen to talk with me.

The word was, in the late 1960's he'd had trouble with his hands and had to stop drumming. He eventually was arrested for using and dealing drugs, and then treated repeatedly, supposedly for depression, with electro-shock therapy, which effectively erased his past.

Roy "Pinky" Herschleb died at age 57. I later asked his friend, Greg, if he knew why he had asked me to the Prom that year. Greg gave me a one line answer and walked away. "We thought you had potential." I'm still trying to figure that one out, getting into the mindset of teen-aged boys, and what "potential" they were referring to.

It was just as well. I didn't have time for boys anyway. Since I was in fifth grade I'd worked every summer vacation and most holidays as a baby-sitter, maid, or photographer's helper. Then, just before the summer of my 17th birthday, I was offered the best job in the valley.

The Benepe family lived a mile up the road, and had four children, aged 11, 13, 15, and 16. I was hired to entertain them, make meals, and do light housework. It was a great job because I loved to cook, the housework was minimal, and I could take the kids to swim at their private beach on May's Lake every afternoon. The 16-year-old was almost never home that summer, since he worked next door with the grounds-keeper for his Grandmother Stolze's estate. But the next youngest boy became my shadow, always talking, picking my brain, opening up his feelings to the safe, country girl who listened.

With our ages so close, and our boundaries undefined, it was inevitable that the day would come when he crossed the line and backed me into a corner, no one else at home, his intentions not honorable.

"Wait a minute," I said, in a solid, controlled voice. "I'm the best friend you've ever had, and if I were you, I'd think really hard about what you're doing!"

I stared a laser beam through his eyes. He knew I could be more dangerous than any of the Nazi war guns and weapons he had in his extensive collection. He backed off.

Later, when I talked it over with his parents, they were afraid I'd quit the job. But I knew he'd gotten the message, and I needed the money.

For the rest of the summer things were different. The children knew I was hired help. Housework increased, and there were no more long talks. And come September, we all went back to school, they in St. Paul, and I to my senior year at Stillwater.

By the end of November I needed cash to buy Christmas presents. So when Caroline Benepe called and wanted to know if I would help at a large party she'd be giving on the 19th of December, I jumped at the chance.

That day I dressed in a white blouse and black skirt, pulled my side curls into a little ponytail to fall over my shoulder-length blonde hair, and fastened it with a sprig of red holly. I was in charge of the downstairs party, filling hors d'oeuvre trays and empty glasses for the kids of the upstairs party guests. My charges were almost all teenagers, St. Paul Academy boys, who traded lusty stories about Summit girls, and did it loudly enough for me to hear.

That was understandable. I was invisible to them, a nobody, pouring Coke over crackling ice cubes, a ghost who hears orders, but not women's names. Someone who was supposed to be as blind and deaf as they were.

Suddenly their conversation switched from girls to academics in a tone as passionate as the former. They talked of Shakespeare, Einstein, and Calder with excitement and intense interest, playing one-ups-man-ship with obscure intellectual data.

One boy, at the far edge of the group, remained silent until the conversation moved to poetry. It was hard not to notice the cocoa brown color of his enormous eyes, the notch of auburn hair that fell down to cover them when he wanted anonymity, and his large pouting lips.

Jeff Malmquist lived close by, over the hill as the crow flies. From his comments it was obvious he wasn't from old money. He was from old brains. They all listened to him, including the judge's son, the boys I worked for, the ones who had tried public school and returned to private, and other strangers from the city.

I, too, listened.

Poetry was my domain.

Out of nowhere Jeff began to recite T.S. Eliot's The Hollow Men.

The eyes are not here
There are no eyes here
In this valley of dying stars
In this hollow valley
This broken jaw of our lost kingdoms.

Jeff, via T.S. Eliot, was talking about our Valley. How did he know they were all sightless?

Did Jeff feel as foreign in that group as I did? I felt an unearthly, pounding desire to vocalize a response, but at first, I held my tongue. I knew he was thinking of this Valley and this party, but I was an outsider, and it was too much of a stretch to imagine he might also be thinking of me.

But I knew I had to become visible to them.

My mouth started reciting Eliot's poem out loud:

Between the idea
And the reality
Between the motion
And the act
Falls the Shadow.

I knew the shadow. I understood the gulf between what was inside my head and what was real. I had seen the shadow of my father and my grandfather's lives disappear. I had lived in the fog-shadow of being the outsider, no matter where I went.

Then I noticed everyone in the room staring at me as if I were crazy, only one of them knowing that the lines were a continuation of the same poem. Jeff shot his eyes into mine and didn't blink as he continued:

> *Between the conception*
> *And the creation*
> *Between the emotion*
> *And the response*
> *Falls the Shadow.*

I knew that shadow too, the shadow that kept the response from happening. I was carefully trained as a child to hold my feelings in, to keep them secret, like a canker sore inside the mouth, hidden, but never far from pain.

And as he said,

> *This is the way the world ends,*
> *not with a bang, but a whimper.*

I knew the world would never end. My heart beat so loudly I wasn't aware of the intense silence in the room.

For one brief disbelieving moment the private school boys saw me, until decorum was once again established, but with one exception. Jeff pulled up a chair next to mine, and for the rest of the evening helped me fill trays and wash empty glasses.

The next morning in my mailbox I found a handwritten copy of *"Pied Beauty"* by Gerard Manley Hopkins.

> *Glory be to God for dappled things –*
> *All things counter, original, spare, strange;*
> *Whatever is fickle, freckled (who knows how?)*

The following days yielded "love poems" by John Donne, then "wild and lovely poems" by e.e. cummings, Emily Dickinson, and William Carlos Williams, until one morning there was a poem by Walt Whitman called *"The Commonplace"*.

Jeff called me that night and said he had been dropped from the St. Paul Academy carpool because of his continued infatuation with me. The family I worked for felt responsible for our meeting, and they let him know emphatically how unacceptable it was. This Whitman poem, praising not only freedom and toleration, but also praising the commonplace − me − or what I was thought to be, was his defense,

> *The open air I sing, freedom, toleration...*
> *The common day and night − the common earth and waters,*
> *Your farm − your work, trade, occupation,*
> *The democratic wisdom underneath, like solid ground for all.*

He weaseled his parents into letting him drive one of their cars to school, passing by my mailbox early, inserting the daily poems, gradually changing to Jeff−written sonnets, a new one each day, remarkably good, and romantic as spring violets.

This relationship was not destined to be predictable, like any old love−song romance. It sported a succession of events, from stock car races, opera, foreign films and darkly−lit coffee house poetry readings, to parties at mansions on Sunfish Lake and Summit Avenue.

Jeff never tired of watching my awestruck face at each new offering, and was equally amazed at how I somehow fit in, like a chameleon, no matter where we went.

Little by little he learned that I was not as commonplace as he and the others had assumed. My widowed mother had sacrificed much in order to take me to the Bolshoi Ballet and Minneapolis Symphony Orchestra, and paid for eight years of private ballet where I'd learned to dance en pointe. I'd studied bass trombone for ten years with one of the midwest's finest musicians, and from my earliest years I'd eaten at the exclusive restaurants where my Dad entertained.

When spring came, Jeff started telling me about his "cathedral", a place between his house and mine where he'd spend hours writing his thoughts. It was near the sacred Native American burial ground at the top of the Indian Trail, just behind historic Jacob Fahlstrom's old cabin and grave. A sanctuary of arching pines there provided the perfect place to listen to cardinals singing pretty, pretty, pretty, and rest against mossy granite boulders, damp from the icy spray of two springs.

In this cathedral, Jeff told me he didn't believe in God, but he believed in this holy place.

It did feel holy there, and I'd think about Jesus' friend Mary Magdalene, who wanted to listen and think and learn, rather than clean dishes and cook.

I was like that. I wanted to transcend my earthly body, to push the limits of thought and creativity. I'd sing and hum as I picked wildflowers. Jeff would write poetry and then read me the lines.

Soon he began reciting other lines, lines he'd heard from his friends at his all-male school, such as, "If you loved me, you'd...," or "I've learned all about the female body. I know more than you'll ever know. I know how to give you great pleasure."

Pleasure wasn't on my list of goals. Pinky had learned that too. Pleasure was on my list of stay-away-from's. I had learned in my 17 years that life was hard work, learning, more hard work, a little art and philosophy, and more hard work. A stay-out-of-trouble philosophy. Little room for pleasure.

I wrote a poem about my confused feelings. When I read it to Jeff, he showed disinterest.

I tried to share my ideas concerning pacifism and social justice. He'd change the subject. He wanted to give me pleasure.

He wanted me to give him pleasure. He wanted me to listen to his poetry and intellectual views, but not interrupt with my own.

But an invisible body feels no pleasure, gives no pleasure. I had thought he had seen me. I had thought he could hear me.

I witnessed the wounding in his beautiful eyes the morning I told him we were finished.

A pedestal was not a comfortable place for me. I wanted to be treated the same as his male friends – with less dignity and more respect.

What he had learned in his own 17 years and in his boy's school education had not prepared him for me, just as my years of exaggerated work ethic and Victorian survival philosophy had not prepared me for him.

I learned years later Jeff had volunteered for the Vietnam War. I visualized the picture of Joyce Kilmer, the poet, in his WWI helmet. I remembered Kilmer died there. I wondered how a poet fared in Vietnam, if he'd found cathedrals beside the guarded rivers, if he'd felt humiliation at the sight of defoliated valleys.

Did Jeff see what Agent Orange did to the trees? Did he remember the words we had shared from Eliot, and think of those foreign valleys as *"dying stars, a broken jaw of our lost kingdoms"*?

Together for a time, we believed we had formed a new kingdom, with an open door. It had opened wide enough to catch the breeze that blew across both the old farms and the country cottages, sweeping dust from stone walls, bowing fields of clover, warming both formal gardens and ditches full of run-away raspberries.

Wild berries could be tamed, gardens trimmed, but even in this cathedral there had not been any way to brighten the beige of the female cardinal, to compare with her partner's scarlet red. The shadow made sure of that.

> *Between the idea and the reality, between the motion and the act.*

And, anyway, who would have been so full of hubris as to suggest so strange a thing in 1965, when our country's schools were not yet racially integrated, the Ivy League and Catholic colleges were still separated by gender, when women were not yet members of Boards of Directors, when their husbands had to hold the deed on any property, when we were still in the midst of a Cold War that diverted billions of dollars away from human services and into weapons, and where, every Independence Day, the Valley's country women still had to beg rich city-slicker, summer-resident men for the means to celebrate freedom.

Memory

You come back home. You expect skeletons – closets –
old hurts – photos from yellowed scrapbooks.

Then the river's flow calls you – says,
"I've got something to show you. – Walk this way."

Through the polished–wood hotel bar,
a slight whiff of beer still hanging in the morning air,

You leave the century–old walls behind, and turn left.
A man is cleaning the mildewed benches, and you cannot sit,

So you take a detour to an historical marker.
On Easter 1965 the river rose 16 feet above normal.

You flash back to dump trucks emptying piles of sand, sand scooped into
dusty burlap bags held open by prisoners,

Red Cross donuts tasting of sweat, bitter coffee warming overworked
hands, supplying energy you never felt before.

It was a hard–working Easter vacation, when the flood of the century,
cascading snow melt, threatened the town

and you and your prisoner partner took turns, first
holding open the rough bags, and then shoveling sand,

hands calloused and sore, water rising as students,
boy, girl, old, young, convict, and those of us who were free,

built a dike, the flood of 1965 washing away old scree,
and in its stead, leaving heavy bags of shifting sand.

chapter 17
branding

Johnny Jump Up
[*Viola tricolor*]

T hat Sunday in 1950, Dad wasn't as tired as usual. Sundays were hard because he never got home from the nightclub until after two in the morning, and we were all used to tiptoeing around the house until after noon. But that day I guess he was still feeling the elation of being the father of his newly born son.

"Eau Claire," he announced. "I bet you kids haven't seen the beautiful hills around Eau Claire, Wisconsin. Let's head that direction and see if Uncle Leonard and Aunt Sylvia are home."

"Johnny, that's too far to drive with the children," replied Mother.

"Oh, but you know they'd love to see the baby. Roxy, Cindy, don't you want to go for a drive?"

We answered yes, and Mother made that giving-in-again look.

Leonard, Dad's birth mother's brother, was someone the rest of us had never met. It would be a two hour drive if all went well. Roxy and I scrambled into the back seat while Mother held Winky on her lap in front.

We started around the S-curve just beyond Sauers' property, when Dad hit the brakes hard. A doe and two fawns ran in front of the car and narrowly escaped. Mother and the baby lurched forward. My tiny brother hit his head on the rear view mirror.

As Winky screamed, blood dripped profusely down his face. Instead of Wisconsin, Dad drove us quickly to Lakeview Hospital in Stillwater, where Roxy and I again waited patiently in the car, just as we had months before when we had picked up our new-born brother.

This time when Mother and Dad came out of the emergency room, Winky's head looked like a white cloth package tied with a thick, black string.

"What are those x's?" I asked.

"Stitches, Dummy!" Roxy replied.

I should have known I'd get a smart answer from my sister. A month later, when Winky fell and hit his head again, and had the stitches replaced, I had the information I needed, and didn't reveal my ignorance.

His head healed, but in place of the gash, a smooth pink scar formed a perfect V, devoid of hair. When anyone asked him why he had a V on his head, Winky would reply, "That's my V for Victory," a line coached by Dad. Having been born after the war, my brother had no idea what it meant.

To me it was his brand. V for Valley Creek.

I had seen cows on cowboy shows being burned by the owner's brand, a brand that defined the geography of the cattle's wanderings. My brother was branded into this Valley, born into a home at the place where creeks flow into a V, where Valley Creek Road and the old Indian Trail form a 45-degree angle at his door. I knew he would never leave.

But I don't share that brand.

I have my own brand – a black spot on the inside of my right middle finger. It appeared little by little over sixty years ago, as my left hand repeatedly screwed a pointed pencil further and further, pushing its lead into the exposed flesh of that finger.

In that sixth grade year I marked myself – not a mark that identified the Valley, but a mark more like a vast dark hole in space that sucked me into a new universe.

I understood at age eleven that a penniless girl had no way to escape, so I plotted an elaborate plan, one requiring years, but guaranteed. I would get straight A's throughout school, earn a scholarship, attend a private college, become a teacher, and leave the Valley.

My brand kept me focused. I had little time for parties or long telephone calls. I didn't drink or smoke or use marijuana or have sex. I left those things for those who did not have dreams, those without pressure for scholarship, those who could allow themselves the pleasure of the moment. I was always on task, never forgetting my way out. I still had to contend with black-bottomed feet, cheap, illfitting clothing, a long bus ride to school, and my wandering, music-filled brain. But my long-term plan kept me on track.

Here in this place the deer trails were as familiar to me as the red and purple lines of my own arteries and veins. All the fancy clothes of my town friends were never as beautiful to me as jewelweed growing on the banks of the creek, and my hard-to-find wild blackcaps tasted better than any entree I ever tasted at The Lowell Inn.

But I needed more.

———— ∘O∘ ————

In primary school everyone was my friend. I even remember where they all lived. My first crush, the best looking kid in Mrs. Johnson's first grade, Eddie, lived in a white, historic house in Afton alongside the river.

Second grade was a magical time as our teacher, Miss Kilkelly, read us poems every day after lunchtime recess. And in third and fourth grade I had numerous games of hopscotch with the girls, and marbles with the boys.

But everything changed when I met Pat.

Just before I entered fifth grade, the Rarig family bought 40 acres south of the Grants' place. They began building what to my eyes appeared to be a mansion, on a knoll overlooking Bolles Creek. All I knew was that the father was an important person in the city (executive director of Wilder Charities), and they had two married daughters. There was no way in the world I could have prepared myself for the arrival of their third daughter, an auburn-haired, red-blooded, city-wise, self-propelled beauty who was my age, and who, for better or worse, attempted to control the outcome of all matters.

The first time I met her, I was standing with Judy Hancock, sampling brownies at the 4th of July dessert potluck table. A girl, half-hidden behind a tree, motioned for me to come. I pointed to myself and raised my eyebrows.

She nodded, mouthing the words, "Just you."

I told Judy I had to go to the outhouse, and I walked over to the tree.

"I'm Pat. I suppose Mrs. Grant told you I'd be coming, but anyway, I'm going to be your best friend. She told me it'd be you – so let's get to know one another."

Startled by her audacity, I asked myself what was going on. Should I be thrilled or cool? What had Evelyn Grant told her about me and the others in the Valley? I wasn't one to question friendship, if that was what this was, but it seemed a bit like the friendship they offer in church when they say that God has chosen you and if you don't accept, there are dire consequences. Did I have a choice?

"Do you know who I am?" I asked, wanting to know if she had motioned to the right person.

"Of course. Are you that stupid? Maybe Mrs. Grant was wrong about you."

"Where'd you come from?" I asked. "Nobody said any-thing about anyone to me."

"My dad's always looking for new property," she said. "Thank goodness this time it's close to the city, not on some God-forsaken farm in Wisconsin or something. We're building a house, and I'm going to live here and go to school with you."

She grabbed my arm and looked straight into my eyes. "We'll be on the same bus, and we'll do everything together, just you and me."

I stood quiet for a moment, letting her know I was not the talkative type, then said, "Yah. I saw where they're building that house. Come on – I'll take you over to meet my friends Carol and Judy. They're over by the rhubarb squares – My mom made 'em, and they're the best."

"No. I don't want them with us. Didn't you hear me? I said just you and me. I can tell I won't like them."

Turns out it really was one of those all or nothing choices. Pat or them. I thought, just for today, I'll see what she's like and then decide.

The excitement of our subsequent adventures and the exclusivity of our already-happening friendship made it no choice at all. And in the following months and years I continued to make the same choice over and over again. To share time with Pat Rarig meant I would never be bored.

In some ways I'd always been waiting for Pat. How did she know, or Mrs. Grant for that matter, that I needed something more than dolls and books and playing solitaire?

She told me stories about the city, about the University of Minnesota theater department that her grandfather headed. She took me to exclusive city stores where she picked out clothes and merely mentioned her name, and the bill was charged to their account. We walked to movies from her grandparent's house and ate Chinese afterward.

But my old friends didn't like it at all.

"Do you really have to be around Pat all the time?" asked Judy, who had been born two days after me in the same hospital, and had been my friend since we could walk and talk. "Or are you just under her spell? My mom says she's evil, and you aren't, and some day you'll find that out. And I'll be waiting."

"Thanks, Judy, but I'll be okay." I didn't believe that anyone was evil, especially my new friend. But I should have told her how guilty I felt abandoning her. Instead I said, "You know my dad doesn't like her either, but I think that's because she's just like him. This Valley doesn't own 'em. They both belong to the world out there, and I've got to find out about it."

By sixth grade Pat's body had meandered into adulthood, while mine was still flowing in its straight and extremely narrow path upward. Every boy in the school wanted Pat's attention, as did every boy in the Valley, between 12 and 21.

I answered a ten o'clock phone call one night. "Sneak out your window and meet me at the second bridge," Pat said. The second bridge, a mile down the road, was being patrolled by old Spike Spreeman. He had been developing the creek beneath the bridge into a trout pond for Charlie Bell, and didn't want any kids or teenagers hanging around to scare the trout, or to fish out the ones he had planted. He had posted No Loitering signs on our public bridge.

It made us all so angry we happily carried out our "sit-ins" as often as possible.

"Lance and Chuck'll be there," she added.

That changed my thinking. It wouldn't be public loitering. She had something else in mind. "Sorry. I take your cigarettes for you when your mom walks into the room. I cover for you so she thinks you're at my house. But I don't want any part of those jerks you hang around with. Just because you think they're 'men' doesn't mean they have a brain in their head. I won't do it. Find someone else for this one," and I hung up.

One minute later she called back. "Lemme talk to Roxy."

When my sister hung up the phone she was gloating. "Boy, you're stupid. I knew she'd catch on sooner or later, and now your chance is over," and she slipped out the window.

They were a better match, Roxy being two years older and more physically mature than I was. She had a ballerina's legs and a beauty queen's face. (In 1963 she had become Miss Stillwater and met the great Bing Crosby. His mother had been born in Stillwater's shanty town of ice cutters just before the turn of the century, and he came to see the place of her childhood.)

Around the time I got put on Pat's out-list, a new girl moved to town. Tall, a little shy, she was related to almost everyone in the town of Afton. I had heard my parents talking about her family, moving back home, taking the building on the old farm that had been a chicken house and remodeling it, adding to it to make a new home. At least, that's how I think I heard it.

At the bus stop the next morning I met Pat. "You know that new girl – I heard my mom say they're making a house out of the old chicken coop on her grandpa's farm. Don't you think that's cool – take a building they don't need and make it into something useful?"

"Chicken coop! You gotta be kiddin'!" Pat laughed all the way to school.

I brought a sack lunch to school every day – half a summer sausage sandwich and a small apple. I'd wait at the far end of the cafeteria for my friends to join me at the table with their hot lunches. But that day they all paraded past me, glaring as if I were fresh gum on a newly upholstered chair.

I caught up with Judy after lunch and asked, "What's going on? Have I done something I don't know about?"

She screamed back at me, "How could you? The new girl is trying to make friends and you tell the whole world she lives in a chicken coop! What's happening to you?"

She looked me in the eye. "Never mind, I know what's happened to you. I thought you'd be bigger than her, but you're not. You're just like her."

"Judy, wait. Where'd you hear that? I didn't say she lived in a chicken coop, I was just telling Pat ... darn!"

"What did you say?"

"I just repeated what I'd heard from my mom and dad about how their house is being built around the old chicken house on the farm. Honest to God – I only repeated what they'd said, and I didn't mean to hurt anyone."

"I believe you, but I don't know if anyone else will." She scrunched my arm, acting as if she was my appointed guardian angel. Her gesture was as warm as the wool sweater I wore, knit by Grandma in the popcorn stitch, bright yellow, and covering a body full of goose-bumps. I returned to class.

"Today's vocabulary word," announced Mrs. Wall, "is lugubrious."

There was a snicker in the room.

"There's nothing funny about this word. I expect it to be in ten sentences by tomorrow afternoon."

I already knew what it meant. I already felt what it meant. I could have invented 100 sentences, but instead I aimed the sharpened point of my pencil at the inner flesh of my finger and pressed. I would get out of here. I pressed harder.

Judy must have passed notes all afternoon because by bus-time the sixth grade class divided into the hate-me's and the love-me's.

"I'm with you," Nanette called to me as she boarded her bus. "I know you'd never say something like that. Count on me."

My sister's support was not as forthcoming. "Serves you right," was Roxy's response to my dilemma later when Mother asked what was bothering me. "You're so naïve – always have been. You didn't even know when Chuck had the hots for you. You don't know when to keep your mouth shut, and when to gun it — and by the way — you leave it hanging open way too much. You are such an embarrassment!"

"That's enough, Roxanne!" Mother kept dishing up the tuna hotdish without looking at me. "They'll all forget it by tomorrow. Just do your homework and you'll be fine. And if you can't get that look off your face — you can just stay in your room until you're civil."

Roxy kicked me under the table.

I headed for my room, seething. I took out my homework and wrote:

1. One becomes lugubrious when no one listens.
2. When one is feeling lugubrious one only wants to sleep and never wake up.
3. A lugubrious tear formed in the outer edge of her eye.
4. It is lugubrious when one's friend turns against you.
5. Since these sentences and other circumstances are making me lugubrious, I cannot finish this assignment.

It convinced me that growing up was going to be like one of those mirrors that contorts your body into a stump and pulls your head longwise into a sharp, aching needle. After that day my class never voted for me again as citizen of the week or student of the month. I developed mouthfuls of canker sores and swollen taste buds. At times the intense pain became impossible to ignore and I would locate the taste bud, grip it firmly between my fingernails, and yank it out.

I had a constant knot in my stomach, except for the times when I worked the pencil point into my finger. It wasn't long before I saw a black spot appearing that wouldn't wash away.

As an adult therapist I now understand all these to be mental health issues, from the loss of friendships, feelings of betrayal, and finally, not knowing where to turn for help, since no one else understood the importance of a young girl's feelings.

I never confronted Pat with what she'd done. After all, she was the only one of the "hate-me's" who would talk to me. It continued that way until school let out for the summer. A babysitting job kept me fully occupied for the next three months.

In August, Helen Rarig, Pat's mother, called and asked my mother and me to attend seventh grade registration with them. It was in Stillwater at the consolidated junior high school, and she wanted us to go to the Lowell Inn for lunch afterward.

I'd never been there, but had seen it many times. It was called the "Mount Vernon of the West," and looked like a southern mansion perched at the bottom of the North Hill. Patrons parked their cars in front of its enormous white pillars and young men in strange costumes drove the Mercuries and Cadillacs away.

Inside, young waitresses, done up in puffy-sleeved, tight-waisted dresses, brought us food arranged in small portions on china plates. The room smelled of mint and honey. Fish swam in a small pool at the end of the largest dining room. Guests had the option of choosing their catch and having it prepared to taste. And what a taste it was! The ambience was pure sophistication.

"This is the first step to becoming a woman," Pat's mother said. "Before you know it, you'll be leaving home. Look at you both, so beautiful, so innocent. Let's toast to the future."

So innocent. Did her mother actually live in the same house with Pat?

To my knowledge it's a good thing her mother never found out about an incident a few months later at Hooley's Supermarket. Pat and I walked there quite often after school to get a treat as we waited for the activity bus to take us home. On this day we walked through the aisles together, found nothing we wanted and then exited the automatic doors.

A siren immediately started screeching, and three policemen ran out at us, grabbing the two of us by the arms of our navy pea coats.

"What's going on," I shouted. "We didn't do anything."

"Leave her alone," one of the policemen ordered. "I was watching her and she's clean."

They demanded Pat take off her coat, right there in sub-freezing weather, and when she did, out dropped two pair of nylon stockings.

"Pat! Where'd you get those?" I asked.

The policeman didn't hesitate to answer. "She took them off the hosiery display. I was watching the whole time –

saw her slip them under her coat – and I was also watching to see if you'd do the same thing."

"She'd never do that," Pat said with a sneer. "It'd never occur to her in a thousand years. Let her go home, okay?"

"Young lady," he said sternly to Pat, "just for the books, state your name and age."

I was surprised she told them her real name, but she came up with a whopper lie after that.

"Tell you what," the policeman said, as he looked Pat over, "we'll let you off this time, but we still have to talk to your parents. What's their number?"

Pat put on her contrite face, and spoke quietly and with measured sweetness. "My mother is very sick, and she just lies in bed all the time, so please call this evening when my dad is home, and talk to him. His number is GE 6-8989. (Back then all our phone numbers started with two letters. GE stood for "General," and later the GE turned into 43.)

As we walked back up the steep hill to catch the late bus, Pat giggled all the way.

"You gave 'em Chuck's number, not your dad's. How are you gonna get away with that?" I asked.

"Chuck's voice sounds like a grown man, and you know he'll do it for me. I'll tell him exactly what to say."

Pat mimicked Chuck's voice, "That daughter of mine, I can't believe she'd do something against the law. She knows better than that. We will deal with her harshly, that's for sure. Thanks for calling, Officer."

It worked. The police believed Chuck was her father. Somehow she always found a way.

At Stillwater Junior High School, the pecking order of popularity was immediately apparent. It reminded me of the game we played back then of cowboys and Indians, the cowboy townies with Gatling guns against the rural Indians, who not only tried to defend themselves with arrows, but didn't even believe in the concept of ownership.

The only exception, of course, was Pat, who despite living in the country, defied explanation, and who became the most popular of all the seventh graders.

Even though I was placed in the accelerated tier of classes with almost all townies, I never really became one of them. We all liked and respected each other, but I was never part of their clique.

All I knew was to continue doing what I knew best, getting A's. Pat also concentrated on A's, – Alan, Arthur, and Alex, and thought I should too.

She knew I had a secret crush on Mark Campbell, the superintendent's son. She took over the microphone and announced a spotlight dance for the two of us at the first Seventh Grade Sock Hop. I knew he danced with me only because Pat flirted with him and somehow persuaded him to cooperate. I had seen her at the punchbowl, standing alongside him, directing her hazel eyes upward. I don't know what she promised him, but it wasn't worth it. Everyone knew it was staged.

The DJ played "Put Your Head on My Shoulder," but I knew enough not to.

My Afton love-me friends surrounded me after the dance, saying, "Oh, you two looked so perfect together," and "He likes you! I can tell! Now you've got it made," and they didn't understand my crying, and they didn't know why I walked to the door, found my shoes, and waited for the late bus in the library.

On the bus Pat asked, "Did you have fun?"

"Oh sure," I replied in a monotone. "Thanks for the spot-light."

"Maybe we can double date sometime." She threw her hair back, and laughed.

It doesn't seem right that I let her bully me that way, but in retrospect, I had no confidence in myself when it came to social life. I wasn't as pretty as my sister, my body had not yet developed, I was estranged from my elementary school friends, and it seemed that Pat was the only person I could cling to.

It wouldn't be until our junior year of high school that we actually double dated, and then it was she who went with Mark, and I who accompanied Pinky to the junior prom.

Those school years passed somewhat uneventfully for me, except for my dad's sudden death when I was in eighth grade. What had been a certain kind of low-income living at that point turned into full-blown poverty, requiring a job squeezed into weekends, vacations and occasionally school nights. But I kept up my grades.

Pat increasingly dated older guys from the city, all the while keeping every Stillwater boy interested. By senior year everyone expected Pat to be crowned homecoming queen.

Despite being neighbors, we were seeing less of each other, and even less when I started dating Jeff.

My old friend Judy appeared at my locker the morning of the homecoming queen balloting. "We've all decided to vote for you."

"Who? Who's going to vote for me? For homecoming queen? Me?"

"Yah! All of us from Afton. We've been with you all the way. I was wrong when I said you were under her spell. We cheered for you every time you stood up to her, every time you didn't give in. We're all voting for you."

As Judy left for her classes I shook my head. I hadn't meant to be anything to anyone. I didn't know what I was doing, except getting myself out of the Valley. It had been years since I'd forced that pencil point into my flesh, but the brand was still dark as ever.

I realized it was the Valley kids, the farm kids, the St. Croix Beach kids, the Afton kids I knew from grade school who were my real friends and supporters. But by that time I was already on my way out – already accepted for the next year at Gustavus Adolphus College, far away from home, a private college, with a scholarship.

———— ∘O∘ ————

During my high school years I switched my musical taste to folk music. I still loved the trombone, but I couldn't reach the high notes, and my family wasn't able to buy me a more professional instrument.

Mr. Regis, the band director, who had been a friend of my dad, and who knew that he would have wanted me to continue in band, offered me the school's bass trombone. We didn't have to buy a new instrument, and I only needed to learn how to play the lower notes. It was a good compromise, and I stayed in the concert band, and jazz band, but I spent less time practicing, and more time playing my guitar – the one I got free from collecting S and H Green stamps.

I had heard the words and music of Joan Baez, Pete Seeger, our state's own Bob Dylan, Peter Paul and Mary, and it spoke to me in an intimate way. The chords were simple to learn and I found that folk music, written by everyday people over the last couple hundred years, fit into my pro-peace, pro-love philosophy.

At the same time I was listening and playing the music "of the people", I was exploring this style of poetry as well. I had become involved in both theater and speech contests, and when it came time to prepare a poem to be read at the oral interpretation contests, I spent hours and hours pouring over poetry books to find the right piece that fit my own philosophy, as well as one that might sound beautiful when read aloud.

It was during that time I "met" Carl Sandburg, through his plain, but authentic descriptions of the Midwest. I never failed to win contests when I read his "Four Preludes on Playthings of the Wind." It was musical as I recited:

> *the feet of the rats*
> *scribble on the doorsills;*
> *the hieroglyphs of the rat footprints*
> *chatter the pedigrees of the rats*
> *and babble of the blood*
> *and gabble of the breed*
> *of the grandfathers and the great-grandfathers*
> *of the rats.*

And Sandburg goes on to warn us:

> *And the wind shifts*
> *and the dust on a doorsill shifts*
> *and even the writing of the rat footprints*
> *tells us nothing, nothing at all*
> *about the greatest city, the greatest nation*
> *where the strong men listened*
> *and the women warbled:*
> *Nothing like us ever was.*

The words of Sandburg became part of me. Pete Seeger's "when will we ever learn" became part of me. Bob Dylan's "how many deaths will it take 'til we know that too many people have died" became part of my breath. It's interesting that Dylan now has a Nobel Prize for his writing. I can't separate them, the music from the words. Together they form the two legs I stand on.

And as for the rats, they started scribbling in my walls when I was young and frightened, and they still "babble of the blood and gabble of the breed" at my doorsill, reminding me every day of their mischief. They never seem to stop.

———— ∘O∘ ————

The entire student body was seated in the gymnasium. Mr. Heimerl, the speech teacher, stood at the podium and announced, with his theatrical flair, the names of the five finalists for Homecoming Queen of 1964.

First he called down Faith Foster, a gorgeous, slightly shy girl from Stillwater. Next was Ellen Carlstrom, from Bayport, who I knew from my confirmation class at Bethlehem Lutheran Church. Then he announced another Stillwater girl, Judy Bielenberg, the French horn player in our band. The fourth candidate, Maureen Arcand, was a good friend of mine, who I'd gotten to know only that year since she'd come up through the Catholic school program. He could have stopped at that point. These were wonderful choices, young women who were not only eye stoppers, but athletic, talented and bright. It was the 1960's and we knew we were ushering in a modern era.

"The fifth candidate is from Afton," Mr. Heimerl announced. I looked over at Pat, who had a smile on her face and was about to stand.

"She is a member of the band, the choir, the dance band..."

My heart flipped. There was no one in the dance band and the choir from Afton except me. My face flushed with color.

"The Thespians, The Honor Society, she writes for the Pony Express, and she has been on numerous school committees. Welcome Cynthia Blomquist."

I don't remember if anyone clapped or yelled. It may have been thunderous or quiet for all I know. I numbly walked to the stage and shook Mr. Heimerl's hand. He had been my mentor, introducing me to the joy of oral interpretation of poetry.

Writing this paragraph decades later I can still feel the warmth inside me. I was the outsider, the out-lier, the girl who played trombone, the one who wouldn't drink or smoke, the one from the country who didn't live on a farm, the country girl put into the accelerated classes, the country girl who danced ballet at the talent show, the girl who wouldn't hide her brains.

The girl with a self-made tattoo inside her hand. How was it possible that the outsider had been chosen for this honor?

The next week the student body voted Faith Foster as their queen. She was exquisite. Like my brother, she has chosen to live her life in the Stillwater area, where her roots are.

As for my old Valley friend, Judy Hancock, she sends me a Christmas card and friendly note every year from Wisconsin – this year a family picture of her grandkids. No matter what I did, and through the dozens of places I've lived, she has always kept in touch. Her parents left the Valley for a while to live closer to their great-grandchildren, but returned, and died there. Judy's father, Blackie, is known in the Valley because he built the beautiful nature center at the Belwin Outdoor Education Laboratory.

But my experience with Pat has been different. She doesn't come to class reunions, although her name is never absent from them. I've seen her only one time in the last decades, when we were both 40 years old and Pat had two small babies. She'd married a man with teenagers, helped raise them, and had her own family later.

We met at a Robert Bly reading. We both love poetry and are both professional social workers. We talked afterward as if there had been no time between, and then we walked away.

Her card at Christmas always gets returned. I know she lives in Florida, but I can't seem to get the address right. The really strange thing is that both she and my childhood friend, Carol Appleby, live in the same Florida town. Carol doesn't write either. But I managed to call her once and she related to me a story about how Pat had come up to her in a restaurant and asked if she was from the Valley. They talked for a short while. They both had children the same age. But that was the end of it.

Clearly, neither Carol nor Pat feels the tie to the Valley that I tried in my childhood to tattoo and burn out of existence.

I'm in Oklahoma now, married to a doctor, my college sweetheart. I have two grown children, who at critical times in their lives attended Stillwater Public Schools, (and for a time one of them attended St. Paul Academy) and who have walked down their own shadowed valleys, forming both sweet and bitter memories of their youth. I write poems and short stories, and I counsel people of all ages who are having trouble with the ambiguities in their own lives.

And I stare every so often at a black tattoo, dark enough to recall a young girl's pain, but hidden away inside my fist, seen only by me, and only when I choose to open my hand to the past.

The dark point pulls me into the mind of that pre-adolescent wrestling with the future. Whether this tattoo can be read as marking my coming of age, or a brand that says, this is who I am, it remains to this day a single, black point positioned in my palm just inches away from my life line.

Orientation

You meet your friend's roommate.
You ask about the photo on the mirror,
his face unknown, yet familiar.

Her brother, she says. You stare.
You know you will marry this man
recognized from your dreams,

the future imprinted on the moment.
This picture on the glass is beautiful,
but you do not say what you know.

*

That old picture was a trickster,
a photo revealing hope, but no pain,
puzzling as a silent movie

without captions, moving forward in
jerky strains, to a tune of romance
and violins.

*

You view your fiftieth anniversary portrait
of wizened lovers grown old,
and close your eyes,

avoiding over-exposure,
of what the future might hold,
allowing love to be blind.

chapter 18

essence

Butter-and-Eggs
[*Linaria vulgaris*]

I knew this face. I had seen it in my dreams, in my good dreams, the ones that helped me wake up feeling peaceful, after the nightmares were over. During freshman orientation at Gustavus Adolphus College, Ann Parkhurst, a friend from home (who eventually married my preschool friend, Steve Wolff) introduced me to her new roommate, Darlene, from Illinois.

As Dar, an athletic girl with a great sense of humor, set up family photographs on her dresser and mirror, I glanced at one, a college-aged boy with natural blond hair and high Scandinavian cheekbones.

I could tell from the resemblance he was related to Darlene. His eyes were not just deep-set, they were cavernous, but also full of compassion and mystery. And the way they were positioned in the photo reminded me of the Mona Lisa. They stared directly at me.

I had reached my goal of leaving the Valley and getting a full scholarship to a private college. By that time I had developed a rather utilitarian, do-what-needs-to-be-done philosophy. I chose Gustavus, a Lutheran college, composed mostly of American Swedes. My dad had been proud of his Swedish heritage, and reminded us often that his two middle names, Gustave and Adolph, were the names of an heroic king of Sweden, a warrior who slaughtered so many in war that when he became king, he ended war for all time in Sweden.

The college was only a few hours from home and its chapel spire still peeks out of the trees on the top of a huge hill in St. Peter, Minnesota. The Minnesota River runs through the town on its unexpected path north to join the Mississippi.

In high school I had dated guys who were dark-haired and dark-eyed, light-skinned and blue-eyed, and other variations of the German, Scotch-Irish, and Scandinavian boys who lived in my community. Many times I asked myself what characteristics I wanted in a boyfriend. I didn't care about looks, or at least didn't require any specific looks. I decided I wanted a scientist who had a humane heart. But my dreams at night told a different story. They always had the same person in them, an intense blond, with deep, deep set eyes, who was tall, thin, and athletic.

My throat tightened as I looked again at the photograph. I could barely say, "Who is this?" I hoped Darlene couldn't hear my heart beating past its capacity.

"My brother, Ed. He's a senior here." She must have noticed the way I stared at the photo, because she said, "He's got a girlfriend, so don't get any ideas."

I blurted out, "I can dream, can't I?" I'd already been dreaming, but now I could call him by name.

"Yah, but you have to know he's really smart. I mean really! Wants to be a doctor. I don't even try to understand him."

"Really smart, huh?" She had no idea it was just what I was looking for.

"Just applied to Harvard Medical School."

"Harvard? Think he'll get in?" I asked.

"Yup. I told you he's so smart I don't understand him. I mean it." She knew she wasn't getting her point across to me (that I wasn't his type) so she said, "Smart, as in … doesn't party … doesn't smoke … doesn't drink. That kind of "boring" smart. Get it?"

I got the picture, but it didn't turn me away. It intrigued me.

That night about thirty girls, including me, gathered in a circle on the floor, lined up along the parlor walls of Sohre Hall, and discussed our first day of freshman orientation. "I can't believe how far it is between buildings. Imagine how cold it's gonna be on this hill come winter?" one girl complained. The group shivered.

Another girl laughed, "Yah, but just imagine what great shape we'll be in by the end of the semester."

"Except everybody says we gain ten pounds the first year, maybe more than that with … what do they call the food service lady?"

"Ma Young," someone answered.

"Her food's incredible."

Ann said, "Especially her almond pie. Have any of you tried it yet?"

"I never tasted anything like that in my life. It's unbelievable," I said.

"Boy, there's nothing like that in my mom's recipe book!" said another. The whole room laughed.

In just that one day I had eaten the three best meals of my life. I started thinking that college life may change me in more ways than I had imagined.

Then a timid voice said, "I don't know if I'm ready for this. Today I heard one of the upperclassmen say the word 'existentialism' and I about fainted."

"Yikes!" Darlene exclaimed. "Existentia ... what?"

I had studied this philosophy in my senior year at Stillwater High School in a controversial and extraordinary class called Honors Contract. Instead of separate English and history classes, the fifteen hand-picked students had a two hour humanities course that included both English and history, and also philosophy. It met only four days a week. On Fridays we didn't have to come to school at all, but could spend the day in the Twin Cities at museums, bookstores, concerts, or doing research for our year-end project. Since most of us didn't have access to cars, we'd come to school on the bus, sit around the large tables in the library's conference room, and discuss politics, religion and philosophy.

"Existentialism," I said. "It's no big thing, Jean Paul Sartre's idea about every human being existing alone in the world, as if you were on an ice floe, and that every action you make is a choice which leads to your essence. It's one of the philosophic responses to the barbarity of the World Wars."

Silence engulfed the room, silent as that day in the swamp when we had strung up the effigy of Old Annie, years before. My heart sank as I realized I had said the wrong thing, or what others called TMI, too much information. It wasn't the first time I had piped up when I was supposed to play dumb. That's why I had gotten my Junior High nickname, "Scholar", for using my brain when I was supposed to defer to the smart boys in class. This was my first day at college … and I had done it again.

The discussion didn't continue. Everyone was tired. I walked to my room, but couldn't sleep that night.

Two weeks later Darlene appeared at my door. "My brother, Ed, remember him? Well, he just broke up with his girlfriend, and he called and asked if there were any interesting freshmen."

"Oh my gosh! Come in. I'll shove over these books and you can tell me all about it."

"I gave him your name. Figured when you knew that existentia-something-or-other you'd be a good match for him. So he'll prob'ly be calling."

Both excited and scared, later, when that phone call came, I felt as though I was in fact on an existential ice floe. It was a float I gladly accepted.

She was right about all of it. He turned out to be the most intelligent human being in the universe, and the most lovable. He graduated in May, and we arranged to work together at a Lutheran summer camp in Wisconsin until late August. He was the lifeguard and I was a camp counselor. It was a grand summer, especially when we sang songs accompanied by my guitar. I taught him to sing the harmony on a few folk songs, and we were the hit of the weekly talent show.

In September he left for Boston and Harvard Medical School. Every day that fall a charming and romantic letter from Massachusetts urged me to transfer from Gustavus Adolphus to Boston University to be near him.

It seemed like it should be an easy decision. However, my Minnesota college had awarded me a full scholarship, and Boston University had no scholarships for transfer students. But in my mind the only important thing was to get there. I forged Mother's signature on the BU college form, sent in the application for the winter semester of 1967, and waited for a reply. When the acceptance to Boston University's College of Liberal Arts arrived, there was no going back. I left for Boston against Mother's better judgment.

In Minnesota there had been no waiting in line for anything. But at BU everything was different. It took good shoes and an iron will to get to the front of the line, especially the registration line. After waiting over an hour I finally got my turn.

"Next."

I stepped up and answered politely, "Cynthia Blomquist, College of Liberal Arts."

The woman with tired eyes, seated at the registration table, looked under the B's. "Nothing here." She looked again. "Spell your last name."

"B L O M Q U I S T. Is something wrong?"

She continued to leaf through scores of papers.

"I'm a transfer student from Minnesota. Here's my acceptance."

"You can throw that away. I need your receipt." She positioned her elbow on the table and lifted her hand in my direction, expecting me to put the receipt in her palm.

"What receipt?"

"For this semester's tuition."

"But I haven't paid it yet. Do I have to pay before I can register?"

The woman lifted her head, stared into my eyes, and sneered at me. "Of course you do. Don't waste my time. Get your receipt and then go to the back of the line."

No one had given me instructions about when or where I needed to pay. At Gustavus I had never thought about tuition. It was taken care of through my scholarships. My spacey, four-leaf-clover-finder brain had gotten me to Boston, but hadn't finished the arrangements. There was no way I would be able to write a check for the whole semester's tuition. Until then I hadn't even thought about how I would pay the tuition.

"Where do I go to pay?" I asked.

"Couple blocks down Bay State." She pointed past the chapel.

In a panic I ran the four blocks to the bursar's office. I had to think fast. Room and board and tuition were more than twice that of Gustavus, and I had only one small scholarship from the Tozer Foundation that transferred with me. At the front desk I asked if they could make some kind of monthly arrangements for me, so I could use my social security check, that came in the mail regularly every month since my dad's death. The man behind the desk assured me that this wouldn't be possible. This was not done.

But I couldn't go back home. I didn't have a place at Gustavus any more. My Minnesota roommates had given me a going-away shower, where they presented me with a beautiful wool skirt and sweater to keep me warm in Boston. They didn't want me to look like the ragamuffin I was, when I had visited Ed at Harvard over Thanksgiving.

I stood in the entryway of the bursar's office about to explode, my face getting redder and redder as my brain came up with dead ends. I had only a few hundred dollars in the bank from working at the summer camp. I'd used the rest of my savings to get myself and my trunk out to Boston. My mother barely made ends meet from her Beauty Shop business, and she still had my brother at home to care for.

———— ∘O∘ ————

After Dad died, five years before I went to college, Mother had continued working as a receptionist at the chiropractic office of Dr. Jim Wallace, where Dad had relocated his practice after first working in St. Paul. After a few months, she decided to leave. She explained that she didn't like being at work when her three kids arrived home from school on the bus. I'm convinced she just couldn't work there any more, with all the memories of my dad, good and bad.

I don't know who she might have talked it over with, but one day she announced to us that she would be enrolling at the Ritter School of Beauty in St. Paul in hopes of becoming a beautician, and opening a shop in our basement. Our four monthly social security checks, Mom's and one each for us kids, were used to pay her tuition and transportation into the city. Not much left over to live on.

Those years had been sparse. Roxy and I used babysitting money for any clothes we needed. For meals we relied heavily on Mom's garden, my foraging for wild berries and asparagus, and Winky's fishing in May's Lake, both summer and winter.

She was so proud when she passed all the tests and graduated from Beauty School, and within months opened a beauty shop in our basement. It was perfect. She worked full time to earn a living, and was also home when the three of us arrived from school. In addition, she was able to use her exceptional creative and social skills. That shop became a community clearing house and all around gossip center, as well as her place to dish out the best haircuts and styles in the Valley. And she had one client we had to keep secret, who was so famous that Secret Service agents often accompanied him.

That story begins with Mother's new husband, Jim, who grew up in Elmore, Minnesota, near the Iowa border. He played on the football team there with an upperclassman named Fritz Mondale. Unfortunately, they got to know one another better because on one muddy day Fritz slipped and, as Jim puts it, "left cleat prints firmly in my back." Fritz apologized, and then frequently checked on Jim, to make sure he was okay.

Shortly after Mom and Jim were married, Jim was at the airport boarding area in Washington D.C., waiting to fly home to Minnesota. Senator Walter (Fritz) Mondale saw him there, and asked if he was the Jim he had played football with. Jim was a huge man, and his chiseled face and big smile hadn't changed much over the years. They shook hands and had a great laugh about the cleat print, and then boarded the plane, Senator Mondale in first class, and Jim in the back. After the seat belt sign went off, Fritz walked to the back of the plane and asked Jim to come sit by him in first class, and tell him all he'd been up to since high school.

"Been a farmer, got tired of that, and now I work as a guard at Stillwater Prison."

"Guess you use all those football moves with them, huh?" the Senator replied. "I can see you showing your muscles, and then talking 'em down."

Jim had regaled us with this story every year at the start of football season. That tiny town's football team was out-of-proportion important to a small-town farm kid.

"Yah, they don't give me no trouble, that's for sure," and Jim laughed. "But you know, I went and took them college courses I was supposed to take to get to be lieutenant, and

I got on top of the list for advancement," Jim sighed, "and then a new commissioner came in, and tore up the list. I've been waitin' five years to get promoted, and it's not happenin'."

"Well that's not fair. Can I help?" the Senator offered.

"Woah! Oh no! I'll get stuck down so deep in a gopher hole I'll never get out. They'll send me to guard duty on the 4th tower. Please don't do that."

"No, that's not right," he said. "I'll write a letter to the commissioner, and then I'll make sure nothing bad happens because of it."

A week later Jim was called into the warden's office.

"And just how is it you happen to know the senator?" he asked.

Jim went into the whole story of playing football and the cleat marks and ...

"That's enough. I got it," the warden said. "Oh, and congratulations. You're now number one on the lieutenant list."

A month later Jim was promoted.

On that plane ride, too, the senator found out that Jim was living in rural Afton (in the Valley). Fritz also lived in Afton during his senate and vice presidential years. Since the Mondales kept a home in Washington D.C., their Minnesota residence was with his in-laws in Afton. In fact, Mother, Jim and the senator all voted for him in the same booth at Afton Village Hall.

The Mondales continued, during his vice presidency, to keep their Minnesota residence in Afton, where my mother often trimmed the hair of many of the members of the Mondale family.

One particularly memorable night the phone rang at midnight.

"Hello," she sleepily replied. "Yes, Mrs. Adams? Of course, come right over. I'll have the light on."

"Who's coming, Dorothy?" Jim asked.

"Mrs. Adams, you know, Joan Mondale's mother, called and asked if I could see Ted tonight."

Her country beauty shop was isolated in the Valley, so they could come at odd hours and keep their privacy.

"Ted Mondale?"

"Ya. He hates getting his hair cut, and keeps putting it off until Grandma can't stand it any more."

A car door slammed, and muttering from a teenage male voice came wafting in the windows.

"He'll get over it. He's a typical teenager. He knows he has to have it short, but he just likes to complain."

Mother descended the steps to her beauty shop, closed the curtains at the end of the stairs and said, "Well hello, Mrs. Adams, and you too, Ted."

This was the era of long hair, and Ted did not come willingly for his monthly trim. Being the son of the Vice President of the United States may have had its advantages, but it also took away significant choices.

"Dorothy, sorry to call you so late," said Mrs. Adams. "But by tomorrow morning the press will be all over this family."

"Oh?"

"It's good news. At least I think it's good news," replied Mrs. Adams. "Fritz has just this hour decided to run for president."

"And guess who has to look 'presentable'?" Ted piped in.

"Well, for sure!" Mother replied. "This is an honor, Ted. Someday you'll understand."

And this time, instead of just trimming Ted's long golden locks, he got them cut considerably shorter.

I started to intensely observe this national public servant who lived only a stone's throw away. It seemed that Walter Mondale embodied the rules of the Valley. Help people where needed, empower people where needed, but make sure whatever was needed was really needed. He answered questions with grace, not doubletalk (in his incredibly thick Minnesota accent). I saw his availability to the people of Minnesota, even though airplane fares back and forth to Washington were expensive. And I witnessed the way he valued his family. Even Minnesota Republicans agreed that Walter Mondale wasn't in public service to judge, or to profit. His mission was to serve. He didn't wait for the right thing to happen, he helped make it happen.

Hubert Humphrey too. I never met him, but I remember Jim's stories about how Hubert, as a senator, had been there for his family and his neighbors when they needed help. It was interesting to have been familiar with two Vice Presidents of the United States.

Then, of course, there was the other Minnesotan in the 1960's, Senator Eugene McCarthy, the peace candidate for President. He too spoke my language, in my own Minnesota accent. My natural proclivity detested violence in all its forms, and when I heard Eugene McCarthy talk about the immorality of war, and the Vietnam War in particular, I listened closely. I found myself asking question after question.

Mother and Dad and my grandparents were all registered Republicans. In those days people assumed you would fall in line with your parent's thoughts. That's why my neighbors, the Bradshaws, influential in the state Republican Party, asked me to attend the state convention as their guest. I accepted and listened carefully. That summer I was also a candidate to Girl's State. (I believe that was one year after Bill Clinton, representing Arkansas at Boy's State, shook the hand of President John Kennedy.) When I was elected mayor of my Girl's State town, I first discovered that my political thoughts and actions leaned more to the left than to the right.

In the end, these three famous Minnesota Democrats won my heart. My interest in politics is so strong ever since, that I could not imagine missing voting in an election. That interest has led to a political activism, which in the last three decades has included helping draft and push through Louisiana legislation for its first child passenger safety law, and working on conservation projects through the Stillwater, Minnesota public school system (an outdoor nature classroom) and the St. Croix Valley Sierra Club (acting as conservation chair to help defend the "wild and scenic" St. Croix River).

Back in the 60's, before I started my semesters at Boston University, my mother asked only one thing of me, that I would not participate in any protests when I lived in Boston. She, like the majority of adults in those days, saw student protesters as a nuisance, as unlawful and ungrateful. I had sneaked around her while applying to BU, and I figured that the least I could do for her was to honor that promise.

In my mind, however, I was always with the protesters. So when the United States was about to enter the first war with Iraq, my son and daughter joined me in protesting at the federal building in Minneapolis. And my husband joined me in standing at a busy street corner several weekends in a row in Tulsa, Oklahoma, to protest entry into the second Iraq War.

A dandelion isn't always a weed. Sometimes it's a toe tickler, or a beautiful flower in a child's bouquet, or even the reflection of butter on your chin.

Rules are like dandelions. It's difficult for a young person to sort them out. I came from a home with fewer rules than most and married a man from a home with more rules than most.

I have spent years trying to determine which are weeds and which are flowers.

Watching and listening to the double talk and sometimes lies of politicians, especially during the Vietnam, Watergate and Trump eras, exposed me to a whole different set of rules. Lucky for me, I concentrated on Walter Mondale, who showed me that relativity was neither good nor bad, but a trait needed in the important art of compromise, and judging cases on their own merits.

I think that's what love means, no rigid rules.

That kind of political balance paralleled what I saw in art. Six years of ballet and toe dancing instruction taught me the beauty a well-balanced form could take, but no matter how beautiful a ballerina *en pointe* could be, it hurt. Every time I stuffed my toes into those hard cardboard toe-shoes and danced to the tune of the "Sugar Plum Fairy," I had to grit my teeth for art's sake.

Balance is a combination of will, coordination, concentration, hard work and pain. I began to see that achieving a delicate balance between accepting and asserting, between traditional rules and new thought, between sacred and secular, between faith and pietism, involved painful choices and questions.

I came to understand that what I needed was to find a place in between all of those poles, a path that felt familiar, a path lined with dandelions wandering through the gray nuances of truth.

———— ∘O∘ ————

"Dear God," I prayed, as I collapsed onto the floor outside the bursar's office. "I'm not leaving this building until I come up with some way to figure out how to pay my room and board and tuition. Please. You gotta help me."

Then I recalled seeing a movie where Jimmy Stewart demanded to talk with the man's boss when he didn't get what he wanted. It sure wasn't what I had been taught to do in Minnesota, and certainly wasn't what a proper lady would do. But what did I have to lose? It was worth a try. I walked calmly back into the bursar's office and found the man I had originally addressed.

"Sir, could I see your boss? This is very important."

"Certainly. Wait here."

I couldn't believe it. No argument. Certainly. Wait here.

It didn't take long before a middle-aged man came out of a back office, introduced himself and said, "Follow me."

He led me to his spacious office and pointed to a comfortable leather chair opposite his desk. I could see the street full of students outside.

"Now, how may I help you?" he said.

I had seldom been treated with such respect. I felt like an adult, his equal. I knew I wasn't, but the atmosphere made it easy to talk. Even if this maneuver didn't work, I decided I liked this university.

I told the man about my fine academic career, and my not-so-fine financial situation, about my steady boyfriend at Harvard Medical School, and why I had just transferred in. (I didn't tell him my mother was against this transfer and had only reluctantly wished me well.)

I finished my spiel by saying, "But you know, as far as Boston University is concerned, you REALLY don't want to lose me as a student. I promise I will be a credit to this institution if you'll just work with me on these payments."

He twirled his pen for a few moments and then started writing a note on official paper. "You've convinced me. We've never done this before, but I believe you are a good risk. I'll have the bursar write up monthly coupons for you that you can include with your payments."

I stood to shake his hand. "Oh, thank you so much. You won't regret this. Really. You'll see. Really!"

As far as I know I was the only student that year, and for a long time afterwards, allowed to pay monthly tuition payments and still register for classes. Thankfully Mother, too, helped with the monthly payment since my social security check didn't quite cover the bill. The next year was easier because I worked as a Resident Assistant in the dorm, which paid room and board and some toward tuition.

Selling Christmas trees also supplemented my income. None of us knew, years earlier when we had planted those one cent pine trees, that they would become a financial life-blood for us. During the month of December we cut and sold hundreds of trees, choosing to thin out every other one, so that the remaining pines had more space to grow. We made money and beautified our back acres at the same time.

In the below zero weather, as I tramped out to the back hill to saw another tree and lug it out and tie it to a customer's car, I'd whistle Christmas carols and remind myself over and over that it allowed me to be in Boston with Ed, and to get a good education as well.

———— ∘O∘ ————

I've always thought of that decision, forging Mother's name and going to college in Boston, as a jumping–off– the–cliff–with–no–safety–net experience. Definitely alone on a melting ice floe. No Gloomy Lutheran would have done it. It was deceitful.

But how was that different from the Old Testament story where Jacob, the second born of twins, outwitted his hairy brother Esau, by using Esau's empty stomach as a bargain- ing tool, and taking away Esau's birthright? And Jacob was even honored, as part of God's holy covenant with Israel, for doing it.

Historically, the story is probably much deeper than that. Esau represented the hunter/gatherer way of life, and Ja- cob represented the new, rival, farmer/shepherd way of life. The name Jacob derives from "heel" or "he supplants", and describes the time in history when farming and shep- herding took over from hunting and gathering.

Anyway, I am a little bit farmer, a little bit shepherd, very much the gatherer, and have nothing of the hunter in me.

I still love to wander and find the sleeping places of deer in woodland meadows. I collect wildflowers and asparagus, wild berries, four–leaf clovers, agates and stories.

Jacob knew what he wanted and was decisive in getting it. Maybe he too was raised in a crusty, seemingly-useless Valley, with neighbors who saw its beauty and worked to keep it that way, a Valley whose limestone and sand hills were both stable and shifting, a Valley that nestled its inhabitants (complex characters and families full of sibling rivalry) in a loosely woven nest, and flung them out when they were ready.

In my eighth decade, after having roamed and rambled through life, I have down-sized into a home that stares at trees full of bird feeders and woods behind them (as my mother and grandmother had done).

Often I unconsciously stop mid-sentence, and raise my hand to silence those around me, to fully listen to an exquisite chord playing on the stereo.

I pause to absorb the sacred sound before moving on, reminiscent of my father.

And one Sunday, not long ago, I found myself pulling up the sleeve on my sweater (just as my dad always did) to see my arm hairs rise, as my choir friend, Michelle, sang an angelic solo.

I have learned to enjoy the myriad styles of music that reflect our human souls and tell our stories, whether it's all about the drumbeat or about the silence between the beats, whether it's about the chord or the dis-chord, the notes or the lyrics.

I don't tolerate secrets.

I value everything my diverse family teaches me, whether learned from joy or pain.

And I proclaim the words written by Woody Guthrie's son Arlo, when he sings "I pass my peace around and round, cross hands of every hue. My peace, my peace is all I've got that I can give to you."

—————— ◦O◦ ——————

The Valley is a character in this book, and so it needs an ending as well.

The schoolhouse-turned-house that Carol lived in has burned to the ground. The knoll now stands empty, full of prairie grasses and yellow toadflax.

The swamp across the road, where I used to gather cowslips, was drained forty years ago into a round lake with a round island. The "cathedral" up the Indian Trail now has a mini-mansion and five acre yard, as does most of the Valley.

I no longer live in the Valley, and my visits are limited since my mother died. Her husband Jim moved from the old farmhouse she and my dad bought in 1947 to northern Minnesota, to be close to his own grandkids. He later entered a senior living center, and has passed away as well. My brother too has sold his house in the Valley, and moved across the river.

The city and its suburbs have bumped into this beautiful rural place, and are angry they cannot fully enter it. Sixty years ago a law was passed that every home in Afton Township needed at least five acres upon which to build.

My family agreed with Grace Stoltz, the architect of that policy and Valley futurist, who wanted to preserve its beauty intact. No one realized that the Valley's wild areas might still be in jeopardy, because of a proclivity for large grass lawns. But most new residents of the Valley have built their homes behind a wall of trees, and have tried to preserve the natural setting.

Some residents complain about Belwin Outdoor Nature Laboratory, the non-profit nature preserve that has bought up miles of land in the Valley. At first everyone loved the idea, because it raised the value of their own property. But now, as the non-profit continues to buy more tax-free land, some of the residents are feeling burdened by their always-hungry, ever-growing neighbor that doesn't share evenly in paying for schools, roads, parks and police.

I find it hard to complain. Belwin is an extraordinary place that preserves native prairie and native lore. It encourages city and suburban kids to freely explore its woodland trails, listen to the gnawing of beavers, and feel part of the earth.

A mischief of mice, a herd of deer, a flock of geese all know how the land heals, how it changes more slowly than we change, how it endures without judgment, absorbs our steps without complaint. It grounds us at the same time as it nourishes the tall trees into which we climb.

Field mice will always look for hollow walls in which to build their winter nests, but only a few curious ears will attend to their mysterious scratching.

Hard As Rock

Widowed at 36 with three kids
and a mortgage, Mother had only enough life
insurance to pay for his funeral.

Food, brought by neighbors,
lasted a week, so I took to gathering
wild berries and asparagus,

as my little brother caught fish,
standing on a rocky shore
or hovered over a hole in the ice.

She grew up on a farm too far
from a high school to attend,
so she left home for the city –

only sixteen, on her own,
she studied secretarial stuff,
learning to be helpful to men.

When she worked for my dad (and his wife)
Mom got pregnant, helped him divorce her,
got married to him,

then watched his charm with women,
using music to lure them like cobras,
ruin any chance at happiness.

And finally when he died, so young,
the government told her my dad had
another family, and three kids.

Called herself a horse-trader,
always landing on her feet, because
she was smart when no one

told her she was smart.
She was outspoken at a time
when it wasn't appreciated.

Mother was tough,
and taught us to be tough,
when women were soft.

She hit a lot of hard rock before
the last rock that killed her,
falling on her own stone steps.

afterword
# of mice and men

Clover
[*Trifolium repens*]

In summer, when field mice tunnel in the violet, vetch-blossomed meadows, and eat and sleep in the open air, I don't mind them.

But when autumn comes to the North Country, and its fields ice over, mice, feeling entitled, enter our warm houses, nibble our leftover crumbs, and scratch messages to one another within our inner walls.

They know we hate seeing them, so they hide their nests between the walls, tunnel in the loose insulation, and come out at night, while we sleep. Every once in a while an old mouse dies between those walls and emits a rotting stench, which can't be removed. It seems, even mice keep secrets.

But we're beginning to understand them better too. In the March 7, 2023 issue of "Current Biology", an experiment at Harvard Medical School examines the differences in behaviors of male and female mice. Male mice had been almost exclusively used in neuroscience research, because the scientists assumed that the females would be "broadly affected by their cyclic variation in hormones."

What they actually found was that the female mice were more controlled in their behavior between themselves, and between them and the males, and the male mice were significantly less stable in those behaviors.

I know that humans lie and then keep secrets, when we are certain the hidden information will either hurt someone, or more commonly, get us into trouble.

The male Blomquist clan was experienced at hiding reality, avoiding the truth, lying by saying nothing at all, and generally exhibiting less stable behaviors.

Only recently did I learn that my great-grandfather, Lars Blomquist, had been an orphan in Sweden. Instead of being sent to an institution, he had been indentured to a Swedish farmer, who worked him like a slave.

As soon as Lars was legally allowed to leave the farm, he moved to the big industrial city of Stockholm, where he met a single, young woman, Annie Ringman, who also lived and worked in that district, and had a fatherless baby named Gustave.

Unfortunately for Annie, her frail baby died. Soon after that, Lars married her, then immediately immigrated to America. It seems as though Lars needed to leave the country in a hurry.

It was hard to find a job in America, where he was referred to as "Dumb Swede."

Annie became pregnant while moving from place to place with Lars, until finally their son, whom they also named

Gustave, was born, not in a home or hospital, but in the train station of a small railroad town called Dassel, Minnesota. My grandfather would be their only child.

Lars, a closed-mouth but hard-working man, had not revealed to his wife that he had a lover, and possibly another child, back in Sweden. One sorrowful day, a few years later, he collected their savings, bought a ticket back to Sweden, and left his penniless wife, and toddler Gus, with a woman on the west side of St. Paul, called Mrs. Palmer.

Lars returned after a year, but things didn't improve much. And to ease his sadness and painful memories of youth, he turned to alcohol. I assume, at some point, he was kicked out of his house, because my great-grandfather, Lars, lived out his older years with my Grandpa Gus and his family, and both my grandfather and my dad were exposed to Lars' alcoholic mean streak.

As far back as I can find, secrets and lies were the hidden mischief passed on to generations.

My Grandpa Gus had his own painful secrets. Why had he never told my dad about his biological mother, who had died shortly after Dad's birth?

Or that Gus was left to raise a baby for five years on his own in the days before government hand-outs?

Or that when he found Ethel, despite the fact that she was the first female to ever earn a mathematics degree from Hamline University, she thankfully agreed to give up any pursuit of professional work, to become Johnny's mother?

And when my dad found out about his biological mother, Grace, why had Gus told him that he was lucky he never knew her? What kind of inner pain must he have felt, to say something so vicious?

And why was Grandpa Gus so adamant about my Dad not following his musical talent?

I can only assume that Grandpa's pain was never verbalized, instead hidden deep as a field mouse nest in the spidery vetch.

Thinking back to the Grandpa I remember, I could see in the wide lines of his forehead, that never became uncreased, that his heart was probably full of disappointment about his son, despair about years of poverty, a gnawing feeling of inferiority toward his educated wife, the loss of a child, Bruce, to the flu epidemic of 1918, and then living again, in his own home, with his alcoholic, abusive father, until Lars died.

———— ∘O∘ ————

I know about my great-grandfather's alcoholism because Dad often referred to it.

Dad was a musician in the days when musicians drank too much, smoked excessively, and used drugs freely. He used to say that police parked around the corner of night clubs, waiting until they closed, to nab "happy" band members who were driving home impaired. But they never caught my dad, because he didn't use alcohol or drugs. He had seen too much intemperance from his Grandpa Lars.

But my dad, Johnny, had his own painful secrets. He'd had a daughter by his first marriage, Grace, that he had been forbidden to ever see again after age 9. My mother eventually told us that Johnny was heartbroken about never again seeing Grace. But we didn't hear about it until Grace herself came looking for her dad.

And he never told us that he was still married to Grace's mother when he got his secretary (my mother) pregnant. I only learned that piece of information from my Aunt Jeune (his half-sister) a few years before she died.

Dad even hid his age from my mother, telling her he was 3 years younger than he actually was, dying at age 48, not 45.

And he never told any of us that he was married to a woman, named Irene, for the last 12 years of his life, at the same time he was married to my mother for his last 15 years.

I only learned lately that Irene and John had actually driven to Iowa, in February of 1948, gotten married, and received a real marriage license, despite John not having been divorced from my mother. All three of her children used my father's last name Blomquist, without hesitation.

I guess this earns Dad the moniker of "rat", not just mischievous mouse. But it's hard to dive too deeply there.

I finally contacted Irene's daughter, J. We had seen, via genetic testing on Ancestry.com, that we were likely half-sisters, and we agreed to speak.

J. was surprised when I asked her questions that made her dad seem less than perfect. I asked her how she could possibly think of him as a full-time father, when he slept every night at our house, and was with us on all holidays. She answered that she was 5 years old when he died, and wouldn't have known if he didn't sleep there.

It's hard to learn about these old scratching memories more than six decades afterwards. They feel as fresh as if Dad had left us yesterday. As if he had told me "You are the one I trust," just yesterday, and then had a massive heart attack.

He didn't leave my dreams for nearly 40 years, until my son started studying music at the university. One strange night, Kent spoke to me and said that he had felt the leaves blowing around in circles as he was walking back from the music building at college, late at night when there was otherwise no wind.

And he said to me, "It's a little strange, but I had a feeling that your dad came to me, and told me he's proud of me."

It didn't seem strange to me. The same night, Dad left my dreams, as if released from a net, free to go on to someplace better.

———— ₒOₒ ————

More than 60 years after Dad left, I have found myself having to rethink how our holidays were spent.

I knew that every Christmas Eve, when we drove to Grandma and Grandpa Knoblauch's house, he drove a different car, because, he said, "I have to leave after supper, to go play for the diners at the St. Paul House."

That was where he worked on other nights.

But, with a tight throat and gut-feeling of betrayal, I have now come to wonder if the St. Paul House was even open on Christmas Eve, and did he actually drive to the other Blomquist house to celebrate with them?

I think the answer is yes.

I now believe Johnny was afraid of losing his children if he divorced Dorothy, the way he had lost Grace with his first divorce.

I don't know what the laws were like then concerning custody. But I believe that he did not want to abandon us.

And there's more. One last secret.

When I asked J., my half-sister, if she had ever met her grandparents, my Grandma and Grandpa Blomquist, who lived in St. Paul, she had an interesting answer.

"No, Grandpa Gus hated my mother, so I never met him."

What I finally understood at that moment, was that Grandpa knew all about my dad's marriages.

I had always thought, after meeting my older half-sister Grace, that Grandpa had been angry with my dad because he had married a Catholic, and then divorced her by agreeing to never see Grace again.

That would have been enough. That reasoning would have made sense to me, and it always had. But the only irrational prejudice those two men agreed on was against Catholics.

But now I understand that my grandfather also knew about Dad's bigamy. Or his lies. Whatever you would want to call it.

And Grandpa Gus hated Irene for being the third wife.

How could Grandpa bear this knowledge and not tell my mother? I'm sure there was no way he would turn Dad into the police, or anything of that sort. But he couldn't tolerate his son's behavior either.

I guess that's why they didn't speak.

And my guess is that he was not ready to face Irene if she was at the funeral, and so he didn't go.

I assume she did attend, and that's what J. remembers. But she didn't bring her three young Blomquist children.

And J. knew her father had died, but Irene told her that her dad had died on the operating table, after suffering a heart attack at work.

It was true, he had his heart attack at work, but he had driven all the way home to our house.

Johnny had died in Mother's arms.

———— ◦O◦ ————

Sometimes the truth is so horrible, you can't absorb it all.

Grandpa finally drove out of the city, to the cemetery in Bayport, and visited my dad's grave three months after the funeral.

There, Gustave Adolph Blomquist felt shaky. His legs collapsed under him, and he found himself kneeling in the dust in front of his son's cold gravestone.

What went through his mind I'll never know, but within a few moments, his arm stiffened with pain as his heart seized. Gus drove directly to a hospital in St. Paul, where he, too, died of a heart attack.

Grandma Blomquist moved to Kansas, along with her sister Blanche. Both lived there, next to her daughter, my Aunt Jeune, and family.

Grandma died in June 1969, and was buried in Minnesota alongside Gus, on the morning of June 7th.

My wedding day.

I sobbed at Grandma's funeral, then dried my eyes as I drove back home, to get ready to meet my future husband at the altar.

I was raised to be a tough girl.

When, years before, Dad had us sleep at our burned-out house, and told us we needed to be strong, I now realize he was already "married" to Irene, with three other children, and must have known that there would be emotional pain in the future, for all of us.

———— ∘O∘ ————

I wonder now where Lars picked up the name "Blomquist", loosely translated as "flowering branch". As an orphan, did my great-grandfather inherit it, did he assume his over-seer's name, did the officials at Ellis Island change it?

In Swedish, did the name mean that there was wildness in us? There were flowers and there were sturdy branches?

My dad had always done his best at cultivating new blos-soms near our Valley home; better than he had ever done at raising mink.

There are a lot of us wild Blomquists around the world. Maybe children Lars had with his lover – we might never know. Roxanne, Wink, and I, J. and her brothers, Grace, and all of our children and grandchildren. All part of that blooming garden.

Some of us inherited Dad's cornsilk hair, some of us hold inside a crippling strength, some have become healers.

Others continue the music that runs through our blood.

But the elders are all gone now, Lars, Gus, Dad, Mom, J.'s mom, Grace's mom, my other grandparents, aunts and uncles, community members, Old Annie, and all the peo-ple whose stories I have told.

All of us were hurt, and healed, in different ways.

That tough girl who wasn't allowed to cry, hardened all of her feelings. I wanted to be an actress, but I couldn't let out real emotion. It was easier to study directing, and teaching. That girl too lost relationships because she wouldn't allow intimacy. I endured too many deaths; father, grandfathers, classmates, friends. Everyone called me "mature." They didn't know. That kind of strength, like a steel bar instead of a waving palm, is interpreted incorrectly.

My dad and grandpa, both gone over 60 years now, left behind their creative efforts. Grandpa designed the die forms and poured the brass for a candelabra and a fish ashtray that I still display. He taught Dad to whittle wood, and I had two small, carved, wooden men, one made by Dad, and the other by Grandpa, that are now standing guard in my son's home in Germany. The school song for Northwestern College of Chiropractic, written by my dad, is sung each year at graduation. And his favorite jazz and classical music is still prominent in my brain.

Johnny's love of photography, with his precious Leica camera, is represented by a framed black and white photo he took of a steam engine pulling a train. Its rising steam becomes the face of a man. Over the years I have discovered other, hidden faces, in the mist.

Mother and Grandmother Knoblauch constantly whisper to me through my garden flowers, and add cheer to my day through the wren singing outside my kitchen window. I still read and cherish the leather-bound poetry book from my mathematician Grandma, that she gave me on my 7th birthday.

And mice are still living in my garden. Every generation makes their own mischief.

I have learned to love the fields of wildflowers and lavender ivy-like vetch, where the mice run freely, and the black and yellow bumble bees buzz around them, collecting honey.

Its sweetness sometimes overwhelms me, and I get caught up in the vines that often catch my boots and trip me. But

I have learned that if I land in the clover, I can lie there and search for four-leafers.

If I fall into wild strawberries, I'll eat until I'm full, and pick the rest to pair with wild rhubarb for pie.

Nothing in the world is richer than picking strawberries and blueberries with my granddaughter, the Oklahoma wind in our straggly hair, our blue-stained fingers ripe with juice.

Instead of screaming at the sight of a spider on the bushes, she identifies it, along with the name of the hawk she hears overhead. She loves the garden and the wilds as much as I do, and without knowing it, she has received the wisdom and love of generations before her.

She is strong, like salt, that makes whatever it touches taste better. She is as beautiful as the wildflowers she collects.

We are explorers, and will run and tunnel with the cleverness of mice.

about **the author**

Cynthia Blomquist Gustavson is a prize-winning author, poet, musician, as well as a pioneer in the field of poetry therapy. She has degrees from Boston University and Louisiana State University, and has lectured extensively around the world about writing, poetry therapy, and personal development. She has held senior positions on several national Boards of Directors, and has a lifelong history of advocacy work for equal rights, environmental protection, and other important causes. She has settled in Tulsa, Oklahoma, where the Lutherans drift south, and where the heat drifts north.

Haiku

The blue-faced river
exhales into white rapids
after holding breath

Printed in the USA
CPSIA information can be obtained
at www.ICGtesting.com
LVHW062325071023
760301LV00008B/45

9 781613 431511